MEDIA OWNERSHIP
and
DEMOCRACY
in the
DIGITAL
INFORMATION AGE

**Promoting Diversity with First Amendment
Principles and Market Structure Analysis**

MARK COOPER

*Director of Research, Consumer Federation of America
Center for the Internet & Society, Stanford Law School
Associated Fellow, Columbia Institute for Tele-information*

Center for Internet & Society
Stanford Law School

Acknowledgments

Many of the concepts in this book are the result of a twenty-year Vulcan mind-meld with Gene Kimmelman of Consumers Union. Steve Cooper provided the initial drafts of most of the material in Chapters 3 and 4 and reviewed numerous drafts of the entire document. Dean Alger provided materials for Chapters 2 and 3 as part of comments filed by the Consumer Federation (et al.) at the Federal Communications Commission. Bob Brandon and Melanie Wyne relentlessly demanded simple English in a series of documents which make up most of the chapters of this book. Susan Punnett tirelessly edited the manuscript. The Ford Foundation provided significant support for the research through its funding of the Consumer Federation of America's *Digital Society Project*. Cover design by Jeff Middour.

ISBN 0-9727460-9-9

Mark Cooper
1424 16th Street, N.W.
Washingtion, D.C. 20036
mcooper@consumerfed.org

Contents

iv

About the author

Dr. Mark Cooper, Director of Research at the Consumer Federation of America and a Fellow at the Stanford Law School Center for Internet and Society and the Columbia Institute for Tele-Information, holds a Ph. D. from Yale University and is a former Yale University and Fulbright Fellow. He is the author of numerous articles in trade and scholarly journals on telecommunications and digital society issues and three books — *The Transformation of Egypt* (1982), *Equity and Energy* (1983) and *Cable Mergers and Monopolies* (2002).

About the Center For Internet & Society

The **Center for Internet & Society** (CIS) is a public interest technology law and policy program at Stanford Law School, part of the Law Science and Technology Program at Stanford Law School. The CIS brings together scholars, academics, legislators, students, hackers, and scientists to study the interaction of new technologies and the law and to examine how the synergy between the two can either promote or harm public goods like free speech, privacy, public commons, diversity, and scientific inquiry. The CIS strives as well to improve both technology and law, encouraging decision makers to design both as a means to further democratic values.

PART I: LEGAL PRINCIPLES AND ANALYTIC FRAMEWORK

I. A Bold Aspiration for the First Amendment

Ownership of Electronic Media and The Freedom of Speech

The Current Debate Over Media Ownership Limits

This book presents a critical view of the current state of commercial mass media in America. It examines the media through the lens of the public policy debates about limits on the number and type of media outlets that a single firm can own. The focal point is the Federal Communications Commission's (FCC) policy that prevents a television station from owning or being owned by a newspaper in the city in which it holds its broadcast license. Additionally, this book devotes some attention to policies that prohibit television station owners from holding licenses to more than one TV station in a city and limit the number of TV stations they can directly own across the nation.

Some of these policies have been adopted pursuant to explicit Congressional mandates; others have been implemented under the FCC's broad responsibility to promote the public interest. All of these policies rest on the premise that because the ability to broadcast over the airwaves in an area is limited by interference, most citizens will not have direct access to electronic, broadcast voices. Broadcast frequencies - the limited resource – have been allocated by licenses. Broadcast licenses are severely limited compared to the number of people who would like to be broadcasters. Because electronic voices are so scarce and powerful, the licenses have been subject to limits and obligations. The purpose of ownership limits is to promote diversity and localism in the broadcast media. Other public policies that have been imposed on licenses include obligations to air certain types of programs, like children's or public affairs programming, and obligations to set aside time or capacity for community programs or political debate.

The ownership limits have recently received considerable attention because the FCC reviewed all of its rules limiting media ownership[1] in the context of what the Chairman of the FCC, Michael Powell, calls a "Copernican Revolution" for media.[2] The Chairman's colorful comparison is not much of an overstatement. The mass media are the primary means through which citizens gather news and information.

3

TV, in particular, is the primary vehicle for political advertising. At the same time, digital media are at the center of the information economy and the emerging multimedia environment in which consumers and citizens will not only listen and watch, but must also be able to express their opinions and views. The stakes for citizens, consumers and the nation are huge – no less than the viability of democratic discourse in the digital information age.

Some of the limitations on ownership were reviewed because the Appeals Court for the District of Columbia had overturned prior rules.[3] This applies to the limit on the number of TV stations a network can own directly nationwide and the number of stations an individual entity can hold a license for in a single market. Other rules were re-examined because of a provision in the Telecommunications Act of 1996 that requires a biennial review of all FCC regulations.[4] This applies to rules affecting broadcaster ownership of newspapers and radio licenses.

Chairman Powell seized on these as an opportunity to eliminate the rules.[5] The "Copernican Revolution" in regulation that he meant to advance reflects his belief that a technological revolution has already transformed the American mass media marketplace. For example, *The Washington Post* offered the following observation on things to come under the headline *Narrowing the Lines of Communications?*

> It is only a matter of time before nearly all barriers to cross-ownership in the media industry are lifted … In major metropolitan areas it may be possible, even common, for one giant corporation to own the dominant newspaper, the cable television monopoly, a local broadcast station, several radio stations and even the dominant Internet access provider.

> The decisions will give added support to FCC Chairman Michael K. Powell, who views such restrictions as anachronisms in an era of Internet, broadband and satellite technology … Any excess concentration, Powell argues, can be handled by the Justice Department in its traditional role as enforcer of the antitrust laws.[6]

Chairman Powell's views are only the latest in a long line of efforts to redefine media policy in narrow economic terms and reduce democratic discourse to commercial success and popularity. This book shows that Chairman Powell's view is wrong on both of its fundamental premises. It is wrong about the state of the media industry and wrong on the purpose of the law he swore to implement.

The Chairman's view of the industry over which he presides is far off the mark, based more on hope and hype than reality.[7] The dissemination of news and information in America, particularly local news and information, is still dominated by local television stations and newspapers. Local media markets are already highly concentrated. Even at the national level, the ownership and control of television programming, especially news dissemination, is concentrated. A relaxation of ownership limits can only make matters worse.

The Chairman's desire to reduce all matters to antitrust is also off base and reinforced by his disregard for the public interest standard of the Communications Act. He made his dim view of the public interest standard clear in one of his first speeches as a Commissioner when he declared that:

> The night after I was sworn in, I waited for a visit from the angel of the public interest. I waited all night, but she did not come. And, in fact, five months into this job, I still have had no divine awakening and no one has issued me my public interest crystal ball.[8]

The chairman's desire to transform the public interest under the Communications Act into competition under the antitrust laws ignores half a century of First Amendment law and jurisprudence. As discussed at length throughout this book, the Supreme Court has adopted a broad view of the First Amendment in the age of electronic broadcast media, declaring the goal to be "the widest possible dissemination of information from diverse and antagonistic sources."[9]

The goal of First Amendment policy under the Communications Act is broader than the goal of competition under the antitrust laws. In merger review, antitrust laws seek to prevent the accumulation of market power while merger review under the Communications Act seeks to promote the public interest. Media mergers must pass both reviews because Congress and the courts recognize that media and communications industries play a special, dual role in society. They are critical commercial activities and deeply affect civic discourse. They affect both consumers and citizens. While economic competition is one way of promoting the public interest, the Communications Act and the courts identify several others. Under the Act, the needs of citizens and democracy take precedence.

The extremely narrow view that the Commission took in its order is captured in fundamental judgments it made about policy and methodology.

Nor is it particularly troubling that media properties do not always, or even frequently, avail themselves to others who may hold contrary opinions. Nothing requires them to do so, nor is it necessarily healthy for public debate to pretend as though all ideas are of equal value entitled to equal airing. The media are not common carriers of speech...

The decision of whether to do weighting turns on whether our focus is on the availability of outlets as a measure of potential voices or whether it is on usage (*i.e.*, which outlets are currently being used by consumers for news and information). We have chosen the availability measure, which is implemented by counting the number of independent outlets available for a particular medium and assuming that all outlets within a medium have equal shares. In the context of evaluating viewpoint diversity, this approach reflects a measure of the likelihood that some particular viewpoint might be censored or foreclosed, *i.e.*, blocked from transmission to the public. [10]

Rather than promote the widest possible dissemination of information from diverse and antagonistic sources, the Powell-led Commission defines its job as merely preventing the complete suppression of ideas. This narrow view of freedom of speech will not support a vibrant democracy and the radical relaxation of ownership limits to which it gives rise will result in concentration of ownership at the local level, consolidation of media into national chains, and conglomeration of different types of media outlets. Concentration of media ownership reduces the diversity of local reporting and gives dominant firms in local markets an immense amount of power to influence critical decisions. Consolidation in national chains squeezes out the local point of view. Conglomeration of media outlets undermines the watchdog role that the print medium plays with respect to television and vice versa.

By combining structural analysis of commercial media markets with qualitative analysis of media market performance, this book demonstrates the misguided nature of the decision to essentially eliminate the limits on ownership. It shows that previous decisions to relax rules led directly to concentration, consolidation and conglomeration, which had harmful effects on the quality of journalism and democratic discourse.

The Expanding Debate Over Media Reform and Justice

For the average citizen, rule makings in Washington are distant and arcane, to say the least, but there are indications that this omnibus assault on media ownership limits may not pass with the public indifference that greets most FCC decisions. The Democratic members of the Commission forced a wider public vetting of the issue by holding public hearings across the country, two of which the Chairman attended. Hundreds of thousands of ordinary citizens took the time to voice their opposition to relaxation of ownership limits.[11]

Deep concern about the impact of the commercial mass media on American democracy long antedated the change in the rules.[12] That concern will only grow as the wave of takeovers and swaps unleashed by the relaxation of ownership limits brings highly visible mergers to cities and towns across America. The official endorsement of concentration, consolidation and conglomeration embodied in the virtual elimination of the public interest standard that has existed for over half a century may mark the start of a vigorous movement for media reform.

Ownership limits on commercial mass media are important constraints because people still turn to these outlets overwhelmingly as their primary source of news and information. Thus, the dissemination of news and information to the vast majority of citizens, the blood that flows through the heart of American democracy, will continue to come from the commercial mass media for the foreseeable future. The effectiveness of ownership limits is finite. These limits can place some constraints on the accumulation of media power by individual media owners. They can disperse viewpoints somewhat and preserve the institutional independence of print and TV media. There are limits to the effectiveness of these policies because the commercial mass media are so powerful. Therefore, ownership limits are only part of a much broader media reform that is needed.

A much wider distribution of the right to broadcast through unlicensed use of the airwaves is technologically possible and should be promoted. Giving every citizen an electronic voice through unlicensed use of the broadcast spectrum would lay the base for a truly "Copernican Revolution."

Public interest obligations should also be imposed on the holders of broadcast licenses to ensure that some of the huge profits created by these licenses are used for informative and high quality content. This

7

would ensure wider distribution of this content and capitalize on the powerful and expansive reach of the electronic media.

Community media, which provides much greater access for and is much more responsive to average citizens, should be developed. Noncommercial outlets and public broadcasting need the resources and independence to provide an alternative channel of high quality, objective content. As community and noncommercial media gain a stronger base, they can take on a key role as a forum for democratic discourse and as a watchdog, checking not only government and corporations, but also the commercial mass media.

OUTLINE

The book is divided into four parts. Part I presents the legal principles and analytic framework. The remainder of this chapter discusses the principles of First Amendment jurisprudence. When the Supreme Court formulated its bold aspiration for electronic speech it explained why democracy needs a media structure that strives for "the widest possible dissemination of information from diverse and antagonistic sources." Because First Amendment rights are involved, the court is also very careful to explain why the First Amendment and economic rights of media owners must serve the public interest. The chapter contrasts the forthright aspiration embodied in current law to the very narrow view taken by the Chairman of the FCC and the major media companies. It concludes with a review of public opinion about these issues.

Chapter II provides a theoretical explanation of why market forces alone will not create a forum for political discourse that meets our democratic needs. It shows that, left unchecked, key economic supply characteristics of mass media in the electronic age will drive the industry toward large entities in highly concentrated markets. The economic needs of these large national corporations will result in bland, homogenous fare that does not meet the needs of citizens in a large, heterogeneous nation. The chapter reviews a vast body of empirical evidence that supports the deep concerns that over-reliance on unfettered commercial mass media will fail to meet the needs of citizens for democratic dialogue.

Part II presents qualitative analyses of trends in the media – hyper-commercialism, concentration, consolidation and conglomeration in the dominant media. These have had a significant impact on democratic discourse in the last two decades of the twentieth century. The qualitative analysis explains why one should care about the ownership structure of the media.

Chapter III reviews some evidence of the qualitative impact on print journalism of mergers across media types as well as the consolidation of ownership of print journalism into national chains. Chapter IV reviews the major electronic media. It begins with the criticism of the role of television in the deterioration of political deliberation in the past several decades. It then reviews the hope and hype surrounding the Internet and discusses the technical, economic and social limitations on the role of the Internet in improving democratic discourse. It concludes with an application of the analytic framework to the coverage of the war in Iraq.

Part III presents quantitative analysis of media markets. While structural limits on ownership must rest on concerns about the qualitative impact of concentration, consolidation and conglomeration in the media, structural policy must also rest on a quantitative assessment of media markets and institutions. Ownership restrictions should be imposed only where there is a reasonable basis to conclude that without such limits democratic discourse will be weakened. Part III takes the view that market structure analysis is a proper basis for ownership policy as long as the analysis is rigorous and the policy rests on high First Amendment standards.

Following the general practice in the antitrust literature, Chapter V starts by defining the space in which news and information are disseminated in terms of its "product" and geographic characteristics. It introduces the formal measures of market structure derived from the field of industrial organization and utilized by antitrust authorities. It looks at the demand side – what consumers watch, read and listen to. The data demonstrates that on the demand side of the market, video, print and audio are distinct media products. They have very different characteristics and usage patterns. It shows that there are distinct national and local markets in which different products are supplied. At the same time, with respect to the production of local news, there are strong similarities between the print and TV markets, so that mergers between firms producing news pose a problem on the supply-side of the market.

Chapter VI reviews the supply side of the market. It examines the revenue and business models for broadcast, cable, newspapers, radio and the Internet. For each industry it applies the formal concepts of market structure analysis to assess the level of concentration in media markets. Applying these concepts, it finds that by routine antitrust standards virtually all of the national and local media product markets are concentrated and most are highly concentrated. The chapter also examines examples of past decisions to relax limits on media ownership to ascertain what is likely to happen should the proposed relaxation of the current rules be implemented. Looking at the relaxation of the TV duopoly rule in the late 1990s, the deregulation of cable in the 1980s, the increase in the radio ownership limits in the Telecommunications Act of 1996, and the repeal of the Financial and Syndication Rules in the early 1990s, the answer is overwhelmingly clear: 'If you let them, they will merge.'

Part IV presents structural policies for media ownership. Chapter VII proposes an approach to media ownership limits based on rigorous market structure analysis and high First Amendment standards. It adopts the principle that the FCC should not encourage media markets to become concentrated or allow mergers involving TV stations in markets that are highly concentrated. It measures market concentration in traditional antitrust terms and offers methodologies to take account of the impact of each type of media and the audience of every media outlets. These simple principles would allow cross-ownership mergers in only 10 markets where about 20 percent of the national population resides, while allowing TV mergers to take place in about 20 markets.

Chapter VIII presents a critique of the FCC's proposed rules. By failing to take audience size into account and assigning far too much importance to radio and weekly newspapers, the FCC bases its rules on a completely distorted picture of media markets. In the FCC analysis of New York City, for example, the Dutchess County Community College educational TV station has more weight than the New York Times. After two years of evidence gathering, the FCC appears to have resorted to politically motivated deal making[13] for the sole purpose of getting the most deregulation possible from a partisan majority. The FCC order gives blanket approval to newspaper–TV cross ownership in about 180 markets serving 98 percent of the nation. The number of markets in which TV-TV mergers are permitted is tripled from approximately 50 to 150.

NOT A TOASTER WITH PICTURES OR PEANUTS AND POTATOES

Democratic Debate v. Commercial Media Markets

The narrow economic view that Chairman Powell would like to impose on the debate over media ownership and his utter disdain for the public interest standard of the Communications Act[14] hark back to Mark Fowler, the first chairman of the Federal Communications Commission in the Reagan administration, who declared that television "is just another appliance … a toaster with pictures."[15]

The owners of media outlets and some of their champions would like to reduce the First Amendment to the status of "a toaster with pictures," and there is no doubt that hyper-commercialism has come to dominate both television and the Internet. Fortunately, neither Congress nor the Supreme Court has accepted that outcome as the best for democracy or as an appropriate reading of the First Amendment in the age of electronic media.

The Federal Appeals Court for the District of Columbia, which has sent the rules back to the Commission for further review and instructed the FCC to provide better justification for its rules, has clearly stated that public policies to promote a more diverse media landscape are constitutional, even if they reduce economic efficiency. The notion that the courts have demanded that the FCC remove or substantially relax media ownership rules is simply wrong. The fact that the Court of Appeals has demanded a coherent analytic framework based on empirical facts does not necessarily indicate that a relaxation of the limits on ownership is warranted. To the contrary, the court recognized that the limits could be loosened or tightened.

The D.C. Appeals Court continues to accept the proposition that "the Congress could reasonably determine that a more diversified ownership of television stations would likely lead to the presentation of more diverse points of view."[16] It went on to outline the logic of ownership limits. "By limiting the number of stations each network (or other entity) owns, the … Rule ensures that there are more owners than there would otherwise be."[17]

The court also accepts the trade-off between diversity and efficiency.

An industry with a larger number of owners may well be less efficient than a more concentrated industry. Both consumer satisfaction and potential operating cost savings may be sacrificed as a result of the Rule. But that is not to say the Rule is unreasonable because the Congress may, in the regulation of broadcasting, constitutionally pursue values other than efficiency – including in particular diversity in programming, for which diversity of ownership is perhaps an aspirational but surely not an irrational proxy. Simply put, it is not unreasonable – and therefore not unconstitutional – for the Congress to prefer having in the aggregate more voices heard.[18]

In *Fox Television Stations, Inc. vs. FCC*, the above reasoning is applied to a rule that increases the number of voices in the nation without increasing the number of voices in a local market. If such a rule can pass constitutional muster, if properly justified, rules that are aimed at increasing local voices, as are many currently under review by the FCC, stand on even firmer ground.

In fact, the aspiration for the First Amendment is much broader than "a toaster with pictures." It was given its modern formulation by Justice Black in 1945 in the seminal case, *Associated Press v. United States.*[19] He concluded that the First Amendment **"rests on the assumption that the widest possible dissemination of information from diverse and antagonistic sources is essential to the welfare of the public."** For the framers of the Constitution, diversity was a force to be tapped for the strengthening of democracy. Cass Sunstein points out that the uniquely American approach to a republican form of government held the view that "heterogeneity, far from being an obstacle, would be a creative force, improving deliberation and producing better outcomes... Alexander Hamilton invoked this point to defend discussion among diverse people within a bicameral legislature, urging... 'the jarring of parties... will promote deliberation'."[20]

Indeed, the governing Supreme Court decisions make it clear that freedom of information and the press transcend mere economics. Justice Frankfurter put it explicitly in concurring in *Associated Press*,

> A free press is indispensable to the workings of our democratic society. The business of the press, and therefore the business of the Associated Press, is the promotion of truth regarding public matters by furnishing the basis for an understanding of them. Truth and understanding are not wares like peanuts and potatoes. And so, the incidence of restraints upon the promotion of truth through denial of access to the basis for understanding calls into play considerations very different from

comparable restraints in a cooperative enterprise having merely a commercial aspect.[21]

Since then, the Supreme Court has reaffirmed this view with respect to newspapers and has unflinchingly applied it to all forms of mass media, including broadcast TV[22] and cable TV.[23] Simply, the needs of citizens cannot be reduced to the needs of consumers. Therefore, "we should evaluate new communications technologies, including the Internet, by asking how they affect us as citizens, not mostly, and certainly not only, by asking how they affect us as consumers."[24] Competition and economics in the commercial market may help to meet both sets of needs – needs as consumers *and* citizens. But, when the two come into conflict, citizens' needs for democratic discourse should take precedence over the commercial marketplace of the mass media.[25] The goal of media policy should be to promote a vigorous forum for democratic discourse.

I refer to the "forum for democratic discourse" rather than the "marketplace of ideas," because the marketplace metaphor is far too commercial. While the basic concept underlying the marketplace of ideas is sound - ideas competing for attention and support in an open public arena - the picture of a marketplace fails to capture the fundamental qualitative difference between the nature of action and interaction in the commercial marketplace and the forum for democratic discourse.[26] I want to draw a sharper distinction between democratic discourse and commercial media.

The objective of the commercial marketplace is to exchange goods and services to improve efficiency and produce profit. The objective of the forum for democratic discourse is to promote a "robust exchange of views" that produces "participation, understanding and truth."[27]

The aspiration for the First Amendment embodied in contemporary Supreme Court case law provides a properly bold vision. Freedom of the press and a robust exchange of views are complex, qualitative goals, which are inherently less tangible than a simple concept of profit or loss. That they are less precise, however, does not make them less important.[28] The fact that the goal is intangible should not prevent us from striving to define it with greater rigor.

Indeed, many of the wounds that the FCC has suffered in the D.C. Court of Appeals are self-inflicted. The Commission has failed to articulate a coherent and consistent vision, letting "a variety of cross-cutting objectives...obscure... the most important role that government regulations designed to enhance media diversity can play: thwarting the creation of undue concentration of media power, thereby advancing the project of democratic deliberation."[29] Those who would abandon the goal of promoting diversity in favor of promoting efficiency are misguided.[30] Structural limits remain the best means for promoting diversity in civic discourse.

> Uncontrolled centralization of media power presents a threat to liberty no less acute than the uncontrolled centralization of political power. Concentrated media power is utterly unaccountable to the citizenry. Similarly put, those who control the electronic media could, with sufficient concentration of media power, effectively displace citizens as the de facto rulers…

> Structural regulation – limiting the number of stations that a single entity can control, divorcing ownership of print media from ownership of broadcast media within the same community, limiting the number of stations that a single entity can own or control within a community, or licensing stations on a community-by-community basis… are mechanical in operation… They are also viewpoint-neutral. The Commission is not picking and choosing among potential speakers in drafting or applying these rules.[31]

Participation in Democratic Debate

The distinction between the commercial marketplace and the forum for democratic discourse becomes readily apparent when we respond to the advice frequently given by the most ardent advocates of pure economics to the complaint of mediocrity in the media. When the poor quality of the media product is brought up, they give a good free market response – "If you do not like what is on the tube, turn it off." An okay answer for consumers is very bad for citizens. It may be perfectly acceptable for consumers to be forced to vote with their dollars and turn off commercial entertainment, but it is not acceptable for citizens to be turned off by the poor quality of civic discourse, and then have no comparable alternative to which they can turn. As Justice Brandeis explained in his concurrence in *Whitney v. California*,

> Those who won our independence believed that the final end of the State was to make men free to develop their faculties; … that the greatest menace to freedom is an inert people; that public discussion is a political duty; and that this should be a fundamental principle of American government.[32]

The desire for active participation and the duty to discuss have important implications. Justice Brandeis' admonition against turning citizens into passive 'couch potatoes' needs to be given its full weight in constructing media ownership policy.

In particular, citizens must enter the debate not simply as listeners or viewers, but also as speakers. One goal is to ensure that they are well informed, receiving good, diverse information. Another even higher goal is to have them engage actively as participants in civic discourse.[33] The First Amendment implications of policies should not only be about how much citizens have to listen to, but also about their opportunities to speak and be heard. Sunstein puts it as follows:

> with respect to a system of freedom of speech, the conflict between consumer sovereignty and political sovereignty can be found in an unexpected place: the great constitutional dissents of Supreme Court Justices Oliver Wendell Holmes and Louis Brandeis… Note Brandeis' suggestion that the greatest threat to freedom is an "inert people," and his insistence, altogether foreign to Holmes, that the public discussion is not only a right but also a "political duty"… On Brandeis's self-consciously republican conception of free speech, unrestricted consumer choice is not an appropriate foundation for policy in a context where the very formation of preferences, and the organizing processes of the democratic order, are at stake.[34]

In fact, in each of the Supreme Court cases dealing with electronic media, the court has lamented not that there is not enough to hear or see, but that the number of electronic voices possible is far smaller than the number of potential speakers. Starting with an early radio case, *National Broadcasting Co. v. United States,* the Supreme Court found that "its facilities are limited; they are not available to all who may wish to use them; the radio spectrum simply is not large enough to accommodate everybody."[35] A quarter of a century later, with regard to television, *FCC v. National Citizens Commission for Broadcasting* again examined the disproportional relationship between potential speakers and electronic voices.

> Because of the problem of interference between broadcast signals, a finite number of frequencies can be used productively; **this number is far exceeded by the number of persons wishing to broadcast to the public.**[36]

In *Red Lion Co. v. FCC,* the unique nature of electronic speech was underscored when the court noted that "where there are substantially more individuals who want to broadcast than there are frequencies to allocate, it is idle to posit an unabridgeable First Amendment right to broadcast comparable to the right of every individual to speak, write, or publish."[37]

In fact, in the *Sinclair Broadcast Group v. FCC* decision, which dealt with local media markets, the court went to considerable lengths to reject Sinclair's claim that its First Amendment rights had been harmed by the duopoly rule.

> [B]ecause there is no unabridgeable First Amendment right comparable to the right of every individual to speak, write or publish, to hold a broadcast license, Sinclair does not have a First Amendment right to hold a broadcast license where it would not, under the *Local Ownership Order,* satisfy the public interest. In *NCCB* the Supreme Court upheld an ownership restriction analogous to the *Local Ownership Order,* based on the same reasons of diversity and competition, in recognition that such an ownership limitation significantly furthers the First Amendment interest in a robust exchange of viewpoints. The Court states in *NCCB* that it "saw nothing in the First Amendment to prevent the Commission from allocating licenses so as to promote the 'public interest' in diversification of the mass communications media.[38]

The general principle that First Amendment policy should draw people into civic discourse applies with particular force to minority points of view. In the commercial model, popular, mainstream, and middle of the road ideas will almost certainly find a voice, one that is likely to be very loud. However, the unpopular, unique, and minority points of view will not. Profit maximization in increasingly centralized, commercial media conglomerates promotes standardized, lowest-common-denominator products that systematically exclude minority audiences, eschew controversy, and avoid culturally uplifting but less commercially attractive content. Sunstein makes this point forcefully by noting that a "principle function of a democratic system is to ensure that through representative or participatory processes, new or submerged voices, or novel depictions of where interests lie and what they in fact are, are heard and understood."[39]

The idea of a duty to discuss and the need for a vibrant democratic discourse lead Sunstein to warn that the passive satisfaction that the media can induce is not an adequate standard for democracy. He argues that the mere fact that citizens keep watching the available fare with various levels of satisfaction and dissatisfaction does not demonstrate the success of the media market from the point of view of democratic discourse.

> Much of the time, people develop tastes for what they are used to seeing and experiencing... And when people are deprived of opportunities, they are likely to adapt and to develop preferences and tastes for what little they have. We are entitled to say that the deprivation of opportunities is a deprivation of freedom – even if people have adapted to it and do not want anything more.[40]

Similar points hold for the world of communications. If people are deprived of access to competing views on public issues, and if as a result they lack a taste for those views, they lack freedom, whatever the nature of their preferences and choices.[41]

Information Dissemination, not Entertainment

The narrow economic view of media leads FCC Chairman Powell directly to a failure to recognize the distinction between entertainment and information and between variety and diversity. He has expressed skepticism that there is a viewpoint expressed in most television programming, and accordingly, skepticism as to whether ownership limits serve any public benefit. As the Chairman stated in *USA Today*,

> [t]his is some sort of *Citizen Kane* idea that our thoughts will be directed to particular viewpoints. But the overwhelming amount of programming we watch is entertainment, and I don't know what it means for the owner to have a political bias. When I'm watching *Temptation Island*, do I see little hallmarks of Rupert Murdoch?[42]

Actually, even at the level of entertainment, the Chairman is not entirely correct. The decision of what is entertaining and what values are promoted in society is clearly embodied in the commercial decision underlying "Temptation Island." It stands for the proposition that paying people money to put their relationships in jeopardy under a voyeuristic lens constitutes good programming. It is highly unlikely that such a view would come from programming on the Pax network, or even on some of Fox's affiliates, as long as they remain independent and can choose not to air programming that offends their local community values.[43]

Additionally, what gets seen and not seen is quite clearly reflected in Rupert Murdoch's values, such as his decision not to include CNN and the BBC in his cable offerings in China because they have, for example, offered unflattering portraits of the Chinese government's stand on human rights issues. Murdoch understood that his ability to continue broadcasting in China was at stake and made a business decision to exclude such programming,[44] just as Comcast chose not to allow antiwar commercials to be aired on its systems.[45]

The most important point is that even if the economic media marketplaces were composed of significant numbers of small firms competing aggressively with one another, an unfettered commercial mass media market might not lead to the vibrant forum for democratic discourse that our Constitution attempts to promote because diverse sources of information are not the object of commercial competition. It favors entertainment at the expense of information. Owen Fiss articulates this point well when he notes that:

> None of this is meant to denigrate the market. It is only to recognize its limitations. The issue is not market failure but market reach. The market might be splendid for some purposes but not for others. It might be an effective institution for producing cheap and varied consumer goods and for providing essential services (including entertainment) but not for producing the kind of debate that constantly renews the capacity of a people for self-determination.[46]

Concentration of ownership may foster entertainment variety, but it undermines diversity of information and journalistic enterprise.

> It is certainly true that a person with two radio stations within the same market will probably select different program formats for each station whereas divided ownership might lead to competition within the same format. Suppose, however, that Disney owned both stations. Would the stations' news bureau report on Disney misdeeds with the same salacious alacrity of a competing local station unaffiliated with Disney? It seems rather unlikely.[47]

Limits on Ownership to Promote Diversity

As the D.C. Appeals Court noted, diversity of ownership is a critical aspect of diversity of information. In *Associated Press*, the Supreme Court also recognized that limitations on private interests to promote freedom of the press were permissible.

> Freedom to publish means freedom for all and not for some. Freedom to publish is guaranteed by the Constitution, but freedom to combine to keep others from publishing is not. Freedom of the press from

governmental interference under the First Amendment does not sanction repression of that freedom by private interests.[48]

Democracy theorists and legal scholars have identified a range of benefits of dispersed media ownership including "the salutary effect of ensuring a local media presence... the ancillary effect of dividing up ownership rights to the mass media... and... the effect of dispersing media power among multiple owners."[49] Increasing the number of independently owned media outlets plays a critical role as a deterrent to negative behavior. Edwin Baker argues that,

> A society's capacity to maintain its democratic bearings or its ability to resist demagogic manipulation *may* be served by a broad distribution of expressive power, especially media-based power. Such a distribution may be harder for a demagogue to manipulate or control or may be better able to deter political abuses because of being more difficult to control. On this account, the value of a wide distribution of media ownership lies not in any particular media product that this ownership produces on a day-to-day basis (such that the value will be reflected in market sales) but the democratic safeguards that this ownership distribution helps provide.[50]

The antagonism that the bold aspiration for the First Amendment seeks to achieve fosters accountability. As Ronald Krotoszynski and Richard Blailock put it, "[j]ust as divided political power fosters accountability – a central tenet of federalism – so too, divided media power fosters accountability."[51]

Baker argues that the promotion of diversity should not simply be applied to owners, but also to forms of ownership. He argues that

> [O]ur system of free press expression must include a plurality of speaker types, including commercial mass media, government subsidized noncommercial media, independent publishers, political and nonprofit associations, universities and individuals. To some extent, each of these speaker types offsets, complements, and checks the rest.[52]

In fact, one of the great weaknesses of the simplistic economic approach to media ownership is its failure to recognize that information is not just a commodity in which one source of information from one type of media can substitute for another. Institutional diversity – different types of media with different cultural and journalistic traditions and different business models – plays a special role in promoting civic discourse. Unique perspectives provided by different institutions are highly valued as sources of information.

Judge Learned Hand painted a picture of diversity that was properly complex, noting that a newspaper "serves one of the most vital of all general interests: the dissemination of news from many different sources, and with as many different facets and colors as possible" because "it is only by cross-lights from varying directions that full illumination can be secured."[53] As a recent law review article puts it:

> [I]t is problematic, or as Judge Learned Hand asserted "impossible," to treat different news services as "interchangeable..." A newspaper reflects the biases and views of its writers, editors, and perhaps owners. One newspaper may downplay and truncate a news wire story, while the other newspaper may carry it as a headline. These are non-fungible commodities. Thus, the marketplace is not about consumers switching from one homogenous product to another. Rather, it is the net increase in consumer welfare from having many competing news sources and editorial voices... Unlike restraints on ordinary commodities (where consumers may turn to less-desirable alternatives but the overall societal impact is not significant), for restraints in the media, the alternative may be inherently unsatisfactory and the costs imposed on society may be significant.[54]

A narrow view that all media information is fungible fails to recognize the unique role of newspaper reporting as a fourth estate: checking waste, fraud, and abuse of power by governments and corporations. It ignores the difference between national and local news markets and the tendency of nationally oriented media, which maximize profit by presenting programming attractive to national audiences and national advertisers, to homogenize the local point of view out of existence.

> These courts have recognized that news comes from many sources: newspapers, television, radio, magazines and more recently the Internet. These sources all arguably compete for the public's attention. But these courts have found that both the format and nature of information in local daily newspapers distinguish them from news and entertainment provided by other sources. Daily local newspapers provide a "unique package" of information to their readers. National newspapers lack the local news and advertising. Radio and television are primarily dedicated to entertainment and their news content lacks the breadth and depth of daily newspapers.[55]

The narrow view also fails to recognize the unique importance and role of television in the political process in a different way. Television is special because of its immense power to influence public opinion[56] and the role it plays in elections. "Because of the speed and immediacy of television, broadcasters perform these public forum-type functions even more than general interest intermediaries in the print media."[57] The broad language that the Supreme Court used in justifying the imposition of obligations on television, with a direct link back to the admonition of Brandeis, bears repeating. As Sunstein puts it,

> [T]he Court said "assuring that the public has access to a multiplicity of information sources is governmental purpose of the highest order, for it promotes values central to the First Amendment." The Court also emphasized the "potential for abuse of... private power over a central avenue of communications," and stressed that the Constitution "does not disable the government from taking steps to ensure that private interest not restrict, through physical control of a critical pathway of communications, the free flow of information and ideas.[58]

An unsophisticated view of media outlets pays no attention to the size of the organizations that produce news and information or their geographic orientation, in the process losing all perspective on citizens' ability to gain access to the media. As corporate scale dwarfs individual resources, citizens are cut off from the means of communication. *Associated Press* certainly expressed a concern about the sheer size of news organizations and the influence that could result.[59]

The narrow view of the public interest taken by Chairman Powell – which concerns itself with the promotion of commercially successful entertainment variety – sells the First Amendment short. The Supreme Court and the founders of the republic had a much bolder aspiration than that. As Sunstein argues, the lifeblood of democracy is the process of participation in the forum of discourse made up of diverse arenas for discussion and debate.

> We have seen that the essential factor is a well-functioning system of free expression – the "only effective guardian," in James Madison's words, "of every other right." To be sure, such a system depends on restraints on official censorship of controversial ideas and opinions. But it depends on far more than that. It also depends on some kind of public domain, in which a wide range of speakers has access to a diverse public – and also to particular institutions, and practices, against which they seek to launch objections. Above all, a republic, or at least a heterogeneous one, depends on arenas in which citizens with varying experiences and prospects, and different views about what is good and right, are able to meet with one another and to consult.[60]

The Need to Improve Democratic Discourse

Demographic Changes

There is a final, fundamental way in which the simplistic, strictly economic view that counts only the number of entertainment channels undervalues civic discourse. It fails to consider whether there is a need for a more effective means of public debate. Counting the number of outlets without reference to the population they serve or the issues they must deal with ignores the needs of the citizenry for information. If citizen participation in civic discourse is to continue to be or become more effective, a substantial improvement in the means of communication at the disposal of the public—far beyond commercial mass media influences—must be promoted through public policy. Policy must recognize that this aspiration for civic discourse must be placed in the social, economic and political context in which citizens live.[61]

While it is certainly true that there is a great deal more information available to more educated citizens today than twenty-five or fifty years ago, it is also true that they need more information. The population has grown in size and diversity. Mobility, globalization of the economy, internationalization of communications, and social fragmentation place greater demands on the communications network to enable citizens to be informed about increasingly complex issues, to express their opinions more effectively in civic discourse and to remain connected to their communities.

The broad parameters of change in American society over the past three decades are so profound that we can safely conclude that a much more diverse set of media institutions and outlets is needed to disseminate information. I focus on the past three decades because many of the rules governing the structure of media ownership were adopted in the early 1970s. For the purposes of this analysis, I start with the household as the consumption unit. TV markets are defined in terms of households. The bulk of newspaper distribution is home delivery.

The number of households has increased by 67 percent in the past two decades. This is twice as fast as the increase in the population (see Figure I-1). This reflects a dramatic change in the composition of households units. The number of married families has declined, while single parent households have increased sharply.

Figure I-1: The Typical U.S. Household Has Changed Dramatically

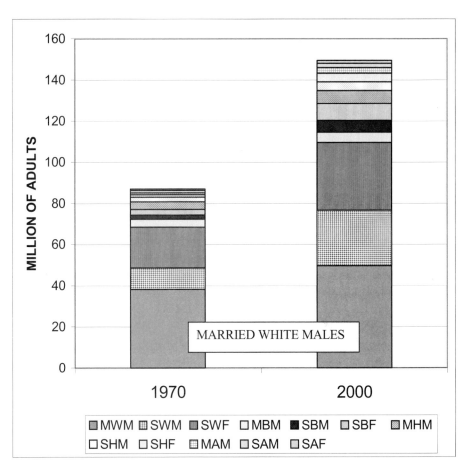

Sources: U.S. Bureau of the Census, *Statistical Abstract of the United States: 2001* (U.S. Department of Commerce, 2001), Table 50. *Statistical Abstract of the United States: 1986*, p. 35. Hispanic and Asian household make-up is held constant between 1970 and 1980.

At the same time, there has been a dramatic change in the racial and ethnic make-up of the population. The share of Hispanics and Asian/Pacific Islanders has doubled. Combining these two trends produces a stunning increase in the diversity of the population.

While the population has become increasingly diverse, it has been drawn more tightly into a more complex world (see Figure I-2).[62] In 1970,

Figure I-2: The U.S. Has Become Much More Deeply Embedded In The World Economy

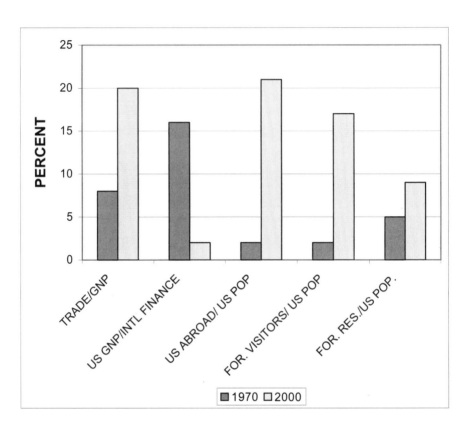

Source: U.S. Bureau of the Census, *Statistical Abstract of the United States: 2001* (U.S. Department of Commerce, 2001), Table 1, 647, 1258, 1259, 1297; Statistical *Abstract of the United States: 1986*, p. 406, 407.

exports and imports equaled about eight percent of gross national product. In 2000, the figure was twenty percent. Global financial markets, in which the U.S. is the leading actor, have grown dramatically. In 1970, the goods and services produced by the U. S. economy equaled about fifteen percent of global financial transactions. By 2000, they equaled only two percent.

The most dramatic changes can be seen in the movement of people. In 1970, two percent of the American population traveled abroad. By

2000, that number had grown tenfold to equal twenty percent of the population. Similarly, foreigners traveling to the U.S. equaled two percent of the population in 1970. By 2000, it had increased to equal sixteen percent of the population. Foreign born, non-citizens resident in the U.S. equaled five percent of the population in 1970. Today they equal ten percent and their racial and ethnic make-up has changed dramatically. In 1970, they were predominantly Europeans. Today they are predominantly Hispanics and Asians.

Technological Change

While the demand side of the media market has become much more complex, the supply side has become much more powerful. The power of digital communications is being greatly enhanced by improved video images with impact heightened by real-time interactivity and ubiquitous personalization. Dramatic increases in the ability to control and target messages and track media use could result in a greater ability to manipulate and mislead, rather than a greater ability to educate and enlist citizens in a more intelligent debate. Individual members of society need new communication skills and access to technology to express themselves and evaluate the information presented by more powerful messengers; citizens need a new kind of "media literacy."

The new technologies of commercial mass media are extremely capital intensive and therefore restrict who has access to them. The size of media organizations presents a growing mismatch between those in control and average citizens.[63] A small number of giant corporations interconnected by ownership, joint ventures, and preferential deals now straddles broadcast, cable and the Internet. Access to the means of communication is controlled by a small number of entities in each community and these distribution proprietors determine what information the public receives.

Notwithstanding the growth of new media, the dominant mass media – commercial television – remains extremely scarce in an important sense. The number of channels available is quite small compared to the number of citizens. Sunstein argues that even in cyberspace, where web sites and home pages are extremely plentiful, there is scarcity of another key element of the communications process: attention.[64]

At this point in time, the hope that new technologies will strengthen civic discourse is just that—a hope. Claims that dramatic changes have already rendered policies to promote diversity obsolete are premature and unsupported by the evidence. There has been far less fundamental change in the forum for democratic discourse than meets the eye.

At the same time, while the Internet has opened possibilities for new avenues of civic discourse, it has not yet even begun to dislodge the commercial mass media from their overwhelmingly dominant role. There is also a strong trend of commercialization and centralization of control over the Internet that may restrict its ultimate impact on civic discourse.[65]

SELLING FIRST AMENDMENT PUBLIC INTEREST PRINCIPLES SHORT

Chairman Powell's decision to define his job as promoting economic efficiency and profits in the entertainment industry and reducing the public interest to variety in entertainment programming sells short the aspiration the Supreme Court articulated for the First Amendment.

The broadcast networks embellish these themes, rejecting the scarcity argument declaring that "the 'scarcity doctrine' is and always has been a factual and economic absurdity."[66] The "widest possible dissemination" principle of First Amendment jurisprudence is reduced to a shadow of its bold aspiration,

> What really matters with ideas from a political point of view is whether they can be suppressed. But given the importance of interpersonal communications, it is extremely difficult to suppress ideas – they can "leak out" even through small or economically minor media outlets.[67]

This view of civic discourse leads directly to a rather remarkable conclusion: the size of the audience does not matter. As their expert put it, "In short, the audience of a media outlet is unrelated to the outlet's significance in the marketplace of ideas."[68] The media companies have put forward a remarkably simple strategy for hiding the extremely concentrated condition of media markets; they tell the FCC to simply ignore it. [69]

Obviously, if you are a prime time programming giant that reaches into tens of millions of homes each night seeking to eliminate regulations that prevent you from growing larger, it is convenient to claim you have no more significance than the web site of the local astronomical society,[70] which gets a handful of hits a month. It may be convenient, but it does not make much sense. Yet, that is exactly how the network broadcasters recommend the FCC analyze media markets. The ability of a citizen to whisper a counter argument over the backyard fence is equal to the powerful electronic media that broadcast the owner's point of view to millions of viewers.

The media owners' utter disdain for the First Amendment policy repeatedly enacted by the Congress and supported by the courts is evident in their rejection of the policy to promote localism in the media. As their leading expert puts it, "Why should the government seek to promote local content as opposed to, and especially at the expense of, any other category of ideas?"[71]

Congress has long recognized that local decisions like school board elections, policing, zoning, refuse collection, and fire and rescue deeply affect the quality of life and need to be aired in the media to have an informed democratic debate. Congressional elections are also local affairs that receive little detailed attention in the national media. The empirical evidence indicates that their concern that national media will neglect local issues is well grounded. The national chains may not like the policy of promoting localism, but it has a sound basis in social reality and law.

The role of the FCC is further restricted in the industry view by insisting that the economic impact on consumers should be the sole focal point of analysis, not the impact on the citizen's freedom of speech.

> Whether ownership concentration poses harm to competition or to consumers is precisely the question on which the Commission should focus, and it is exactly the question upon which the antitrust laws and their enforcers focus.[72]

In the narrow economic view, the importance of ownership disappears since, "it is the tastes and demands of audiences, not the wishes of broadcasters that determine the extent of content diversity in a competitive marketplace."[73] The empirical evidence simply does not support this view. Not only do owners actively take points of view on key issues, but economic processes drive them to under serve and undervalue preference minorities.

Moreover, since the role of citizens and civic discourse are read out of the Communications Act by the broadcasters, we should not be surprised to find that the distinction between entertainment and news and information is eliminated.

> [T]he commission's sometime preoccupation with news and public affairs, as distinct from entertainment programming... makes even less sense than localism. First, broadcast news is entertainment – it has to be, at least in part, in order to attract audiences that can be sold to advertisers.[74]

In this view of the world, the commercial purposes of the broadcasters overwhelm the role of the media in civic discourse. People cannot possibly watch television to become informed. They can only watch it to be entertained. If the Commission accepts this view of its First Amendment charge under the Communications Act, it should not be surprised to find that it has no role since "it will duplicate the work of the Antitrust Division, which would be a waste of public resources."[75] Although entertainment certainly can contribute to civic discourse and it certainly shapes social and cultural values, news and information provide the critical inputs for public decision making about key public policy issues.

The twisted logic of the broadcast networks stands economic analysis on its head. Rather than count the audience or market share of each firm, they simply equate all outlets, regardless of the disparity in the reach or audience. Proper economic analysis counts these sources according to their market share.

The extreme position of the networks leads them to another absurd conclusion. For example, they say that any web site that "could plausibly offer content specific to the Milwaukee DMA"[76] counts just as much as the most powerful broadcast station. A cursory glance at the Internet web sites the broadcasters list would no doubt show that the content was not "specific" to Milwaukee. Further, over half of the web sites on the list are, in fact, the web sites of local media outlets. Being the same owners, they bring little new to the table. Virtually all of the remainder is highly specialized, with little capacity or inclination to produce general news and information. None have the ability to announce events with the broad impact of the electronic media.

In their analysis, the network broadcasters equate WTMC, the NBC affiliate in Milwaukee that leads the broadcast market, to the following web sites: Milwaukee Aquarium Society, Milwaukee Astronomical Society, and the Milwaukee Curling Club. Interestingly, Journal Communications, which owns WTMC, the number one TV station, also owns the Milwaukee Journal, the largest newspaper in the Milwaukee DMA, and two of the top radio stations in the Milwaukee area. The failure to recognize any difference between huge media conglomerates and minuscule web sites defies common sense, is inconsistent with economic analysis, and has no basis in media jurisprudence.

This approach to the analysis of market structure in the marketplace of ideas certainly suits the interests of owners of the high-rated prime time shows, but it is simply not a realistic view of the role and function of broadcast TV in contemporary society. One need only observe the behaviors of political candidates to recognize that all media outlets are not equal in democratic discourse. Candidates spend huge sums of resources on TV advertising, which consumes the vast majority of their campaign budgets.

PUBLIC OPINION ABOUT THE MEDIA

Fortunately, it is not only the courts and congress that reject the narrow economic view of the electronic mass media; the public does too (see Figure I-3). Although the FCC Chairman and the head of the Mass Media Bureau have expressed their disdain for public input on important policy issues,[77] as reexamination of the rules governing media ownership and the flow of information over communications networks plays out, it is critical that policy makers recognize that the public has a vision for democratic mass media and advanced communications networks that is much more consumer and citizen friendly than the apparent view of the Chairman and the majority at the FCC. The hundreds of thousands of cards and letters sent to the Commission by concerned citizens indicate a great deal of public interest in preserving ownership limits.[78] Public opinion surveys over the past several years demonstrate that the public's view of media concentration and digital communication networks stands in sharp contrast to the narrow view being pushed by the industry and the Chairman of the Federal Communications Commission.

Ironically, the Lou Dobbs *Moneyline* show on CNN ran an online poll asking whether "too few corporations own too many media outlets?" Ninety-eight percent said yes.[79] Hearst, one of the publishers seeking relaxation of the rules, conducted a poll that asked whether the current rules should be modified.[80] The respondents voted almost seven to one in favor of keeping the rules. The paper cautioned that the sample might not be representative, which is true of the Lou Dobbs poll as well. Scientific samples yield similar results.

- In contrast to recent FCC proposals that express little concern about increasing concentration in the media and telecommunications industries, the public is troubled by the growing concentration of the media.
- In contrast to FCC Chairman Powell, who has expressed skepticism over the usefulness of the public interest standard mentioned 112

FIGURE I-3: The Public Opposes Greater Media Concentration and Supports Public Interest Obligations on Broadcasters

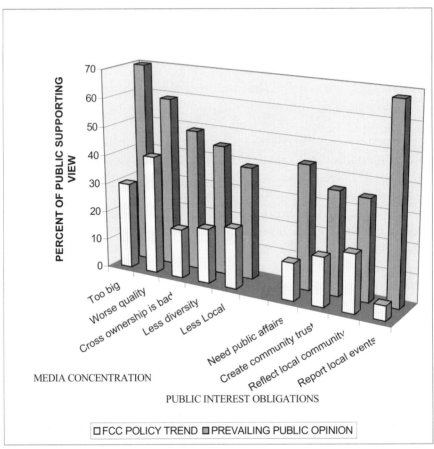

Sources: Digital Media Forum Survey Findings on Media Mergers and Internet Open Access, September 13, 2000. Consumer Federation of America, Media Policy Goals Survey, September 2002; Mergers and Deregulation on the Information Superhighway: The Public Takes a Dim View: Results of a National Opinion Poll (Consumer Federation of America and Center for Digital Democracy September 1995); Project on Media Ownership, People for Better TV, Findings of a National Survey, Lake Snell Perry & Associates, May 1999. Percentages may not sum to 100 due to rounding and the fact that "Don't Know" responses are not included in the Figure.

times in the Communications Act, the public expresses strong support for public interest obligations for both television and the Internet.

Across a range of questions, public concern over growing media concentration appears to have increased since the mid-1990s when the passage of the Telecommunications Act of 1996 deregulated media and triggered a wave of mergers.[81] By a wide margin (70% vs. 30%), survey respondents believe that media companies are becoming too large. This concern reflects their belief that mergers between media companies do not lead to better content and services (58% vs. 41%). They believe that mergers result in higher, not lower, prices (50% vs. 12%) and worse, not better, quality (36% vs. 14%). Consequently, they think it should be harder, rather than easier, for media mergers to be approved (55% vs. 32%). They are strongly opposed to very large mergers, like the AT&T/Comcast merger (66% vs. 12%).

The public also opposes mergers across media types, such as between broadcast stations and newspapers. Asked whether such mergers would be good or bad for their communities, respondents felt it would be bad by a three to one margin (49% to 17%). Asked whether such mergers would be good or bad for the country, their negative reaction was even stronger. Between 55 and 75 percent of respondents said mergers would be bad, compared to fewer than 15 percent who said mergers would be good. These cross-media mergers are a source of concern because respondents felt there would be less, not more, diversity of editorial points of view (43% vs. 18%) and that diversity of points of view in covering local news would decrease, not increase (39% vs. 21%).

Concern about the impact of mergers on the quality and content of programming reflects a deeply seated concern among consumers. They do not feel that television accurately represents the average consumer (60% vs. 28%). Almost one half (47%) does not trust the information they find in the news. Another Lou Dobbs *Moneyline* poll a few days later found that 45 percent of the respondents were skeptical of the media, 42 percent were mad as hell about its performance, and only ten percent thought the media did a good job.

Respondents deem it important that shows reflect the cultural and ethnic make-up of the community (very important = 35%, somewhat important = 42%, not important at all = 23%). Similarly, they deem it important to have public affairs programs that discuss local issues (very important = 43%, somewhat important = 43%, not important at all = 13%).

They find it very important (68% = very, 25% = somewhat) that local news and events are reported.

The public supports a range of public interest obligations. Almost two-thirds of respondents believe that broadcasters will just maximize profits if not directed to air public interest programming (63%). Substantial majorities of respondents believe broadcasters should provide public service programming and services. For example, approximately 70 percent of respondents say broadcasters should be required to provide more educational programming, and that figure rises to 85 percent when the new digital spectrum can be used for this purpose. The public supports a community trust fund to support public programs (very important = 36%, somewhat important = 43%; not important at all = 17%).

The support for community-oriented activities with respect to television has transferred to the new communications media – the Internet. Respondents express support for public interest obligations extending to the Internet. They would like some sections of the Internet to be commercial free (82%) and protected from commercial development (77%). They believe some of the space on the Internet should be devoted to public forums (72%) and non-profit groups (68%). They believe service providers should give free advertising to charities (65%) and regularly post public service announcements (59%).

Thus, the Supreme Court's bold aspiration for a more diverse media is shared by the public, as is the recognition that the media should bear public interest obligations. This is as far from a toaster with pictures as one could get.

II. MEDIA ECONOMICS AND DEMOCRATIC DISCOURSE

The previous legal discussion sets out the public policy issues by emphasizing the ways in which civic discourse transcends mere economics. This section takes the argument one step farther. It demonstrates why economic characteristics of mass media production result in "market failure." Even if a marketplace of ideas were all we wanted, the commercial mass media would not produce it. In other words, the problem is not that 'good' economics makes for 'bad' civic discourse. In fact, vigorous, atomistic competition is generally considered supportive of democracy. The problem is that the structural tendencies of media markets make for 'bad' economics, which reinforces the tendency of failure in the forum for democratic discourse.

THE TYRANNY OF THE MAJORITY IN THE MASS MEDIA

Competition, Democracy and the Shortcomings of Mass Media

Vigorously competitive markets are not antithetical to democratic processes. Indeed, economists stress that there are political reasons to prefer atomistically competitive markets. F. Michael Scherer and David Ross, among the most prominent analysts of industrial organization, note that analysis should begin with the political implications of economic institutions.[82] Specifically, they ask, "Why is a competitive market system held in such high esteem by statesmen and economists alike? Why is competition the ideal in a market economy, and what is wrong with monopoly?" They provide a series of answers, starting from the decentralized, objective processes that typify atomistically competitive markets and check the power of large entities.

> One of the most important arguments is that the atomistic structure of buyers and sellers required for competition decentralizes and disperses power. The resource allocation and income distribution problem is solved through the almost mechanical interaction of supply and demand forces on the market, and not through the conscious exercise of power held in private hands (for example, under monopoly) or government hands (that is, under state enterprise or government

33

regulation). Limiting the power of both government bodies and private individuals to make decisions that shape people's lives and fortunes was a fundamental goal of the men who wrote the U.S. Constitution.[83]

Other economic characteristics of atomistically competitive markets that converge with democratic principles are the autonomy and freedom of entry that such markets imply.

> A closely related benefit is the fact that competitive market processes solve the economic problem *impersonally,* and not through the personal control of entrepreneurs and bureaucrats...

> [Another] political merit of a competitive market is its freedom of opportunity. When the no-barriers-to-entry condition of perfect competition is satisfied, individuals are free to choose whatever trade or profession they prefer, limited only by their own talent and skill and by their ability to raise the (presumably modest) amount of capital required.[84]

Thus, atomistic competition promotes individualistic, impersonal decisions with freedom of opportunity and relatively low resource requirements for entry. These are ideal for populist forms of democracy.[85] Lawrence Lessig points out that at the time of the framing of the Constitution the press had a very atomistic character.

> The "press" in 1791 was not the *New York Times* or the *Wall Street Journal.* It did not comprise large organizations of private interests, with millions of readers associated with each organization. Rather, the press then was much like the Internet today. The cost of a printing press was low, the readership was slight, and anyone (within reason) could become a publisher – and in fact an extraordinary number did.[86]

The problem in contemporary mass media markets is that they have moved quite far from the competitive form of organization. In fact, the pursuit of efficiency through economies of scale and network effects has pushed many contemporary industries toward oligopoly or monopoly. This is a source of concern and requires constant vigilance in all commercial markets. Efficiency that results from large economies of scale also leads toward small numbers of competitors and can degenerate into inefficient abuse of monopoly power.[87] In media markets, where the impact reverberates so powerfully in the forum for democratic discourse, these tendencies must be prevented from distorting civic discourse.

An Economic Theory of Discrimination

It has long been recognized that the technologies and cost structure of commercial mass media production in the 20th century are not conducive to vigorous, atomistic competition. Print and broadcast media have unique economic characteristics.[88] To the extent that economics is a consideration, economic competition in commercial mass media markets cannot assure diversity and antagonism.[89]

The conceptual underpinnings of the argument are well known to media market analysts.[90] On the supply-side, media markets exhibit high first copy costs or high fixed costs.[91] On the demand-side, media market products are in some important respects non-substitutable or exhibit strong group-specific preferences.[92]

The "welfare" effect of these characteristics is to cause the market to fail to meet the information needs of some groups in society. This results because groups express strong preferences for specific types of programming or content. Programming that is targeted at whites is not highly substitutable for programming that is targeted at blacks, from the point of view of blacks. If fixed costs and group preferences are strong, producers must decide at whom to target their content. Given the profit maximizing incentive to recover the high costs from the larger audience, they target the majority. The minority is less well served.

Figure II-1 demonstrates the strong differences between blacks and whites in their preferences for programming. Similarly, preferences differ sharply across groups defined by gender, age, race and ethnicity (Hispanic). The Figure shows the ranking among whites and blacks of the top ten shows viewed by whites, the top ten shows viewed by blacks, and the six news shows ranked in the top twenty among whites. In all, we have 25 shows, fifteen that are highly ranked among whites and fourteen that are highly ranked among blacks. There is little overlap between the two groups.

The easiest way to appreciate the difference is to note that nine of the top ten ranked shows among blacks do not even rank in the top fifty among whites. The most popular fifteen shows among whites have an average ranking of 57 among blacks. The top ten shows among blacks have an average ranking of 85 among whites. The difference in preference for the popular news shows is similar. The average ranking for the six news shows analyzed among whites was fourteen; among blacks it was 53.

FIGURE II-1: Most Popular TV Shows Differ Between White And Black Audiences

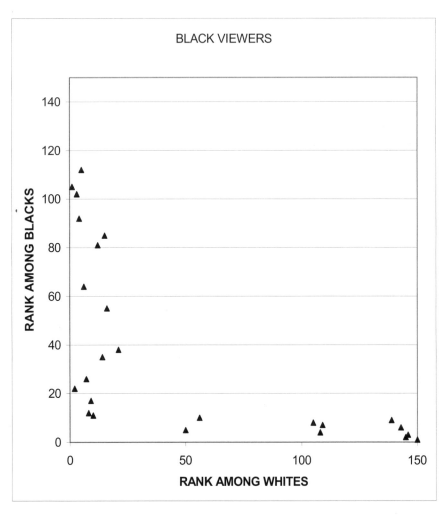

Source: Goldberg, Bernard, *Bias* (Washington, D.C.: Regnery, 2002), pp. 150, 155.

The tendency to under serve minority points of view springs in part from the role of advertising in the media.[93] Advertising as a determinant of demand introduces a substantial disconnection between what consumers want and what the market produces. First, to a significant extent, because advertisers account for such a large share of the revenue of the mass media, the market produces what advertisers want as much as, if not more than, what consumers want. Second, because advertising in particular, and the media in general, revolves around influencing people's choices, there is a sense in which the industry creates its own demand.[94] The tendency to avoid controversy and seek a lowest common denominator is augmented by the presence of advertisers, expressing their preferences in the market.[95]

As articulated and empirically demonstrated by Joel Waldfogel, this might be termed an economic theory of discrimination "because it gives a non-discriminatory reason why markets will deliver fewer products – and, one might infer, lower utility – to 'preference minorities,' small groups of individuals with atypical preferences."[96] Discrimination results not from biases or psychological factors, but from impersonal economic processes.

> A consumer with atypical tastes will face less product variety than one with common tastes…. The market delivers fewer products – and less associated satisfaction – to these groups simply because they are small. This phenomenon can arise even if radio firms are national and entirely non-discriminatory.

> The fundamental conditions needed to produce compartmentalized preference externalities are large fixed costs and preferences that differ sharply across groups of consumers. These conditions are likely to hold, to greater or lesser extents, in a variety of media markets – newspapers, magazines, television, and movies.[97]

This poses a fundamental challenge to the validity of the assumption that markets allocate resources efficiently.

> Friedman has eloquently argued that markets avoid the tyrannies of the majority endemic to allocation through collective choice. Mounting evidence that minority consumer welfare depends on local minority population in local media markets indicates that, for this industry at least, the difference between market and collective choice allocation is a matter of degree, not kind. It is important to understand the relationship between market demographic composition and the targeting of programming content because related research documents a relationship between the presence of black-targeted media and the tendency for blacks to vote.[98]

Figure II-2 shows graphically how the tyranny of the majority works in media markets. When there are large fixed costs, a limited ability to cover the market and strong differences in preference for programming, profit maximizers serve the core audience and neglect small preference

FIGURE II-2: Conceptualizing The Tyranny of the Majority in Media Markets

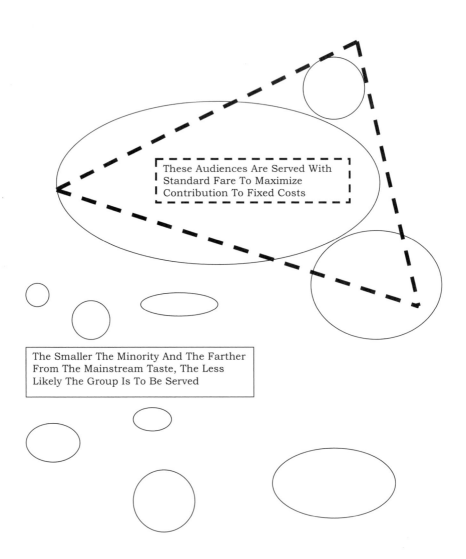

These Audiences Are Served With Standard Fare To Maximize Contribution To Fixed Costs

The Smaller The Minority And The Farther From The Mainstream Taste, The Less Likely The Group Is To Be Served

minorities. The larger the minority group and the closer its taste to the majority, the more likely it is to be served.

The tyranny of the majority in media markets is linked to the tyranny of the majority in politics because the media are the means of political communication.

We present evidence that electoral competition leads candidates to propose policies that are supported by proportionately larger groups and that members of these groups are more likely to turn out if they find the proposed policies more appealing. In addition, we show that candidates find it easier to direct campaign efforts at larger groups because many existing media outlets cater to this audience…

Channels of communication that are used to disseminate political information rarely exist for the sole purpose of informing potential voters. The number of channels that candidates have at their disposal reflects the cost structure of printing newspapers, establishing radio stations, and founding political groups. To the extent that these activities carry fixed costs, channels that cater to small groups are less likely to exist. The welfare implications – if one views the decision to vote as the decision to "consume" an election — are analogous to those of differentiated markets with fixed costs.[99]

The Impact of Market Failure on Civic Discourse

The impact of market failure is felt in three areas: owner influence, loss of local perspective, and erosion of checks and balances and other positive externalities of vigorous civic discourse.

Baker presents a lengthy discussion of the political implications of the monopolistic media market. The first point is that it results in market power, traditionally measured as monopoly profits.[100] For media markets, however, economic profits can be used (dissipated) in another important way. Media monopolists can use their market power to influence content or policy directly.

The weak competition that results from the first copy/non-substitutability characteristics allows owners to earn monopoly profits and to use monopoly rents to pursue their personal agendas. The claim that ownership of the media does not matter to the selection and presentation of content is not plausible.[101] Whatever their political preferences, media owners are in a uniquely powerful position to influence civic discourse. They can use both the economic resources made available by their market power (as can monopolists in any industry) and the unique role of the media to pursue those preferences.

Nevertheless, within this type of competition, products' uniqueness or monopoly status often permits considerable margin for variation while still remaining profitable. The "potential" profit of the profit maximizing strategy can be realized and taken out as profit – which is what the corporate newspaper chains are accused of doing. However, the market itself does not require the profit maximizing response as it does in models of pure competition. Rather, the potential profit can instead be spent on indulging (or "subsidizing") the owners' choices about content or price.[102]

One set of behaviors that is particularly problematic involves undemocratic uses of media market power in pursuit of the private interests of owners through manipulation, co-optation and censorious behaviors.[103] This can undermine the watchdog role of the press or distort coverage of events, when it suits their interests. The chilling effect need not be conscious or overt. Powerful media owners tend to be very visible figures in their political and policy preferences. Employees and institutions instinctively toe the line and self-censor out of an instinct for self-preservation, which dampens antagonism in the media.[104]

Even though this is not Waldfogel's central concern, when he looks at the question of ownership, he finds support for the view that ownership matters beyond "simple" economics. Waldfogel finds in his study of radio markets that "black owners enter in situations that white owners avoid."[105] He continues to consider possible explanations for this behavior and offers a hypothesis that relies on owner preferences,

> A second possibility is that black owners enter for "ideological" reasons, which means they are willing to forego some profits in order to provide a particular sort of programming. This hypothesis would rationalize the observation that black-owned and targeted stations have fewer listeners, on average, that [sic] their white-owned counterparts (in markets with both white and black-owned, black-targeted stations). Black owners' willingness to accept smaller returns could explain why greater black ownership increases black-targeted programming: additional black owners are willing to enter low-profitability market niches (programming to small black audiences) that whites would not enter.[106]

Perhaps Waldfogel puts the word "ideology" in quotes to blunt its negative connotation. Baker presents the policy implications in terms that are familiar and relevant to the arena of diversity policy in civic discourse.

> Choice, not merely market forces, influences quality. Choice explains the variation both within and between ownership categories. Moreover, quality may provide some efficiencies and management qualities that sometimes increase the enterprise's potential for profits or quality. However, the incentives for executives (editors and publishers) in chain

firms as well as the added pressures of public ownership are likely to be directed toward focusing on increasing profits. Possibly due to price of membership or involvement within a community that leads to dedication or desires to form status in that community, local ownership might be sociologically predicted to lead to greater commitment to and greater choice to serve values other than the bottom line.[107]

Baker argues that the experiences of civic discourse for minorities and the public at large are deeply affected by ownership. Large, monopolistic structures make it more difficult for opinion leaders within minority or niche communities to gain experience in the industry.

> [A] *complex democracy* may benefit society as a whole… And a complex democracy may require media entities that not only provide particular content but that are experienced as being owned, or at least controlled, by different groups or by people who identify as and are identified by others as being members of or having allegiances to particular groups. If so, the ownership pattern called for by this democratic theory would have significant positive externalities, but an antitrust analysis would remain blind to the costs of any merger that undermines this distribution.[108]

Baker links the need to have policies that promote viewpoint diversity to the tendency of the commercial media to under serve the less powerful in society.[109] In order for the media to meet the needs of these groups, it must inform and mobilize them.

> [P]luralist democracy hopes to generate fair bargains as a result of groups' pressing their interests. In this process, the media should perform several tasks. First, the press should provide individuals and organized groups with information that indicates when their interests are at stake. Second, the media should help mobilize people to participate and promote their divergent interests… Third, for pluralist democracy to work, information about popular demands must flow properly - that is, given the practical gap between citizens and policy makers, the press should make policy makers aware of the content and strength of people's demands.[110]

That these needs have traditionally been centered in localism is understandable. The primary referent for identity and community has traditionally been and remains significantly local.[111] The link between localism and de-concentration of the media seems obvious. Changes in electronic media distribution technologies have not significantly altered this fundamental relationship.[112] Waldfogel finds important localism effects operating in the media that support this view. He finds that the preference externality operates in non-prime time programming because it is subject to greater local control and therefore can be more responsive to local market conditions.[113] Concentration of national and local markets into national chains reinforces the tendencies of media owners to ignore local needs.[114]

Left unrestrained, the marketplace will produce fewer watchdog activities conducted by less rigorous institutions. The public at large benefits from the watchdog function beyond the value that individual media firms can capture in their market transactions (advertising revenue and viewer payments). Baker uses investigative journalism as an example. Abuses are less likely to be uncovered and more likely to occur because the deterrent of the threat of exposure will be diminished.[116]

> One item both news entities "sell" is expose's on the content of investigative journalism. Not just the readers or listeners but all members of the community benefit from whatever reform or better government or improved corporate behavior that occurs due to these stories. This journalism can create huge positive externalities. The paper's limited number of purchasers cannot be expected to pay the full value of this benefit - they have no reason to pay for the value received by non-readers. Even more (economically) troubling, a major benefit of the existence of news organizations that engage in relatively effective investigative journalism is that this journalism deters wrong doing by governmental or corporate actors - but deterred behavior produces no story for the journalism to report and hence for the media entity to sell. The paper has no opportunity to internalize these benefits of its journalism - an economic explanation for there being less of this type of journalism than a straight welfare economics analysis justifies.[115]

The positive externalities that Baker identifies with respect to the watchdog and experiential functions are part of a larger category of externalities associated with information products, particularly civic discourse content. Information products, to a significant degree, are seen as possessing attributes of public goods. Sunstein makes this broader point in regard to television.

> Even if broadcasters did provide each viewer with what he or she wanted, a significant problem would remain, and from the economic point of view, this is probably the most serious of all. Information is a public good, and once one person knows something (about for example, product hazards, asthma, official misconduct, poverty, welfare reform, or abuse of power), the benefits of that knowledge will probably accrue to others.[117]

Note that two of the central issues mentioned by Sunstein are positive externalities in the political arena on which Baker's analysis is centrally focused: official misconduct and abuse of power. These are but two of many externalities of information production.[118]

The central fact that all of these discussions share is that market forces provide neither adequate incentives to produce the high quality media product, nor adequate incentives to distribute sufficient amounts of diverse content necessary to meet consumer and citizen needs. Sunstein states the general proposition as follows:

> Individual choices by individual viewers are highly likely to produce too little public interest programming in light of the fact that the benefits of viewing such programming are not fully "internalized" by individual viewers. Thus, individually rational decisions may inflict costs on others at the same time that they fail to confer benefits on others. In this respect, the problem "is not that people choose unwisely as individuals, but that the collective consequences of their choices often turn out to be very different from what they desire or anticipate."[119]

To most media analysts in our democracy, institutions play a critical role in mediating between individuals and the political process. Some draw the link between the institution and the investigative role.

> Democratic governance requires a free press not just in the sense of a diversity of expression. It requires the *institution* of a free press. It requires media with the financial wherewithal and political independence to engage in sustained investigative journalism, to expose the errors and excesses of government and other powerful political and economic actors...

> Our best hope for democratic governance in this world is far messier than the ideal republic of yeomen. It requires mediating institutions and associations, private and public concentrations of wealth and power, and varied mechanisms to maintain multiple balances of power within government, within civil society, and between government and civil society.[120]

> One of the central benefits of promoting deconcentrated and diverse media markets is to provide a self-checking function on the media. The media needs to be accountable to the public, but that function cannot, as a general matter, be provided by government action in our political system. It can best be provided by the media itself, as long as there is vigorous antagonism between sources of news and information.[121]

Baker finds that one function of structural policy is to promote institutions that have different structures[122] and are driven by different institutional imperatives.

> Finally, the market does not measure preferences for nor produce sufficient amounts of noncommodified media products. Thus, it is likely (but not certain) that self-conscious people would favor rules or subsidies that tilt production toward more diverse noncommodified media...

> Thus, media policy should favor structural rules that allocate or encourage the allocation of decision-making control over content creation to people with commitments to quality rather than merely to the bottom line (e.g., the content creators themselves or decentralized control by people involved in the media enterprise). This goal, for example, supports a drastic revitalization of antitrust enforcement in the media area, with the policy being guided by First Amendment concerns that go beyond traditional market analyses. It also supports the following: the long-standing FCC policy of favoring license grants for applicants whose principals live in the community or, even better, whose principals are themselves involved in management; tax policies that favor family ownership rather than sale to conglomerate interests; labor laws that favor a stronger editorial voice for media workers; business organization laws that favor media ownership by workers or non-profit organizations; and access rules or provision of communications facilities (e.g., public-access channels) that provide greater opportunities to communicate for individuals and noncommercial entities.[123]

OWNERSHIP MATTERS

The empirical evidence available in the academic and trade literatures overwhelmingly supports the concerns expressed about the emergence of a hyper-commercialized, concentrated mass media. Commercialism can easily overwhelm public interest and diverse content.[124] Concentration drains resources from journalistic enterprises.[125] Empirical evidence clearly suggests that concentration in media markets– fewer independent owners — has a negative effect on diversity.[126] The evidence to support this conclusion includes both annecdotal examples and statistical studies. The economic interests of media owners influence their advertising, programming choices, and how they provide access to political information.[127]

Conglomerates are driven by advertisers, who exercise influence over content.[128] Dangerous abuse of this influence ranges from favorable newspaper reviews of a broadcaster's programming[129] or loss of coverage,[130] to positive editorials/opinion articles about the business interests of a broadcaster or politician.[131] Such favoritism would be more difficult to prevent if cross-ownership were broadly permitted.[132] When the two largest sources of news and information – television and newspaper – come under the same ownership roof, there is special cause for concern about business pressures that could undermine the forum for democratic discourse.[133]

Bias-Bashing Among the Most Prominent American Journalistic Icons

The "biases" of owners are frequently known, as a flap about Rupert Murdoch's news operations at Fox television attests. The close political connection between Fox's Roger Ailes and the Republican Party was underscored by his admission that he had sent a public policy memo to the Bush Administration.[134] The response from Fox to these "charges" explained in a 2002 best seller by Bernard Goldberg says mountains about the slanting of TV news and commentary across the board.

> This is how Roger Ailes… explained it in a *New York Times Magazine* piece in June 2001: "There are more conservatives *on* Fox. But we are *not* a conservative network. That disparity says far more about the competition." In other words, if Fox is alleged to have a conservative bias, that's only because there are so few conservative voices on the air at ABC, CBS, NBC, CNN and MSNBC. There certainly *is* a conservative "attitude" at Fox, a conservative sensibility. [135]

Goldberg ends his discussion of bias in the TV media, which begins with and focuses on an op-ed piece about liberal bias in the TV media he had published in the *Wall Street Journal,* with a discussion of bias in the print media in a second op-ed on the editorial pages of the *Wall Street Journal.*

> Consider this: In 1996 after I wrote about liberal bias on this very page, Dan [Rather] was furious and during a phone conversation he indicated that picking the *Wall Street Journal* to air my views was especially appalling given the conservative views of the paper's editorial page. "What do you consider the *New York Times*?" I asked him, since he had written op-eds for that paper. "Middle of the road," he said.
>
> I couldn't believe he was serious. The *Times* is a newspaper that has taken the liberal side of every important social issue of our time, which

is fine with me. But if you see the *New York Times* editorial page as middle of the road, one thing is clear: You don't have a clue.[136]

There are many who would debate the "liberal" bias of the *New York Times*, but it is clear that there is little love lost between the *New York Times* and Mr. Ailes and his supporters. Within a week of the revelation of Mr. Ailes' memo to the White House, the *New York Times* chastised Ailes in an editorial, pointing out that giving advice to the President

> would be fine, were Mr. Ailes still in the business of advising political candidates, but as a top executive of a news organization he should know better than to offer private counsel to Mr. Bush.

> Mr. Ailes' action seems especially hypocritical for someone who has spent years trumpeting the fairness of Fox and the partisanship of just about everybody in the news business. Fox's promotional slogan is: "We report, you decide." But the news channel has a Republican tilt and a conservative agenda.[137]

In fact, Paul Krugman (certainly a Democrat, if not a liberal) writing in the *New York Times*, repeated Al Gore's complaint that the "liberal media" had gone very conservative.

> This week Al Gore said the obvious. "The media is kind of weird these days on politics," he told The New York Observer, "and there are some major institutional voices that are, truthfully speaking, part and parcel of the Republican Party.

> The reaction from most journalists in the "liberal Media" was embarrassed silence. I don't quite understand why, but there are some things that you're not supposed to say, precisely because they are so clearly true.[138]

Michael Kelly, a conservative columnist, could not let the Gore/Krugman complaint pass without comment.[139] He cites about a dozen "major surveys on the political beliefs and voting patterns of mainstream print and broadcast journalists" from 1962 to 2001, which show about a three-to-one ratio (46 to 15) of liberals to conservatives. He answers the rhetorical question, "Does a (still) largely liberal news media (still) exhibit a largely liberal bias?" with a resounding "Sure."[140] He cites S. Robert Lichter, president of the independent Center for Media and Public Affairs, who observes that,

> [J]ournalists tell the truth – but like everyone else, they tell the truth *as they see it*. Even the most conscientious journalists cannot overcome the subjectivity inherent in their profession, which is expressed through such everyday decisions as whether a topic or source is trustworthy.

The important and unavoidable lesson is that editorial preferences are deeply embedded in commercial mass media not only on the editorial pages, but also on the news pages. In a sense, this is the essence of the concept of antagonism. Rather than claim that many outlets owned by a single entity will present a neutral, objective, or balanced picture, public policy should recognize that diversity and antagonism of viewpoints comes from diversity of ownership. Indeed, Lichter entered the fray with a letter to the editor pointing out,

> In some cases, the coverage of social and political issues clearly coincides with the perspectives of journalists. But such correspondence is not guaranteed, and it cannot be reliably predicted to operate in particular instances.[141]

Systematic Evidence on Systematic Bias

The demonstration of owner and editorial bias is not only qualitative or anecdotal. An article from the June 2002 *American Political Science Review* makes it clear that ownership (embodied in the editorial position of the outlet) matters in reporting the news.[142]

> One of the essential elements of an impartial press in the United States is the "wall of separation" between the editorial pages and the pages devoted to the news. While the political beliefs of newspaper owners and editors are clearly articulated on opinion pages, their views are not supposed to infiltrate the reporting of the news. The analysis presented in this paper raises questions about this claim. We examine newspaper coverage of more than 60 Senatorial campaigns across three election years and find that information on news pages is slanted in favor of the candidates endorsed on the newspaper's editorial pages. We find that the coverage of incumbent Senators is most affected by the newspaper's endorsement. We explore the consequences of "slanted" news coverage by showing that voters evaluate endorsed candidates more favorably than candidates who fail to secure an editorial endorsement. The impact of the endorsement decision on voters' evaluations is most powerful in races receiving a great deal of press attention and among citizens who read their local newspapers on a daily basis.[143]

Systematic studies of coverage of local issues found that "objectivity violations in all 20 stories were classified as serving the self-interest of the news organization or its parent corporation."[144] National issues reveal that the interests of the owners influence reporting and editorial position.

A study by James Snider and Benjamin Page looked at the decision to allow TV stations to have additional digital spectrum without paying for it, while other parts of the spectrum were being auctioned for other commercial uses.[145] The editorial positions of media corporations that owned newspapers and had significant TV station ownership (at least 20% of revenues from that source) were compared to the editorial stands on the spectrum give-away/auction issue of newspapers owned by companies having little or no TV station ownership. The findings were striking:

> The results on editorials are very strong and highly significant [statistically]; in fact, among newspapers that editorialized on the subject, every one whose owners got little TV revenue editorialized against the spectrum 'giveaway,' whereas every one with high TV revenues editorialized in favor of giving broadcasters free use of spectrum.[146]

The dynamics of the newsroom relationships between editors and reporters create a tendency to produce stories that are unbalanced.

> While partisan balance may have existed over the course of the entire coverage, individual stories were seldom balanced. In fact, the viewer had only a one in four chance of seeing an approximately balanced story, while 40 percent of the time the viewer was likely to see a story that was structurally imbalanced in every measured way. But this research also indicates that this would vary depending on the station and the day the viewer was watching.[147]

Even if consolidated ownership presents a variety of entertainment, it invariably creates a risk of slant, bias, or tilt in presenting critical issues at crucial moments in time. While a precise prediction of how bias might operate may not be possible, the tendency is clear; it is much more likely to operate in the owner's interest.[148]

Direct Financial Interests Affects Coverage

Coverage of the 1996 Telecommunications Act, or lack thereof, leads to a similar conclusion. An analysis of the networks' coverage was conducted by Dean Alger using the Vanderbilt TV News Archive to assess how the three prime network news shows covered the Telecom Act of 1996 – as a whole, not just the spectrum give-away issue – as it went through the congressional process.[149] The analysis found that ABC, CBS and NBC network news combined devoted only 19.5 minutes to the Telecom Act during the entire nine months it was in the process (early

May 1995-early February 1996); most of that was focused on the v-chip and the "Internet Decency Act" side issues. Most crucially and tellingly, there was essentially no meaningful coverage of the elimination or reduction of ownership limits and the probable consequences of such actions for more concentrated control of mass media, nor was there meaningful attention given to the give-away of the extra spectrum for transition to digital, high-definition TV.[150]

Another example is the city of Milwaukee, which has been described as an example of cross-ownership leading to model behavior. A closer examination reveals anything but model behavior, this time involving a publicly financed sports stadium project. Journal Broadcast Corporation operates the *Milwaukee Journal Sentinel* as well as WTMJ-TV, WTMJ-AM and WKTI-FM in Milwaukee. All are leaders in their service area. In comments to the FCC, the Journal noted that "the radio and television stations have been totally independent from the newspaper in both program and editorial content," and that the outlets have been critical of each other.[151] At a key moment, on an issue of great public importance, which directly involved the private interests of the company, that appears not to have been the case.

There was a move for public financing of a new stadium for the area's major league baseball team, the Brewers. The Journal Group's AM radio station has the contract for broadcasting Brewers' games. In late 1994, the CEO of the Journal Group, Robert Kahlor, became head of the Milwaukee committee championing public financing for the stadium, and even registered as chief lobbyist. This was a much-debated issue. Indeed, when it came to a vote in the state Senate (in fall 1995) it was decided by one vote. How did the *Journal Sentinel* media cover this big, contentious issue?

"The Journal Company's newspaper, TV-news shows, and news-talk radio station all marched in lock-step supporting the public financing position."[152] In the case of the newspaper, that avid support appeared from the news pages to sports page columns to editorials. The other two TV stations in Milwaukee, while not such avid boosters, generally reported on the public financing position in a positive fashion. Thus, the citizens of Milwaukee, despite the contentious nature of the issue, did not have antagonistic voices in the main media to rely on. The dominant news outlet, the metro paper, had a financial interest in getting the stadium built, which directed its coverage.

A veteran local media analyst, who had also been a journalism professor for years (David Beckman), noted, "this case is a classic example of how a media monolith defeats the purposes of free and open debate"[153] in the main media that people rely on and which dominate the public arena, overwhelmingly defining the public discourse. No coincidence, say local critics, that WTMJ stations also carry Brewers games. "All four Journal media lost almost all objectivity."[154]

Another case of a sports team and cross-ownership is telling but with different details. The *Dispatch*'s Wolff family is part owners of the Columbus, Ohio pro-hockey team. Besides the usual boosterism coverage of the team connected by ownership to the media outlet (that is now too common), there were proposals to build a new hockey stadium. The overt outcome of this was different from the Milwaukee case. Public financing proposals lost twice in ballot measures. The Wolff family and an insurance company financed the building of the stadium itself. But, since then, the city has given land, easements, clean-up, infrastructure and other assistance subsidized to the tune of "at least $80 million,"[155] which the alternative weekly (*The Other Paper*) has documented in what coverage they could muster. Had a family that owned the TV station received such subsidies in a city with an independently-owned newspaper, the investigative juices of the paper's reporters and editors would have been flowing; front page coverage would have been produced from the one local mass medium that has the resources for in-depth investigation. *The Dispatch* has not, however, covered this huge subsidy. Instead, it was a cheerleader for the team and the stadium. Once again, a case of a cross-owned newspaper and TV station failed the local democratic process.

Note also that the *Dispatch* editorialized in favor of the Telecom Act, saying "The telecommunications bill passed by the senate ... is a worthwhile effort at getting government out of the way and letting the affected companies freely reshape their industries."[156] The benefit to the *Dispatch*/Wolff family's TV station was not mentioned.

TENSION BETWEEN COMMERCIALISM AND CIVIC DISCOURSE IS CLEAR

Happy News at the Lowest Cost

The pressures on commercial mass media to produce high volumes of "happy" or sensationalized news with the fewest number of reporters to support the interests of advertisers or to attract viewers is well documented.[157] As a result, the existence of multiple outlets providing more examples of similar shows does not accomplish the goal of providing greater diversity of points of view.[158]

For Fox, which appears to be following a strategy that emphasizes duopolies,[159] the implications are obvious –

> News staffs at both WWOR-TV and KCOP (TV) were told that there are no plans for changes, consolidations or cancellations at present, although some economies of scale seem obvious. "We don't have to have two news crews at one event," says a Fox executive.[160]

Other Fox duopolies exhibit a similar pattern,

> "[a]ll departments at the station have been consolidated, all under prior KTTV station leadership... The station's newscast was switched in June from an hour at 10 p.m. to a half-hour at 11, to avoid direct competition with KTTV and allow KCOP an hour syndicated-sitcom block at 10.[161]

The problem is compounded by the important role of advertisers in commercial mass media as seen in the results of a "survey of 118 news directors around the country, conducted between June and August 2001 [that] represents a significant proportion of the approximately 850 stations that broadcast news." The survey found that "[i]t is 'getting harder every year' to maintain the wall between sales and news"[162] as pressure builds from owners to produce profits, which undermines quality, and from sponsors to slant the news.

> To meet profit demands, many news directors report they are having to produce thinner and cheaper product by adding news programs while cutting their budgets....
>
> [M]ore than half, 53 percent, reported that advertisers pressure them to kill negative stories or run positive ones...
>
> News directors also reported their TV consultants (outside companies hired by stations to critique newscasts and improve ratings) issuing blanket edicts about what to cover and what not to cover in order to attract the most advertising dollars.
>
> Together the findings and comments raise questions about the journalistic independence of local television news.
>
> Breaking down the sponsor suggestions more specifically, 47 percent of news directors this year said sponsors tried to get them to provide favorable coverage.

And 18 percent of news directors – almost one-in-five – say sponsors try to prevent them from covering stories, a problem that is more acute in smaller markets.[163]

Minority Communities and Unpopular Points of View are Under served

The failure of commercial mass media to meet the needs of citizens is nowhere more evident than in minority communities. Waldfogel has presented strong evidence of a kind of a tyranny of the majority in a number of media markets. These findings have been reinforced by recent findings of other scholars, as a 2002 article in the *Journal of Broadcasting and Electronic Media* makes clear.[164]

> The analyses presented here represent the next step forward in determining the extent to which advertiser valuations of minority audiences affect the viability of minority-owned and minority-targeted media outlets. The results conform to those of previous studies, which found that minority audiences are more difficult to monetize than non-minority audiences…[165]

> Minority-targeted media content suffers from not only the potentially lower valuations of minority audiences but also from the fact that, by definition, it appeals to a small audience. Smaller audiences mean small revenues, particularly when the audience is not highly valued by advertisers…[166]

> Moreover, lower levels of audience size and value both exert downward pressures on the production budgets of minority content, which further undermines the ability of such content to compete and remain viable… The differential in production budgets may be enough for some minority audience members to find the majority content more appealing than the content targeted at their particular interest and concerns. Such defections further undermine the viability of minority-targeted content… The end result is lower levels of availability of minority-targeted content.

A long tradition of more qualitative research also supports the conclusion that minority market segments are less well served.[167] Greater concentration results in less diversity of ownership, and diversity of ownership – across geographic, ethnic and gender lines – is correlated with diversity of programming.[168] Simply, minority owners are more likely to present minority points of view[169] just as females are more likely to present a female point of view[170] in the speakers, formats and content they put forward.

Concentration and Consolidation of the Media Undermines Localism

The important role of the media in informing citizens about local affairs is well documented.[171] Localism suffers a fate similar to diversity at the hands of national chains.[172] It is well documented that the dictates of mass audiences create a largest market share/lowest common denominator ethic that undercuts the ability to deliver culturally diverse programming,[173] locally-oriented programming,[174] and public interest programming.[175] News and public affairs programming are particularly vulnerable to these economic pressures.[176] As market forces grow, these types of programming are reduced.[177] Unfortunately, the coverage that disappears tends to deal with schools, localized government affairs, and other community-strengthening material that enables people to live more secure and educated lives.[178]

Waldfogel's findings on localism, derived from the basic economics of the media, cut across each of the major products.

> The local data indicate, to a greater extent than the national prime time or cable data, both the distance between black and white preferences and the fact that local programming, far more than national programming, caters to those preferences.[179]

While the economics of television give rise to strong concerns about localism,[180] Waldfogel sees indications of similar localism effects in newspaper markets as well, supporting the conclusion that "content origin matters."[181] He describes localism's effect on behavior in the preliminary findings of a study on the entry of a national newspaper into local markets as follows:

> How does national news media affect local news sources and local political participation?
>
> Preliminary results- Increased circulation of national daily affects:
>
> Local paper circulation – reduced targeted audience readership
>
> Local paper positioning – toward local content
>
> Local political participation – reduces voting, less so in presidential years.[182]

A recent study of television news provides powerful evidence of this problem noting that "overall the data strongly suggest regulatory changes that encourage heavy concentration of ownership in local television by a few large corporations will erode the quality of news Americans receive." Among the findings:

> Smaller station groups overall tended to produce higher quality newscasts than stations owned by larger companies — by a significant margin.
>
> Network affiliated stations tended to produce higher quality newscasts than network owned and operated stations — also by a large margin.
>
> Stations with cross-ownership — in which the parent company also owns a newspaper in the same market — tended to produce higher quality newscasts.
>
> Local ownership offered some protection against newscasts being very poor, but did not encourage superior quality.[183]

The growing impact of homogenization in the TV industry, stimulated by the lifting of national ownership limits and restrictions on vertical integration into programming, is also unmistakable.[185] Insertion of local programming is restricted or eliminated. Stories of local importance are driven out of the high visibility hours or off the air.[186] Pooled news services reduce the ability of local stations to present local stories and eventually erode the capability to produce them. The radio industry, which has been subject to the most unfettered process of "rationalization," demonstrates how local content can be homogenized off the air.[184] Below are two examples.

> Radio: "A Giant Radio Chain Perfecting the Art of Seeming Local,"
>
> "In the studio with Evan and Jaron," Mr. Alan began. "How are you guys doing?"
>
> The artists reported that they had just come from skiing at nearby Sun Valley, then praised the local scene ... "Yeah, we've got some good people here." Later, he asked Boise fans to e-mail or call the station with questions for the performers.
>
> But even the most ardent fan never got through to the brothers that day. The singers had actually done the interview in San Diego a few weeks earlier. Mr. Alan himself had never been to Boise, though he offers a flurry of local touches on the show he hosts every weekday from 10 a.m. to 3 p. m. on the city's leading pop station.[187]

"The Trouble With Corporate Radio: The Day the Protest Music Died"

Senator Byron Dorgan, Democrat of North Dakota, had a potential disaster in his district when a freight train carrying anhydrous ammonia derailed, releasing a deadly cloud over the city of Minot. When the emergency alert system failed, the police called the town radio stations, six of which are owned by the corporate giant Clear Channel. According to news accounts, no one answered the phone at the stations for more than an hour and a half.[188]

THE MASS MEDIA ARE CRITICAL TO POLITICAL PROCESSES

Agenda Setting and Influencing Public Opinion

The fact that owners and editors influence coverage is important because mass media influence the agenda of public policy issues and the public's perception of those issues. Consider a Spring 2002 article from the *Journalism and Mass Communications Quarterly*.[189]

This study examined the attribute agenda-setting function of the media, which refers to significant correspondence between prominent issue attributes in the media and the agenda of attributes among audiences. An opinion survey on a local issue and a content analysis of a local newspaper revealed that, by covering certain issue aspects more prominently, the media increase the salience of those aspects among audience members. We also found an important outcome of attribute agenda setting, attribute-priming effects. Findings indicate that issue attributes salient in the media are functioning as a significant dimension of issue evaluation among audience members. This study concluded that the media, by emphasizing certain attributes of an issue, tell us "how to think about" this issue as well as "what to think about."[190]

Does the agenda setting and influence of perception take place during election campaigns on important issues? An article in the *American Political Science Review* in 2002 finds evidence to support this effect in one of the most enduring issues in America, race.[191]

Recent evidence shows that elites can capitalize on preexisting linkages between issues and social groups to alter the criteria citizens use to make political decisions.[192] In particular, studies have shown that subtle race cues in campaign communications may activate racial attitudes, thereby altering the foundations of mass political decision making... Results show that a wide range of race cues can prime racial attitudes and that cognitive accessibility mediates the effect.[193]

While race may be a particularly prominent case of influence over attitudes and agenda-setting, the media plays a powerful role across a broad range of issues.[194]

> Historically, the press has played two crucial roles during elections. First, it has been a conduit of information between citizens and candidates. Indeed, most of what citizens know about candidates comes from the news media....[195]

> Second, the press structures the discourse of political campaigns by emphasizing certain topics over others.[196]

Diversity Is Critical to Supporting Democratic Discourse

As the importance of mass media, particularly TV advertising and news coverage, is affirmed, one may wonder whether diversity is still important to democracy. Diversity promotes democracy by exposing citizens to a broader range of views, as emphasized by Sunstein. Does the mass media play a critical role in promoting this cross-cutting exposure? Recent articles in the *American Political Science Review* give affirmative answers to these questions.[197]

> Exposure to conflicting political viewpoints is widely assumed to benefit the citizens of a democratic polity... Drawing on national survey data that tap characteristics of people's political discussion networks, I examine the impact of heterogeneous networks of political discussion on individuals' awareness of legitimate rationales for oppositional viewpoints, on their awareness of rationales for their owner viewpoints, and on levels of political tolerance... [and] utilizing a laboratory experiment manipulating exposure to dissonant and consonant political views, I further substantiate the causal role of cross-cutting exposure in fostering political tolerance.[198]

> Furthermore, counter-stereotypic cues – especially those implying blacks are deserving of government resources – dampen racial priming suggesting that the meaning drawn from the visual/narrative pairing in an advertisement, and not simply the presence of black images, triggers the effect.[199]

Recent evidence supports the more complex concept of democratic discourse, since mere exposure to information is reinforced by interpersonal communication.[200]

> The key role commonly attributed to interpersonal discussion in democratic societies, of course, stems from its direct impact on various forms of participatory behavior. More important, however, this study

shows that interpersonal discussion plays a role in the reception and processing of political news when it comes to translating mass-mediated messages into meaningful individual action. Consequently, people who are frequent hard news users are significantly more likely to engage in various forms of political action if they talk these issues through with others that are frequent news users who talk to others less often.[201]

DIFFERENT ROLES OF DIFFERENT MEDIA

People use different media in different ways to meet different needs. They spend vastly different amounts of time in different media environments, consume services under different circumstances, and pay for them in different ways. In economic terms, these are separate markets with weak substitution effects. They have different content offered by different means and they differ widely in their impact and effect. The various media are based on different business models and address different advertising markets. As a result, competition between the media is muted in the marketplace and the specialization of each is worth preserving because of the unique functions provided in the forum for democratic discourse.

Identifying Media Functions

The two dominant political media – daily newspapers and television – appear to play very different roles. TV, which is, by far, the leading political advertising vehicle, has a special influence on political discourse,[202] through its influence on political attitudes and behaviors[203] and its prominent place in election campaigns. Television and radio have long been recognized as occupying different product spaces[204] although radio's role may be changing[205] and shrinking in importance.[206] Broadcast does not compete effectively with newspapers in the news function.[207]

TV in general, network TV in particular, has become the premier vehicle for political advertising. The differential impact of television advertising is clear.

> Clearly, television is a unique communications medium unlike any other, including print, radio, and traditional public address. Unlike most other media, television incorporates a significant nonverbal component, which not only serves to suppress the importance of content but also requires little deliberative message processing...

A number of empirical studies have concluded that reliance on information from television leads to less understanding of policy issues than newspapers. Studies also indicate that when people use television for political news, they emerge less informed than those of equal education and political interest who avoid the medium.[208]

Newspapers provide a distinct role. Newspapers devote greater attention to local news and provide a distinct role through broad, deep coverage and investigative reporting.[209] They provide a different type of information service with different impact. In this they have adapted to a role that is distinct from television.

> The news business itself reflects the partitioning in its awards… Pulitzer prizes have been added for criticism, features, and explanatory writing, because those are the aspects of news left for print excellence in television's wake… For while television editorializing can be intelligent and eloquent, and even promote political change, the star treatment accorded to television news personalities removes them from the civic discourse.[210]

Print journalists often assert an allegiance to their almost century-old creed:

> I believe in the profession of journalism. I believe that the public journal is a public trust; that all connected with it are, to the full measure of their responsibility, trustees for the public; that acceptance of lesser service than the public service is a betrayal of this trust.[211]

Television Plays the Central Media Role in Civic Discourse

TV serves a crucial role in providing information. Research attention now focuses on how campaigns affect and are affected by public opinion.[212]

> [V]oters do learn about candidates and their position on issues (policy) from candidate advertising. Research from three presidential campaigns demonstrates that citizens obtain more information from television spots than from the news.[213]

> Television has become society's primary source of information, and local television news is more likely to be used by viewers than national news broadcasts. Therefore, how such election news is relayed on local television is increasingly important in our political system.[214]

> The impact of television is pervasive throughout all elections.[215]

> Presidential elections are unquestionably the main event in American politics…[216] Candidates and campaign consultants believe that

television advertising is pivotal to winning a state-level campaign...[217] Research confirms that television spots influence election outcomes at all levels.[218]

Visual images are important in *priming* the audience; understanding the mechanisms through which the effect operates is growing, as a 2002 article in *Journalism* discusses.[219]

> Claims by political and news elites about the influence of visual images are far more common than actual evidence of such effects. This research attempts to gain insight into the 'power' of visual images, specifically those that accompany lexical-verbal messages in the press... Findings suggest that visual news images (a) influence people's information processing in ways that can be understood only by taking into account individual's predispositions and values, and (b) at the same time appear to have a particular ability to 'trigger' considerations that spread through one's mental framework to other evaluations.[220]

Television impacts not only news coverage, but also, and perhaps even more importantly, advertising and the interaction between advertising and news, as a 2002 article in *American Politics Research* concludes.[221]

> [T]he author examines whether network news coverage of a campaign advertisement issue can reinforce the ad's basic message for the public and alter individual candidate assessments... Results show that general campaign coverage of race and crime issues... influenced individual ideological perceptions... [T]his influence was limited to certain individuals within the population, namely, media coverage affects individuals with moderate levels of political awareness who have weaker initial predispositions. Combined, these results demonstrate that media can exert both significantly and substantively significant influence on the public.[222]

Certainly the huge amounts spent on TV advertising by candidates attests to its importance.[223] The audience that is most susceptible to advertising and news coverage by this account is precisely the audience on which general elections focus – the undecided middle – thereby justifying the spending.[224] Whereas candidates must focus on the committed, active party base in primaries, they must shift their attention to the less aware, less committed middle of the political spectrum to get elected.[225]

Conclusion

Old Theories that No Longer Apply

The FCC presents two theories that argue concentration of the media is good for consumers: Peter Steiner's[226] argument that concentrated media companies provide greater diversity and Joseph Schumpeter's[227] theory that monopolists produce more innovation. The Commission and industry comments that regurgitate these theories present no economic evidence in support of the arguments. The FCC either misrepresents the original idea, or fails to recognize that the assumptions underlying the theories do not fit the media market reality.[228]

The critical assumption underlying Steiner's theory is a relative homogeneity of taste. The theory may have been true when it was first offered fifty years ago, given the make-up of the population and the demographic characteristics of the audience at whom the media were targeted. The empirical evidence of the past decade shows that strong differences in taste result in preference minorities who are under served and undervalued by the commercial mass media. Moreover, as the population becomes increasingly complex, the role of differences in information needs to grow. Even where it can be shown that mergers allow a beat to be added, we find that upscale entertainment is the focus (mining the favored audience) at the expense of news and information. It is time for the Commission to abandon the theory supporting increased concentration in media markets. It no longer fits the reality of the conditions of civic discourse in America, if indeed, it ever did.

The Commission relies upon the Schumpeterian argument on transitory monopoly power to suggest it should allow or promote concentrated media markets to provide resources for investment. The Commission has completely misinterpreted or misapplied Schumpeter's argument.[229] The FCC seeks to justify market concentration, whereas Schumpeter focused on market size. There is no doubt that the dominant commercial mass media firms are already large enough to possess economies of scale. Concentration that increases market power may undermine Schumpeterian processes because it dulls competition, which was central to his argument.

The monopoly rents earned by the innovative entrepreneur must be transitory, lest they degenerate into plain old antisocial monopoly rents. I have pointed out that media industry moguls look and behave much more like traditional anti-competitive monopolists than innovative Schumpeterian entrepreneurs.[230] The underlying technologies have been relatively stable for decades. Strengthening the hand of entrenched incumbents using off-the-shelf technologies hardly seems the way to promote innovation and creative destruction. The Commission's policies are having the opposite effect.[231] Here, as in the case of the Steiner hypothesis, the Commission has simply failed to accept the empirical facts.

Based upon the empirical evidence, the Commission must abandon the Steiner/Schumpeter justification for concentration and monopoly power in media markets. Whether these two arguments articulated over fifty years ago ever made sense for media markets is debatable, but it is overwhelmingly clear they do not fit the facts of 21st century America.

Empirical Concepts of Media Diversity

The FCC has used a variety of concepts of diversity over the years. Diversity and antagonism in civic discourse are complex. Opponents of policies to promote the goals of enriching civic discourse complain that the imprecision of the outcome makes it difficult, if not impossible, to measure success. I believe this reflects the fact that the goal of having an informed citizenry is inherently qualitative and complex. Most social and psychological relationships have numerous highly intertwined causes; there is no reason that knowledge and participation in public policy formation should be otherwise.

The difficulty of defining outcomes in civic discourse is compounded by another important factor. Public policy cannot and should not try to make people listen and learn. The First Amendment properly leans heavily against dictating the content that is made available. Therefore, we cannot direct people as to what they say or restrict their options as to what they can listen to. Ensuring media structures that make voices more accessible is an indirect approach to promoting the goal of minimizing government intervention into content. As Baker puts it, "[S]tructural interventions refer to rules that allocate (or create) authority or opportunities."[232]

I define the richness of civic discourse in empirical terms to include viewpoint diversity, source diversity and institutional diversity.

Viewpoint diversity focuses on the ownership of outlets. Independent ownership of outlets is critical because outlets that are commonly owned are less likely to provide diverse points of view.

61

Owners have a tendency to impose their preferences and biases on the media they control.[233] They may not do so all of the time or on all issues, but at critical moments, when their interests are at stake, they are more likely to do so. Antagonism in viewpoints is fostered by independence of ownership. The number of independently owned outlets is critical to civic discourse for a variety of reasons. Positive externalities flow from having a larger number of outlets. When media outlets are numerous, they are also more accessible. In addition, independent ownership of outlets should be promoted because ownership influences media organizations' structure and content.[234] Simply put, ownership dictates viewpoint.

When independently owned outlets are numerous, they are more likely to be local, but that is not uniformly so. A large number of nationally owned, independent outlets would not automatically ensure that local points of view would be reflected in the media. The Internet appears to be creating greater availability of national and international information, but not local information. Therefore, recognizing viewpoint diversity, particularly local viewpoints, is a goal of public policy that is distinct from ownership diversity. Concentration is the primary concern that underlies viewpoint diversity.

Although the central focus of structural policy is on viewpoint diversity, which is driven by ownership of outlets, it would be a mistake to neglect the concept of source diversity as an independent factor in the effort to promote and ensure vibrant democratic discourse. After all, the ultimate objective of structural policy is to promote diversity of sources.

The difference between source and viewpoint diversity is the difference between production and distribution. Owners' viewpoints are expressed in the content they choose to deliver to the public through the outlets they control. The outlet owners may produce their own content or buy it from independent producers. The forum for democratic discourse will be better served by a multiplicity of sources producing content that reflects owners' points of view. Structural policy can strive to create an environment that promotes independent production by preventing excessive concentration of ownership of distribution or excessive integration between distribution and production. Several of the proceedings ongoing before the FCC (i.e. the national caps on ownership of broadcast TV stations and cable systems) are driven by a major concern over source diversity. Increasing concentration of ownership of outlets and the tendency of outlet owners to also own production companies are threats to the viability of independent sources of content. Concentration interacts with the problem of consolidation into national chains to cause the concern about source diversity.

Institutional diversity reflects the special expertise and culture of certain media, such as the newspaper tradition of in-depth investigative journalism. Institutional diversity is grounded in the watchdog function.[235] The quality of investigative reporting and the accessibility of different types of institutions to leaders and the public are promoted by institutional diversity. Institutional diversity involves different structures of media presentation (different business models, journalistic culture and tradition) and these institutions often involve different independent owners and viewpoints across media. To promote institutional diversity, like other forms of diversity, the institutions must be independently owned. Yet even in independently owned conglomerates, the journalistic ethic can be overwhelmed. Institutional diversity is impacted by conglomeration. Institutional diversity is also extremely important for the broader public policy issue of noncommercial sources of news.

These three aspects of diversity in civic discourse sharpen the conclusion that variety does not constitute diversity. As demonstrated, the empirical evidence indicates that gains in variety do not compensate for losses in diversity. The media's tendency to under serve minority and atypical groups in addition to ownership's influence over institutional configurations and content demonstrate why the claim that concentration in media markets enhances diversity is wrong, or at best irrelevant. The presumed ability of larger firms to provide a little more variety by covering a new "beat" or offering a hybrid format[236] pales in comparison to the much larger loss of diversity and antagonism when media voices merge.

PART II: QUALITATIVE STUDIES OF MEDIA TRENDS

III. PRINT JOURNALISM

This chapter examines the powerful trends that affect the print media and their impact on democratic discourse and political processes. It begins with important trends that can be observed in the cross ownership situations that currently exist around the country, which were grandfathered when the ban was adopted or have been allowed through waivers. It then examines trends within the print media alone.

THE UNIQUE IMPACT OF NEWSPAPER-TELEVISION MERGERS

I have described a complex relationship between newspapers and TV. On the supply-side, the antagonism between TV and newspapers is an important element of promoting civic discourse. At the same time, the operation of newspaper newsrooms produces many stories, especially local, that become an input for TV news. Without the much more intensive and in-depth news gathering of papers, the news product space will be reduced. On the demand side, we observe that newspapers and television are complements. Consumers seek in-depth follow-up of the news headlines that they encounter in broadcast. We want to preserve the antagonism and independent resources that newspapers bring.

To the extent that FCC regulation of the media subject to its authority has the consequence of deconcentrating the production of local news and preserving the antagonism between the print and broadcast media, it should do so. An avenue of integration that would be particularly destructive of the journalistic values in our society or destructive of the competitive and symbiotic relationship between newspapers and broadcast that disciplines the broadcast media should be a source of serious concern to the Commission.

Thus the Commission can legitimately enquire into the impact on civic discourse of conglomeration, concentration and integration in each of the media. Several recent books about newspapers paint an extremely troubling picture. Many analysts believe that the health of both American journalism and the newspaper industry will depend on their ability to successfully achieve three things: diluting what has become an increasingly over-concentrated marketplace; better managing the balance between providing informative, influential news coverage and sustaining a profitable newspaper; and recommitting ourselves to, as Leonard

Downie, Jr. and Robert G. Kaiser of *The Washington Post* put it, "independent, aggressive journalism [which] strengthens American democracy, improves the lives of its citizens, checks the abuses of powerful people, supports the weakest members of society," and, ultimately, "connects us all to one another."[237] Put more simply by Bartholomew Sparrow, quoting former journalist Harold Evans, "[T]he challenge before the American media 'is not to stay in business – it is to stay in journalism'."[238] My suggestion here is that the challenge for newspapers that are drawn into cross ownership situations in which democracy has an important stake is to stay in print journalism.

I will discuss three direct ways in which removal of the ban on cross-ownership would affect print journalism. There is also the concern that the pattern of conglomeration and cross-media ownership in the newspaper industry and the potential for a substantial increase in these developments will result in a qualitatively new type of problem: the potential for fundamental, institutional conflicts of interest.

> The flurry of debate over media consolidation masks an equally, if not more disturbing trend: the conflict of interest inherent in diversified cross-ownership of newsgathering institutions by multinational concerns. A media market in which *The Washington Post* and *Newsweek* join in "strategic alliances" with NBC, Microsoft Corp. helps underwrite the salaries of reporters for MSNBC, and America Online helps capitalize CNN expands the potential for conflict of interest far beyond the individual to the institutional level. Indeed, the cross-ownership and content sharing that typifies American mass media today raises legitimate questions about whether journalists working on such far-flung conglomerates can avoid conflicts of interest on the institutional level, and about what such conflicts do to the notion of an independent press...
>
> Institutional conflict of interest extends the conflict inherent in a commercial press... beyond the immediate concerns of the journalist or even the news organization for which he or she works.[239]

Pressure From Concentration, Vertical Integration and Conglomeration on Journalistic Values

The prospect of mergers between TV stations and newspapers raises concerns about vertical integration conglomeration and horizontal concentration (see Figure III-1).[240] Such a merger is said to be vertical if the news production output of the newspaper operation would become

FIGURE III-1: NEWSPAPER-TV MERGERS AS A MIX OF CONCENTRATION, VERTICAL INTEGRATION AND CONGLOMERATION

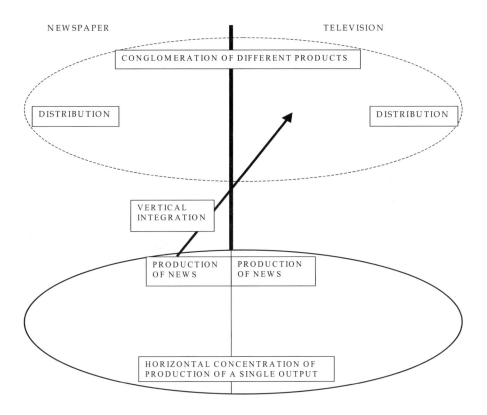

input for the TV distribution activity. It is a conglomerate merger if the new entity spans two separate markets: the print news and the video news market. Both of these changes would have negative effects on the journalistic endeavor of the newspaper.

- The dictates of video delivery would alter the nature of reporting and commitments to investigative journalism.
- The conglomeration in larger enterprises would reduce the journalistic activity to a profit center that is driven by the larger economic goals of the parent.
- Combining the two activities within one entity diminishes the antagonism between print and video media.

The purely horizontal aspect of these mergers also poses a problem. The basic activity of gathering news as an input for distribution is very similar in the print and television media. To the extent large entities control a substantial part of the production of news in an area, these mergers can create market power.

Consider the contrast between journalistic values and the image presented by Tribune Company executives describing how the Chicago Tribune and Chicago television station WGN, among other media properties, view their business:

> Tribune had a story to tell – and it was just the story Wall Street wanted to hear.
>
> In charts and appendices, they showed a company that owns four newspapers – and 16 TV stations (with shared ownership of two others); four radio stations; three local cable news channels; a lucrative educational book division; a producer and syndicator of TV programming, including Geraldo Rivera's daytime talk show; a partnership in the new WB television network; the Chicago Cubs; and new-media investments worth more than $600 million, including a $10 million investment in Baring Communications Equity Fund, with dozens of Asian offices hunting out media investments.
>
> ...There was an internal logic and consistent language to their talk: Tribune, said the four men, was a "content company" with a powerful "brand." Among and between its divisions, there was a "synergy."
>
> ...It was a well-scripted, well-rehearsed performance, thorough and thoroughly upbeat. And the word "journalism" was never uttered, once.
>
> ...Even apart from TV and new media – at the Tribune papers themselves – the editor in chief rarely presides at the daily page one meeting. The editor's gaze is fixed on the future, on new-zoned sections, multimedia desks, meetings with the business side, focus group research on extending the brand, or opening new beachheads in affluent suburbs. "I am not the editor of a newspaper," says Howard Tyner, 54, whose official resume identifies him as vice president and editor of the Chicago Tribune. "I am the manager of a content company. That's what I do. I don't do newspapers alone. We gather content."[241]

In highlighting the Tribune Company, I do not mean to suggest that there is anything wrong with the company's behavior. On the contrary, economic "synergies" may certainly help Tribune improve the quality of its media products. And I do not mean to suggest that other factors, like newspaper consolidation and newspaper ties with other corporate entities, do not also challenge print journalist's ability to follow their creed. However, when the two largest sources of news and information – television and newspaper[242] – come under the same ownership roof, there is special cause for concern about business pressures that could undermine the forum for democratic discourse.

Reducing Antagonism and the Watchdog Role

Except where there is meaningful competition between local newspapers, I believe that lifting the newspaper/broadcast cross-ownership ban would significantly undercut the watchdog role that newspapers play over broadcasters and thereby undermine, particularly in the realm of political speech, Congress' goal of ensuring a vigorous exchange of views.

Industry commenters in FCC proceedings have made an important aspect of the case for us. Their repeated statements that joint ventures are not effective means for capturing economic efficiencies underscore the important role of antagonism. In other words, they claim that independent entities in joint ventures are too difficult to keep in line.

> Tash sees advantages to partnering, including the ability for both companies to maintain separate and independent voices.
>
> "Anything you do ends up being in partners' interest rather than being forced through common ownership," Tash says. "If it's common ownership, you might add up the pluses and minuses and decide it's a net-plus, even if it's a net-minus for one partner. In this relationship, it has to be a net plus for both.
>
> Tash admits that partnerships with other media companies can be tricky. "You can't rely on orders from a common owner to work through issues that arise."[243]

It is exactly that antagonism that the forum for civic discourse needs, but would lose with cross-ownership.

> Down in Tampa, Media General has gone so far as to put its newspaper, the Tribune, in the same building with its local television station and online operation, the better to exchange stories and, ostensibly, resources. (It's still unclear what the newspapers get out of the bargain other than garish weather maps sponsored by the local TV meteorologist.) Tampa's has become the most sophisticated model of this kind of thing, and as such is drawing enormous interest from other newspaper companies.
>
> Under the Tampa model, and presumably in most major city rooms of the future, news decisions for all these outlets are made in a coordinated

way, sometimes in the same meeting. In effect the same group of minds decides what "news" is, in every conceivable way that people can get their local news. This isn't sinister; it's just not competition.[244]

In Tampa, Florida, Media General, Inc. owns both the *Tampa Tribune* newspaper and WFLA-TV. The decision to co-locate the two media outlets led to a loss of editorial and journalistic integrity even before the actual move:

> Others wonder how the cozy, inbred relationship between the newsrooms might affect their coverage of each other. *Tribune* TV writer Walter Belcher offered a chilling example, saying editors forced him to lay off criticism of WFLA for nearly a year prior to the opening of the News Center [which housed the *Tribune* and WFLA news operations in the same space to facilitate their integration], supposedly to avoid ill will between the staffs. "I told them that maybe I should just stop writing about TV altogether," Belcher says with a laugh. "I eventually went back to [covering WFLA] in February, but I still felt like I had to be careful and explain some things more clearly."[245]

Unfortunately, such chilling of free speech in a newsroom is no laughing matter. Nor is it the only example in which Belcher's coverage of WFLA came under scrutiny from joint management. Belcher's coverage was compromised further when managers at WFLA requested that he not write about speculation that a reporter would be leaving the station to follow her husband, a former WFLA reporter who moved to another station in Alabama.

Oddly enough, Media General, in its comments to the Commission, opines that "it is Tampa that to date best illustrates the company's approach to convergence."[246] Given the demonstrable "loss of editorial or journalistic integrity" in Tampa, Media General's showcase example of "the company's approach to convergence" makes a solid case for retaining the newspaper/broadcast cross-ownership rule to prevent the kind of abuses seen in Tampa.

A. H. Belo Corporation (Belo), owner of the *Dallas Morning News* and WFAA-TV, argues in its comments that its joint ownership "has had no noticeable impact on the intense level of diversity and competition in the Dallas/Fort Worth marketplace."[247] That is likely because of Belo's decision that the *Morning News* should cease any TV criticism in order to stay away from critical reporting about its sister station.

> Then there is a question of how the *Morning News* would cover the station. Because the two share Belo as a parent, the newspaper has often been criticized as being too soft on its sibling. But now that the

two were officially partners, the News decided it could no longer cover WFAA objectively. Rather than exclude the one station from its coverage, the *News* halted all TV criticism.[248]

Not only was the *Morning News*'s coverage of WFAA-TV stifled because of the co-ownership, an important media critic for the entire market was also lost. If joint corporate ownership of a newspaper and television station can lead to coverage being dropped to maintain positive internal relations, what other types of coverage could be jettisoned to protect corporate interests?

Consolidating News Production

The driving force behind the push for cross ownership demonstrates that the supply of news involves the production of a single product. A substantial part of the economies that are sought is driven by a desire to use reporters in both activities, to repurpose or repackage their output. It is the reporter producing copy that is the central activity of both TV and newspaper newsrooms. On the supply side it starts as one product.

Media giants like Gannett Co.,[249] Times Mirror Co.,[250] and Hearst[251] that are pushing hard for cross-ownership would find another vehicle to consolidate dailies and weeklies and to slash staffs and pages. Now the TV station would be pulled into this process. In the interest of monopolizing a region or cutting costs, the newspaper Goliaths ignore the needs of the local people – intense, focused coverage of local schools, community activities, and community concerns such as crime and local development.

Tampa again provides a case in point. There is no doubt that the economic goal is to combine the production of news. Economic convergence just needs to overcome the cultural and professional differences that characterize the newsrooms. As a key player in the most vigorous effort to create convergence put it "The single greatest challenge we have is to overcome our [work] cultural differences.[252]

Those pushing convergence from the newspaper side are even more adamant about ridding the operation of the journalistic ethic.

> "An ongoing concern is how to integrate the entrepreneur into a traditional culture," Thelen [the Tampa Tribune's executive editor and vice chairman] says. "This will be a challenge for the company to adjust to. We want to place a high value on experimental risk taking, rather than on the tried and true journalism story."[253]

Reporters caught in the convergence frenzy clearly bristle under the heavy-handed efforts to merge the media.

> But Kathleen Gallagher, a Milwaukee Journal Sentinel investment writer, who often does live 45-second interviews from the newsroom, finds the TV piece "disconcerting." [TV anchors] spend all this time thinking about their product and how they present themselves, and you're interrupting the writing of your story to do [the interview] quickly.[254]

> "The last newspaper story I wrote, I wrote on my own time," says veteran WFLA reporter Lance Williams. "But the fun part of it is there are no restrictions on my story. It is hard to write a minute and thirty-second story. But writing for the newspaper is freeing.

> "My brain was mush by the end," says Barron, who normally runs WFLA's Sarasota bureau. "There were times when I sat down to write a script for TV and would start putting in attribution like it was a newspaper story."[255]

> With a 110,000-daily-circulation lead over the competition, Brown says the *Times* still beats the *Tribune* with basic, hard-core journalism. "I think [convergence] creates a serious distraction, potentially, in how they cover the news," he says. "There is a risk of dilution."[256]

> However, whatever happens, the Tampa convergence experience raises at least two concerns. If journalists spend time contributing to each other's media, when will they have time to gather the news? And more important, will similar media convergence mean that fewer voices produce the news or perhaps, some voices will be lost.[257]

The problem is not limited to Tampa or Milwaukee. Lewis Friedland outlines several processes that have starved local news reporting of resources and cautions that

> To allow further linkages between these two, already powerful movements towards concentration would further damage the already fragile environments of local news.

> What would be the almost certain, immediate effect of allowing newspaper-television cross ownership? The most obvious effect would be a constriction of the supply of local news and a concomitant restriction in the supply of local news sources.[258]

While the general impact of triggering a merger trend will have negative impacts on journalistic values, it is important to note that there are ways in which combinations pose special threats to the preservation of journalistic principles. While mergers tend to starve the journalistic values of the enterprise of resources, in the drive to produce profits for the merged entity, the multitasking[259] and cross selling[260] that typifies combination mergers pose a special threat. They are intended specifically to homogenize the media.

Moreover, because professional lines are breached, it is quite problematic to define activities and preserve professional ethics.

> The alliance between the *Chicago Tribune* and Tribune-owned WGN channel 9 led the American Federation of Television and Radio Artists (AFTRA) to file a grievance against the station after a WGN reporter (an AFTRA member) was asked to write for the newspaper without additional compensation. "I think that with the consolidation of the media, it's a real danger," says Eileen Willenborg, executive director of AFTRA's Chicago chapter. She raises another issue as well. 'You can't spread professionals so thin and still have a professional product." *Tribune* executives declined comment.[261]

> As staff began to work more closely, they discovered a disparity in the pay levels between television reporters and newspaper reporters. Religion writer Bearden used to get extra pay for filing TV stories in addition to her newspaper stories. With convergence, the extra pay will dry up. *Tribune* managers say they know they will have to address the pay issue if newspaper staffers routinely appear on television.

> And then there is the issue of workload. Reporters and photojournalists worry the marriage will mean more work without more money.[262]

> Along with concerns about journalistic quality and time management comes the question of compensation of reporters who perform crossover work, as well as redefining job descriptions and hiring rules for incoming reporters. So far, no staffers have received extra pay for going beyond their regular workload, and many say they would like to see the issue settled before convergence becomes more routine.[263]

These pressures and problems emerge in all mergers. They are heightened because the "fear is that corporate bean counters see convergence simply as a way to 'thin the herd' of reporters rather than using the huge reporting teams fielded by papers to greatly broaden the scope of broadcast stories."[264]

TRENDS WITHIN PRINT JOURNALISM

This section argues that the FCC must consider the qualitative impact of removal of the newspaper-TV cross ownership ban for direct and indirect reasons. The FCC's broadcast licensing authority is the launch pad for ownership policies. However, it does not regulate the print media in any way. Yet, even though the FCC has no direct authority over newspapers, the wave of newspaper conglomeration and concentration into national chains is relevant to the estimation of the impact of the relaxation of ownership restrictions in several indirect ways. The economic "logic" of pursuing profits through conglomeration, concentration and national integration is potent, but the Commission's job is to consider the impact of those economic trends on the quality of civic discourse. It cannot pay homage to pure economics but ignore the end point to which reliance on pure economics will drive civic discourse.

At the simplest and most general level, the extent to which newspapers have experienced the trends more in the past may be an indication of what will happen in other media. Indeed, given the developments in radio during the rapid acceleration of integration of stations into national chains unleashed by the 1996 Telecommunications Act, the general impact of these trends on civic discourse seems clear and should be a major source of concern to the Commission.

Concentration Eliminates Diversity

In *Taking Stock,* Gilbert Cranberg, Randall Bezanson and John Soloski argue that if any one thing is to blame for the deterioration of American newspapers it is the over-concentration of the marketplace.[265] The efforts of the large newspaper corporations to monopolize regions and their respective voices has lead to an entirely profit-driven business model that has in turn de-prioritized product quality and debilitated most news operations' ability to fully serve a free press.[266] Companies like Gannett and Knight Ridder, two of seventeen dominant chains, have taken control of dozens of newspapers, buying out hundreds of competitors, and reducing citizens' access to probing, helpful information that is vital to daily life. Many of the public companies have begun to seek advantages from grouping papers into dominant metropolitan and regional chains and then combining many aspects of the news operations, sharing news among all of the nominally separate papers. This is a strategy of vertical integration through control over content.[267]

This has an immediate and negative impact on any given local news consumer, for he is fed a generic dose of coverage that does not likely inform him of what is going on in his neighborhood. In Wisconsin, for instance, Gannett purchased Thompson's central holdings (eight dailies and six weeklies) to add to the two it already owned there, effectively monopolizing the area.[268] Suddenly, thousands of subscribers lost their essential local coverage.

Similar cases can be found all over the country.[269] CNHI bought eight Thompson dailies in Indiana, adding to the four it already owned there. CNHI and Gannett now account for 40% of Indiana's daily circulation. The consequences of this are clear: fewer voices and perspectives are provided and the ability of the people to "make judgments on the issues of the time," something central to the American Society of Newspaper Editors' *Statement of Purpose*, is hindered.[270]

The statistics at this point are staggering. Chains own 80 percent of America's newspapers and the aforementioned content-sharing has become one of our biggest hurdles.[271] In the Southeast, Knight Ridder shares content between three of its papers, *The Charlotte Observer*, *The State* (Columbia, SC) and *The Sun News* (Myrtle Beach, SC), which are at least one hundred miles away from each other and span two states. The likelihood of coverage being pertinent to individual readers in districts this far apart is virtually nil. In Baltimore, Times Mirror Co. bought a Patuxent chain of thirteen weeklies in the Baltimore suburbs even though it owns *The Baltimore Sun*. If any of those thirteen weeklies were offering opposing viewpoints to the *Baltimore Sun*, the purchase cut citizens' access to this competing dialogue. In monopolizing these mini-marketplaces of ideas, the newspaper corporations demonstrate that they are not committed to upholding their position as *the* "broadly democratic and broadly representative source of information in our democratic society."[272]

Family operated papers are also being swallowed up by the corporate papers who toss fists full of money at them.[273] In Hartford, Times Mirror Co. bought *The Hartford Advocate*, a weekly created for the sole purpose of competing with the Times Mirror-owned *Hartford Courant*, the dominant daily.[274] In Montana, Lee Enterprises bought *The Hungry Horse Tribune* and *The Whitefish Pilot* and began running identical editorials as if the two communities had the same concerns.[275] In Westchester County, NY, Gannett combined ten papers it owned and created one, *The Journal News*, sacrificing successful, respected papers such as *The Tarrytown Daily News*.[276]

Profit at the Expense of Journalism

The frightening reality of this corporate expansion is that these companies, over the past few decades, have shown a declining interest in journalism and an overwhelming interest in profit-maximizing business practices. This 'business over news' attitude has countless drawbacks that have manifested themselves in various forms at hundreds of now-weakened newspapers.

Before identifying the specific ills, it is important to understand the corporate structures and mandates that have undermined America's newspapers' goals. Cranberg, Bezanson and Soloski note that "news has become secondary, even incidental, to markets and revenues and margins and advertisers and consumer preferences."[277] This list of motivating factors sums up where the newspaper chains' allegiances lie. This is due, in large part, to the make-up of the corporate boards that run the newspaper companies. "They draw heavily from industry, finance and law for outside directors."[278] *Taking Stock* research indicates that "of the 131 outside directors on the boards of the 17 dominant chains, only 17 (13 percent) have had experience on the editorial side of a news organization."[279] Furthermore, seven companies "have *no* outside directors with a newspaper background" and "a half-dozen only have one."[280] Without dedicated newspaper people involved in the highest level of management, the publicly owned (and traded) newspaper becomes a stock market entity like any other, and the product, news, becomes an expendable commodity that is "altered to fit tastes" and used to drive shareholder value up, without regard for journalistic integrity.[281]

While *Taking Stock* does concede that "some editors may still dominate corporate conversations about what constitutes news and how to deploy news gatherers," it cautions that "most no longer make such determinations singly or without elaborately justifying the effects on the bottom line."[282] In surveying CEOs of some of these companies, they find a common commitment to shareholders and stock value, not news and readers. William Burleigh of Scripps Howard points to a "suitable return" as his obligation, while Robert Jelenic of Journal Register Co. says his "mandate from the board is to produce longtime shareholder value."[283] The simple omission of news and readers as motivation speaks on how these papers are run, assembled and presented to the public – as money-making machines that subvert their "primary purpose of gathering and distributing news and opinion [in order] to serve the general welfare."[284]

Unfortunately, the fallout is felt across the country. Editors at papers big and small describe the stress caused by major newspaper corporations bearing down on their news operations, enforcing a bottom line principle, and, ultimately, infringing on their editorial role and the newspaper's output. *Taking Stock* cites an editor survey in which ninety percent of editors interviewed affirmed that they felt pressure from the bottom line, many adding that they felt "resignation" and "resentment" because of this pressure.[285] Geneva Overholser, former editor of *The Des Moines Register*, conducted a study for the American Journalism Review and found that "ownership by public corporations has fundamentally and permanently transformed the role of editor," noting that of the seventy-seven editors surveyed, "half of them said they spent a third or more of their time on "matters other than news."[286] *The News About the News* explains that editors who once "spent their days working with reporters…now spend more of their time in meetings with the paper's business-side executives, plotting marketing strategies or cost-cutting campaigns."[287]

The result of the 'business over news' attitude has been the deterioration of the American newspaper. *The Philadelphia Inquirer*, for example, became one of the nation's strongest papers while Gene Roberts was its editor. When Knight Ridder bought the daily, it began slashing staff and putting tremendous pressure on Roberts to increase profits. Roberts soon had enough of the corporate newspaper model and retired with the *Inquirer's* daily circulation at 520,000 and its Sunday circulation at 978,000. Eleven years later, the paper's circulation had plummeted to 365,000 daily and 732,000 Sunday.[288] Surprisingly, Knight Ridder's profit margins rose an astonishing 16 percent (to just under 20 percent) during that time, epitomizing what has become an industry trend: "publicly traded newspaper companies have seen significant growth in their cash flow, despite modest growth in revenues."[289] Hence, although subscription rates are dropping because the quality of the papers is dropping, the chains are still profiting.

In order to accomplish this, the major corporations often hire analysts to determine how much of their newsroom staff and resources they can cut. At *The Winston-Salem Journal* in North Carolina, a newspaper owned by Richmond's Media General, a consulting firm (DeWolff, Boberg & Associates) was brought in to analyze how efficiently the paper's staff was operating. After making the reporters keep "precise diaries on how they spent their time over three weeks, DeWolff, Boberg produced a "grid" describing how much time various journalistic endeavors should take.[290] Based on the placement of a story within the paper, the analysis suggested how much time should be spent working the story (down to the tenth of an hour), whether or not a press release should be used, how many and which types of sources should be used and, of course, how long the story should be. It took three months for the editors to convince the owners that "creative work like journalism cannot be governed by such arbitrary formulas."[291] Nonetheless, Media General laid off twenty percent of its workforce by the time DeWolff, Boberg had completed their consultation.

Knight Ridder had a similar outlook for the *San Jose Mercury News* whose publisher, Jay T. Harris, revealed that "the drive for ever-increasing profits [was] pulling quality down." What eventually drove Harris away from the paper were Knight Ridder's demands that the paper reach "a specific profit margin, an exact percentage figure" that would give them a suitable return. Harris could no longer stomach Knight Ridder's lack of regard for the paper's journalistic responsibilities and left.[292]

Instances of staff cutting by corporate companies have piled up over the past two decades. When Gannett bought *The Asbury Park Press* (boosting its and Newhouse's combined share of New Jersey's circulation to a whopping 73 percent) it immediately liquidated a fourth of the newsroom staff, from 240 people to 185.[293] Next, the news hole was reduced, bleeding out niche local coverage that was vital to a highly subdivided area with many townships and districts. The *Press* had trained itself to adequately serve its varied readership, setting up localized bureaus and printing five zoned editions. Gannett swiftly dropped the *Press* to four zoned editions and in a final swipe at the newsroom staff, the chain increased workloads and took away overtime pay.

The *Press* is one of hundreds of papers wrestling with these new terms of competition, terms that "have little or nothing to do with news quality."[294] MediaNews acquired the *Long Beach Press-Telegram* and immediately cut 128 jobs. Knight Ridder acquired the *Monterey County Herald* and dropped 28 employees on day one. The Journal Register Co. bought the *Times-Herald* (Norristown, PA) and subsequently fired 25 people. Their op-ed page was dropped, the mayor stopped subscribing and within one year the paper was completely detached from Norristown's immediate needs. Time and again, economic pressures have swelled, undermining "traditional journalistic standards and values" and proving that "there is no obvious way to simultaneously shrink a newspaper and make it better."[295]

Happy News

The corporate paper takeovers of the past two decades have also resulted in the 'softening' of news to appease advertisers who want buoyant, happy readers perusing their ads. Avoiding content that some advertisers find boring (mainly government, especially state and local government) or unlikely to give readers the zest they need to buy, has become commonplace as the papers remove hard news sections to add "reader-friendly" content, as Gannett calls it. Their aforementioned *Asbury Park Press* reporters were told that "there will be no bad news in the "Day in the Life stories," and "no aggressive reporting or attempts to expose problems or wrongdoing."[296] Gannett's *Courier-Journal* in Rockford, Illinois was criticized in an evaluation by former editor Mark Silverman for emphasizing "hard-news subjects" and suggested the paper consider "more how-to stories, stories that show how a person or a group of people accomplished something, question-and-answer columns, 'ask the experts' call-in hot lines, and even first-person stories by readers."[297] These are examples of the "prevailing ethos" at Gannett and other corporate newspaper companies – soft news is easy and inexpensive to cover; it is devoid of controversy and is therefore safe; and, most importantly, it makes advertisers happy.

The dilemma here is not that the chain-owned newspapers are adding content. That, in theory, is a good thing. But, in order to make room under the shrunken budgets, other content has to be cut, and it almost always comes out of the hard-news bin. This means that Gannett can easily and profitably remove hard-news reporters at the *Asbury Park Press*, load up on AP story releases, shrink hard-news story length, and add low-cost sections like "Whatever," a teen beat section, and "Critters," a pet section which includes pet obituaries that cost readers at least 50 and sometimes 300 dollars to print.[298] To compensate, the chains do a significant amount of the cutting in the state government bureaus. In 1998, "only 513 reporters" nationwide were covering all state governments full-time. *Breach of Faith* points out that, disturbingly, over 3000 media credentials were issued for that year's Super Bowl.[299]

The corporate departure from state government coverage has come with little or no regard for journalistic integrity or the benefits the public receives from this coverage. Bureaus at hundreds of papers across the country have been slashed. The *Journal-Constitution*, in Atlanta, used to house one of the most prolific state government bureaus in the nation, boasting twelve esteemed reporters. When Cox bought the paper, it was left with three statehouse reporters. Shortly thereafter, the *Journal-Constitution* had slanted, one-sided coverage that did not have the resources to inform itself adequately and, in turn, inform the public sufficiently. When the reporter crunch received bad press, Cox doubled its number of statehouse reporters to six.

In Montana, the *Great Falls Tribune* earned a great reputation for state government coverage, only to have Gannett buy the paper and attempt to shut down the entire bureau in order to rely strictly on the Associated Press. The editors talked new president Chris Jensen out of it, only to find copies of the paper on their desks with "Gs" "marked on any story he considered too governmental."[300] The editor's copy and budget were being cut, to the point where law books that were vital to reporting were no longer being ordered.

Former Georgia Governor Zell Miller's concern is that the turnover of the statehouse reporters and their relative youth and mobility detract from the coverage, coverage that is already being hampered. "They don't have a long view of the leaders," he said. "They don't have context. There's no historical perspective whatsoever."[301] Reaching this low-point in state reporting is the function of nearly two decades of corporate ownership demoralizing the veteran reporters, forcing them to leave for papers where they can truly pursue their journalistic endeavors and substituting young, inexperienced reporters who need jobs – the kind of staff that will do what you tell them. As this cycle permeates the rest of the newsroom, as other departments are slashed, it will become increasingly difficult for chain-owned papers to serve as a free press.

While the phenomenon is most prevalent in smaller markets, it also afflicts some of the largest newspapers, including *USA Today*,[302] *The Washington Post*[303] and the *New York Times*.[304] In order to maintain advertiser relationships, coverage has to be undermined. These instances make it seem as though advertisers have as much say about what is being reported as the reporters do. This is certainly not a healthy journalistic environment.

Under Serving Commercially Unattractive Audiences

Putting circulation quality over circulation quantity is the other major tactic the corporate papers use to cut cost and boost profits. This means that newspapers determine the value of a region with respect to its attractiveness to advertisers. The advertisers are not interested in pitching their products to economic and social groups that they do not normally attract or who fall into unwanted demographics. So, they put pressure on the papers to get their ads to the "right" people for the smallest price.

According to *Taking Stock*, "the practice of cutting circulation has increased in the past two decades, with papers halting circulation to areas where readers don't interest advertisers."[305] The result of this is that the lowest circulation penetration is found "in areas with high concentrations of both low income and minority populations."[306] This leaves the minority and low-income populations under served by the press, with fewer opportunities to access the valuable daily news and entertainment that people in higher "quality" socioeconomic groups are supplied with.

Furthermore, "competition for socioeconomically defined market segments increasingly takes the form of altering the subject matter and shape of news content, delivering the types and forms of information that persons in the socioeconomically defined market prefer."[307] This means that not only are the chain papers physically not getting copies to certain social groups (their tactics will be highlighted momentarily), they are slanting the news they do print to please the readers that the advertisers want pleased. At this point, the low income and minority populations are doubly deserted. The financial motivations of the corporate owners strip the newsrooms of their ability to justly report and inform, and prohibit us from celebrating, mourning and co-existing fruitfully as a culture.

The "deliberate industry strategy to pursue a more upscale readership" has been exposed by researchers at the University of Iowa's school of journalism by surveying directors at the largest 90 U.S. dailies. The research states:

> Interviews…made it evident that lower-income neighborhoods were being disadvantaged by such tactics as requiring payment in advance, refusing to deliver to public housing, door-to-door sales efforts only on days of the month when government checks were due, and denial of discounts. Combined with "aggressive pricing"- that is, charging more – the practices amount to writing off a whole class of potential readers.[308]

These tendencies are reinforced by a relative absence of minorities from newsrooms. Vanessa Williams weaves together the relationship between communities, journalists, news organizations, reporting and democracy that I have highlighted throughout this analysis.

Black and white and red all over: the continued struggle to integrate American newsrooms. It's a play on an old riddle. In this case, the black and white refer to race, although I might add that in recent years the industry, faced with the rapidly changing demographics of the country, must also be concerned with Asians, Hispanics, and Native Americans. The red refers to the heated emotions that color this struggle: frustration, embarrassment, anger.

What does this have to do the news product? Everything. News organizations' continued inability to integrate African-Americans and other journalists of color into their newsrooms and to more accurately and fairly represent racial and ethnic communities threatens the credibility and viability of daily general-circulation newspapers. How can a newspaper claim to be a journal of record for a given city or region if it routinely ignores or misrepresents large segments of the population in the geographic area it covers?...

Our greatest concern about the industry's failure to grasp the gravity of its diversity deficit should be the potential harm to society. Many Americans continue to operate out of misinformation and misunderstanding when it comes to perceptions and relationships between racial groups, between religious groups, between men and women, straight and gay people, young and old people, middle-class and working-class people. The press, by failing to provide more accurate, thorough, and balanced coverage of our increasingly diverse communities, has abdicated its responsibility to foster an exchange of information and perspectives that is necessary in a democracy.[309]

The unique "market failures" discussed in the previous chapter provide the basis for public policy intervention to ensure robust civic discourse. That is, if we were only concerned about the traditional market failures described in the previous section, we might rely on antitrust policy, perhaps with a more rigorous set of structural screens and a heightened concern for vertical/conglomerate issues. However, the unique market failures demand much more public policy intervention to promote such civic discourse.

When entities merge, everyone in the market loses an independent voice, while a small segment of the market gains better coverage. In fact, depending on the distribution of preferences, the least well-served in the market may become even less well-served, if the merged entity drives out sources that are targeted to the needs of minorities and atypical groups. This is particularly true when a national entity buys out a local entity. When the merger crosses institutional lines, it may result in an equally severe loss of institutional diversity.

IV. THE ELECTRONIC MASS MEDIA

THE CRITIQUE OF TELEVISION'S IMPACT ON POLITICAL DISCOURSE

Commercialism

The criticism of the impact of television on the political process takes off from the problem of commercialism,[310] but adds another important layer to the concern about the role of mass media in the erosion of democratic processes. Initially intended to pull people together and provide information to educate and enable citizens to more actively pursue their political and cultural interests, the profit potential of the burgeoning electronic media industry led to a takeover by advertisers and large bureaucratic and corporate institutions.[311] As the entertainment quotient rose and the community-serving quotient declined, viewership was boosted and advertisers were able to "reach huge audiences regularly, and in receptive settings, with messages about products and, generally through those products, with messages about consumption as the centerpiece of the American Way of Life."[312]

With media conglomerates clawing at consumers' tastes by careful observation of their interests and ever more intensive targeting of marketing, they gained strength in controlling public attitudes and action.[313] The electronic media "are mainly employed to measure and monitor information transactions and to package and repackage information products many times over,"[314] effectively dictating what is available to whom.[315]

As the most profitable products (information or otherwise) are made exponentially available since they are safe money-makers, the set of genuine choices narrows. The result is to dull citizens' hunger for new information and consciousness by force-feeding them what they already know how to digest.[316] The power of commercialism is so great that it overwhelms the political function of the media.

> It is assumed that mass media contribute in some way to the political life of citizens, furnishing them with a means of representing themselves and their interest, allowing them a space – a 'public sphere' – within which they can reflect on the conditions of their lives and how these might be changed for the better. But can such an ideal coexist with commercialized media directed at consumers rather than citizens?[317]

> Media rules on capturing audience attention and thus eventually
> market shares dominate the business almost to the exclusion of all other
> principles, and are put into effect without any thought being given to
> the democratic or cultural standards of communication.[318]

As this trend intensifies, life becomes a drone of repetition and
regurgitation, devoid of outlets for expression and the will to consider,
to express dissent and to enact change. The television environment
becomes a source of concern for some at a broad level because of "the
amount of advertising constantly interrupting the visual flow... which
for people growing up in such an environment must, over time, inevitably
lead to a loss of the ability to concentrate."[319]

With respect to democratic theory, the critique of video culture
points toward a "worrisome conclusion: that the citizens of television
societies may be rapidly losing their faculties of political judgment as a
result of... stage-managed, entertainment oriented presentation of
events."[320]

Technology Influencing Social Processes

Many media critics across the political spectrum have argued that
hyper-commercialism combined with the expansion of media outlets
deeply affects the news reporting process, particularly as it covers politics.
On the one hand, there are more television outlets needed to fill more
space.[321] On the other hand, they need to attract more viewers to be
profitable. The media's schedule and perpetual news cycle become the
driving force, emphasizing speed, simplicity and routinization.[322] The
news production process is transformed.

> The problems stem largely from the very nature of commercially
> supplied news in a big country. News organizations are responsible
> for supplying an always new product to large numbers of people,
> regularly and on time. As a result, news must be mass-produced,
> virtually requiring an industrial process that takes place on a kind of
> assembly line.[323]

Tight schedules and competition for attention put their stamp on
the newsgathering and reporting process.[324] Reporting becomes highly
condensed and selective.[325] Planned events and personalities are the
easiest to cover. Short pieces require extreme simplification. Stories
become stylized so they can be easily conveyed.

Time pressures create a tendency to not only run quickly with a
story but to uncritically pass through manufactured news.[326]

Entertainment and aesthetic values dictate the nature of the picture and getting good video images becomes a critical need.[327] Staging gives the news the predictability it needs, but results in typecasting and posing.[328]

Competition drives news to seek blockbuster scoops and to play the big story more intensely and longer, to hold the larger audiences that have been attracted.[329] The search to find and maintain the audience's attention drives the media towards exaggeration and emotionalism at the expense of analysis.

Four types of news are ideally suited to perform this function. **Celebrity personalities** become the centerpiece because of the easy point of focus on highly visible individuals.[330] **Scandal** attracts audiences. The personal travails of prominent figures in titillating scandals are grist for the media mill, attracting attention without threatening the audience. This news may not be happy, but it fills the preference for happy news because it involves someone else's troubles of no direct relevance to public policy or the public's welfare. The **horse race and hoopla** – the game – are another easy way to frame the news and to produce constant updating of who is ahead.[331] Who wins and who loses is much easier to portray than the complexity of what is at stake. **Verbal duels**[332] and loud, often one-sided arguments find audiences[333] more easily than reasoned, balanced debates. Talk show pundits grab attention with extreme positions, usually negative attacks on targets that are not in the room to defend themselves.

Both journalism and politics suffer as a result of this process. Businesses and politicians recognize "the profit potential in marketable information and hence promote the development of technologies that enhance marketability."[334] Pressure applied by corporate ownership has forced news and entertainment to submit to heavy profit-maximizing strategies that foster financial gain at the expense of the democratic ideal. These two incongruent processes align for the personal benefit of a select few. As a result, "There has been an enormous increase in expenditure on public relations by both government and business… These powerful institutions subsidize the cost of gathering and processing the news in order to influence positively the way they are reported."[335]

Politicians conform and cater to the demands of the media and leverage their ability to manipulate their public image. Their interaction with the media becomes a form of extracted publicity in which they strive to be placed in the most favorable theatrical light. Politics, as a result, has been forced to submit to the media's dictatorship over the depiction of its major parties and personalities, creating a "house of mirrors, in which both politics and the media recognize only images of themselves, thereby losing sight of the real world."[336] Journalism degenerates into a photo-op dance[337] between reporters and political handlers in which the spinmeisters have the upper hand.

These spinmeisters become gatekeepers who can punish or reward with access to politicians and who control the scheduling of events. They can stonewall some or give exclusives to others. As a result, "top-down news turns journalists into messengers of the very political, governmental, and other leaders who are... felt to be untrustworthy and unresponsive by significant numbers of poll respondents."[338] The media produces a blend of news and free advertising for the candidates[339] and as with much advertising, the point may be to give a misimpression rather than convey accurate information.[340]

Hence, journalistic values are marred.[341] Dependence on well-connected sources and pressures to get a story out first short-circuit the application of traditional standards of reporting.[342] Discourse degenerates into a stream of stage-managed, entertainment-oriented, issueless politics.[343] Celebrity and scandal replace substance as the central considerations.

The fashion in which stories are selected and the time-frame within which these stories are developed, in accordance with mass media's pursuit of big headlines and profits, have undercut politicians' ability to realize legitimate political agendas.[344] Instead, parties and political players shape their decisions and actions within the framework of how the media will present them.[345]

Alienating Citizens

Regardless of the circumstances surrounding the development of the media-run democracy and whether or not the politicians themselves are largely responsible for allowing its emergence, politicians acquiesce in a Faustian bargain. "In exchange for their 'tactical' submission to the media rules, political actors gain a well-founded expectation that they will be invited to help shape the way the media portray them."[346] This clearly undermines the political process and changes the relative weight of parties and how they function to achieve goals.[347] Citizens are presented with an illusion of policy in election campaigns.[348]

Covering mainly "prestige institutions as an economical and effective way of gathering the news"[349] severely hampers the public's knowledge of the overall democratic landscape and widens the gap between elite and less visible groups in society, supporting the power structure while stigmatizing dissent as extreme and rare.[350] The watchdog function is short-circuited by the close relationships.[351] This awards too much attention to too few political figures and views and sets the stage for politicians to manage their public identities through manipulation of the media's tendencies. Parties and ordinary group affiliation recede, as individuals and lead institutions become the center of attention.

James Curran notes that "the media routinely report the news as discrete events, abstracted from their wider contexts," which promotes "a tacit view of the social order as natural, inevitable, outside of time – 'the way things are'."[352] Without an ongoing dialogue of the conditions that enable the reported events to take place, the public cannot adequately formulate opinions; hence, they cannot act or mobilize in an educated manner. The critical elements of responsibility, causality and connectedness between events are lost.

Public involvement in policy formation suffers not only because of the shift in focus fostered by the media, but also because of the short time-frame demanded by the media. The recognition of the news as being reported 'outside of time' highlights the troubling difference between the media's timeline and the timeline necessary for political agendas to be carried out. "The traditional model of a political party that reaches consensus via extended discussions with many centers of influence in civil society, that allows decisions and programs to mature gradually, has become practically an anachronism."[353]

The policy creation process should rely on a bipartisan system to decipher what is in the best interest of the American people in order to achieve our democratic ideal. However, these deliberations are not given sufficient time to develop as the media's need for decisive headlines encourages quick, extreme stances to be taken. "Abbreviating the time interval normally demanded by the political process down to what the media's production schedule permits means abridging the entire process by deleting the procedural components that qualify it as democratic,"[354] and insisting that politicians rush to get their views to their constituents before they can be swayed in an opposing direction. These circumstances, according to Thomas Meyer, tend to "pin down inchoate opinions and moods into immutable prejudices,"[355] which become fundamental obstacles to achieving a rational, common good. The rapid-fire sequence of simple, emotional snap shots staged to increase popularity replaces discourse as the basis of politics.

Demobilizing Voters

The legal and analytic discussion identified participation as the currency of civic discourse. The discussion in this chapter has shown that the commercial mass media interacts with the political process to shrink the content of public discourse and orient it toward a style that disengages the citizenry from serious public policy dialogue. The inevitable effect is to disengage them from participation in politics. The ultimate effect is to diminish their desire to vote (see Figure IV-1).

There are certainly many reasons for the declining participation in elections, but Thomas Patterson and others argue that the media circus has played an important part.[356] The ascendance of the TV medium is tied to the fundamental difference between newspapers and television. Parties were the pistons of voter turnout and issues were the spark plugs. The narrowing of substance disserves the public, above all in the electoral process. While the nature and number of issues faced by Americans have grown, their primary political institutions – parties – have shrunk. Voters are forced to choose a candidate whom they least dislike, based on non-substantive grounds, which we can easily link to disenchantment and a rapid trickle-down effect of squashing voter turnout. This sheds light on how voter turnout could fall despite a rise in education, registration and civil rights; people are not excited about their representatives.

Presidential elections, along with lower-level elections, have become candidate-oriented, delving into softer, more personal and moral appeals, and moving away from hard-line political affiliation based on honest stances on issues. Public opinion about candidates rests often on meaningless probing (someone's five o'clock shadow, misspoken words during speeches, investigating candidates' pasts) and moral power play, leaving the issues of the election unattended. The issues themselves are not given sufficient care by the candidates, according to Patterson, who says candidates find it easier to speak vaguely and play the public opinion charade. This renders the party identity obsolete, a party identity which previously had encouraged participation by giving supporters a sense of unity that rested on a clear, issue-based platform that sought to achieve a common set of goals.

FIGURE IV-1: Electoral Turnout in the Television Age Has Declined

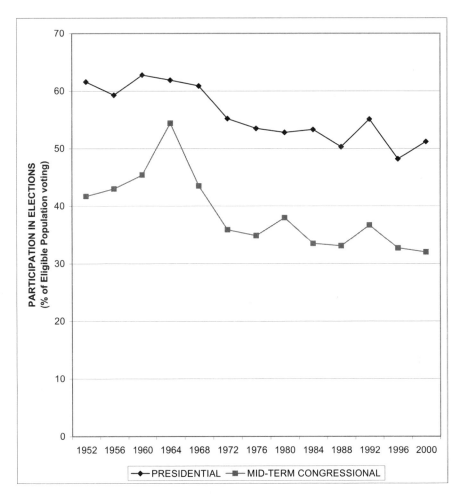

Source: U.S. Bureau of the Census, *Statistical Abstract of the United States: 2002*, Table 395.

Another widely agreed upon obstacle to higher voter turnout is the length of the American presidential campaign. The need for attention in the celebrity environment extends campaigns, but a long campaign does not necessarily ensure an informed electorate. Meaningless events are littered throughout the nearly year-long struggle, too many for Americans to process but few grand enough for Americans to reach for, latch on to, and take something worthwhile away from. The debates have become slanderous and vague with more personality sparring than political discussion. Negative ad campaigns have become the norm, disgusting many Americans who would rather not choose between mudslingers. The negativity breeds distrust of the candidates since suspicion is constantly raised (whether unfounded or not). This keeps people away from the voting booth.

The structure of the campaign is such that the candidates with the most money and previously established party support are heavily favored considering the number of months the money must last. Most Americans do not feel as though they even need to pay attention as the party nomination is essentially made for them. By Super Tuesday, the bulk of candidates vying for candidacy are broke and disheartened. Similarly, front-loading renders many states obsolete, further disenchanting voters as they watch the news and are made to feel as though their late-in-the-campaign-vote is useless. Once the candidates are in place, more state neglect arises. Non-swing states are given almost no attention. Little money is spent bringing people out to the polls, making people feel like their vote counts. Ads run exponentially more in toss-up states; candidates visit and speak in those states at an alarming rate.

Patterson weaves together the central themes in the interrelated degeneration of journalism and politics to point to diminished turnout – negative attack strategies, reduction in hard news and political coverage. In the end, "Americans have grown to dislike almost everything about modern campaigns ... too much money, too much theater, too much fighting, and too much deception... reasons not to participate.[357]

HOPE & HYPE V. REALITY: THE ROLE OF THE INTERNET

Progressives hoped that the Internet would correct the flaws in the development of television and finally deliver on the promise of the electronic mass media to educate, motivate and mobilize the great body of citizens to participate in political discourse in a constructive way.[358] Large media companies now claim the Internet has radically altered the media landscape by making an immense number of choices available to consumers, providing a ubiquitous means of mass communication that competes directly with the commercial media. Consequently, they want more freedom to pursue their commercial enterprise.

After three decades of existence and two decades of presence in civil society, the Internet has not lived up to its hope or hype. It has become more of an extension of two dominant, 20th century communications media than a revolutionary new 21st century technology.

The Internet has become an extension of television, as huge media giants harness its ability to "push" their commercial messages on the public. The one-to-many function has been quickly exploited for its commercial value. The Internet has also become an extension of the telephone, a "pull" medium. "One-to-one" communications through e-mail and instant messaging are the dominant uses of the Internet in terms of time. These functions have been driven by commercial interests as well, as they bundle e-mail addresses and exploit the value of instant messaging to drive adoption.

While it is certainly too soon to pronounce the Internet a failure in civic discourse, it is critically important to understand its limitations and their causes so that public policies can be identified that promote democratic discourse in the digital information age. Indeed, because the Internet is being cited as a justification to deregulate the commercial mass media, it is particularly important to debunk the myth that the Internet has significantly altered or diminished the influence of the powerful push broadcast media has on politics.

The unique, many-to-many potential of the Internet is lagging behind, particularly as a political vehicle. Internet optimists, from the outset, hoped for a hyper-connected populous, capable of reaching out to anybody and anything with a simple set of keystrokes. They predicted intensified participation in the democratic process as a new outlet emerged to access and spread information, one which alleged to make it easier to be heard.

The counter-culturalists who were largely responsible for the advent of the Internet hoped that "cheap computing power in the hands of citizens could be a powerful resource for democracy and a weapon against overbearing government and big business."[359] Cyberspace was a technological gold mine, replete with opportunity and excitement, and brimming with potentially positive results. The idea of an information revolution was based on decentralization and empowerment; two concepts that counter-culturalists hoped would flourish by "reappropriating technological power on behalf of citizens."[360] True electronic democracy, it was hoped, would be created by "the possibilities for interactive and collective communication offered by cyberspace to encourage the expression and elaboration of urban problems by local citizens themselves."[361]

If the architecture of the Internet was geared towards democracy, we might begin to conquer space by connecting citizens to each other "in ways that extend the developmental benefits of civic participation beyond those immediately present."[362] An active, informed citizenry would spark self-organization and participation, two benchmarks of the counter-culturalist dream. Democracy would benefit greatly if we were "encouraging the collective and continuous elaboration of problems and their cooperative, concrete resolutions by those affected."[363]

Underlying this view with respect to information technology is the idea that,

> the government serves as the manager of a commons, working on behalf of the society. No one has the right to alienate a part of the commons for private use. Any use of the information resource is subject to a public interest determination on the part of the trustee, acting on behalf of the entire society.[364]

This old-fashioned concept of democracy – technically, the airwaves have been defined in this fashion almost since the inception of electronic use of the spectrum – informs the shape of the Internet debate by re-establishing the roles to be played by government and society.[365]

To date, the Internet's ability to create a more vibrant forum for democratic discourse has been limited by a number of factors, some inherent in the technology, others the result of public policy. There is growing doubt and concern that the Internet will not fundamentally enhance the quality of civic discourse in America. In a recent article, Peter Levine appropriately asked, "Can the Internet Rescue Democracy?"[366] The answer is not entirely encouraging, and it outlines numerous concerns about the ultimate ability of the Internet to transform politics.

> The fact that the Internet can work as a commons hardly guarantees that American democracy will flourish. It is not clear that even a vibrant commons could serve the functions of political mobilization and socialization that ordinary people need before they can influence public policy. Nor will the Internet *necessarily* operate as a commons; in fact, the odds favor an increasingly privatized and commercialized cyberspace. Nevertheless, one of the most promising strategies for democratic renewal today is to try to keep the Internet a publicly accessible space in which citizens create and share free public goods.[367]

Beyond the problem of creating (or preserving) a commons or public space for civic discourse in cyberspace,[368] Levine identifies some traditional mass media problems that are quickly migrating to the Internet including "inequality, weakened social bonds, diminished public deliberation, rampant consumerism, and the impact of eroding privacy on freedom of association."[369]

Commercialism

By the late 1980s the Internet had emerged as the pre-eminent media alternative.[370] The governments in the nations with a leading role in developing the Internet and its related technologies were committed to free market economics, however, which led, willy nilly to a resurgence of commercial interests on the Internet.[371] Symbolically, the network itself was handed over to Sprint, MCI, WorldCom, PSINet and GTE.[372] Shortly thereafter, the corporate dominance of the Internet was reinforced when a decision was made to allow the leading technology for delivering high-speed Internet services to consumers to be operated on a closed, proprietary basis.[373] The cable companies, who assert the right to choose which video services flow over their wires, were allowed to extend that business model to high-speed Internet services.[374] They operated their advanced telecommunications networks on an exclusive basis, with one exception, where antitrust authorities compelled them to provide access to other commercial interests. The telephone companies have been allowed to follow the same path.

With commercialism as the guiding principle, the extremely powerful commercial thrust of the new media reinforces the central concern of media public policy.[375] New technologies do not alter underlying economic relationships because the mass-market audience orientation of the business takes precedence.[376] Indeed, because the new media markets have moved quickly to vertical integration by dominant incumbents from the old media, the problems of raising capital and acquiring licenses that have afflicted the old media persist[377] and the circumstances surrounding the production and delivery of information inhibit its utility to expand political participation and enhance social and cultural consciouness.[378] A prime concern is that "information is both a commodity and, within a society marked by the general tendency to commodification, information is a form of social control."[379]

Handed over to commercial interests, with dominant media and telecommunications firms in the lead, the Internet became the logical conclusion to the development of electronic media. After seventy years of titillating public tastes through advertising, electronic media could now provide instant e-commerce, to buy on the spot. In the case of digital products, it could deliver immediate consumption and instant gratification.

The resulting e-commerce is an electronic "direct mail on steroids" pumped up by the ability of viewers to click through digitally inserted advertising for purchases.[380] High-powered advertising is targeted at demographically compatible viewers identified by detailed information created by the two-way network on viewing patterns and past purchases,[381] leading to growing concerns that certain groups are not likely to have fair access to the opportunities of cyberspace.[382] The new services may be expensive to deliver because of the cost of appliances, production equipment necessary to produce programming that takes advantage of the new appliance, and also because of the infrastructure necessary to deliver interactive services.[383]

Companies introducing technologies quickly identify the likely early adopters and innovators and orient their product distribution to maximize the penetration within that market segment.[384] It should not be surprising that the target market is resource rich households. There is a very strong base of support for the importance of income and education in the adoptions of high technology innovations like computers and telecommunications equipment.[385] The strong predictors of inclination to early adoption point directly to market segmentation strategies.[386]

Technology Influencing Social Processes

There are other limitations of the Internet as a political space, driven by the nature of the technology. The Internet's characteristic impersonality keeps discussion and action online from achieving what discussion and action face-to-face have achieved in the past.[387] It lacks the ability to give individuals and their ideas the necessary momentum to organize and accomplish their goals. We have long recognized that "these systems have the potential to isolate individuals from one another so much that market driven social atomization erodes the social community."[388]

Online forums have not achieved a breakthrough in democratic deliberation,[389] and online newspapers look like the cyber-versions of the physical world counterparts from which they are a spin off.[390] It is still early and the possibility for new forms of communications emerging cannot be discounted[391] since "people who participate in typical on-line activities sometimes initiate political discussions and organize political actions."[392] But we must be cautious because "participants tend to be distributed across jurisdictions, which makes political organizing difficult."[393]

In fact, critics argue that the time spent in political discussions online may be detrimental because it cuts into the amount of time individuals spend face-to-face, an arena that has proven functionality and promise. "When we communicate using a computer, we can withhold practically all information about ourselves…we can break off contact at will; we can adopt multiple personalities and identities; and we can shield ourselves from the consequences of what we say."[394] It becomes difficult to put faith in online relationships and the time spent promoting ideas[395] because the mechanisms for developing trust and bonds are weak."[396] These are crucial to driving political organizations and communities. In face-to-face political discussions there is a better understanding of how the people involved will be affected, which informs their motivations and intentions.

Similarly, the ease of exit on the Internet undercuts its role as a political platform. In most respects the Internet is a highly selective tool where individuals seek out what they already know or are interested in proliferating. Attempting to change the "prevailing norms" of an online space is particularly difficult because the receivers one encounters will be different every time and the sender will never have any knowledge of its audience at any given moment. "The Web users are unlike visitors to a physical space, because they do not have to hear a civil rights marcher, take a leaflet from the striking worker, or see the unwashed homeless person."[397] Online, people can cleanse their world of all interactions outside of those they explicitly choose, isolating themselves from other ideologies and avoiding "uncomfortable perspectives and stories that might shake their prejudices."[398] Though self-segregation does exist in the physical world, its opposite also exists in abundance. On the Internet, "there is no common space, mass audience or means of addressing people who don't seek out the speaker."[399]

While being involved in discussion online makes an individual more socially active at any given moment, there is concern that over time the social and political activity of our nation will decrease, weaken, and become atomized as a result of the Internet. "The search functions on the Internet make selection too easy and threaten to tip the balance toward hyper-specialization,"[400] furthering the digital divide and enabling "intellectual stratification as experts are able to talk only among themselves and ignore the rest of the public."[401]

The end point of this will be weaker communities where mutual obligation to the consequences and decisions of groups will be non-existent. Volunteering locally has always resulted from the desire to have an impact in the local setting. On the Internet it is difficult to gauge the impact one will have since reliance on other online members and participants is risky and uncertain. Hence, the speed and "access" which promoters of the Internet cite as beneficial is "unlikely to raise the level of participation"[402] because strong, motivating community ties have not subsisted and users are not convinced their work will yield results. Here, Levine writes, "the Internet may have just the opposite effect by insulating us from the kinds of people whom we could serve face-to-face."[403]

Social Alienation

Hannah Arendt argues that "the public realm has been displaced by a mass society of atomized individuals."[404] Underrepresented groups are therefore unable to build communities to achieve their goals and to reap the benefits of democracy. Furthered freedom for the large corporations perpetuates the digital divide between the information-rich and the information-poor. The least powerful "[c]itizens are denied the information they need by the few powerful media companies"[405] which "eliminates a human right and makes it a marketable commodity, a right for those who can afford it."[406]

The equality of the online environment is undercut by the centralized commercial control of its mechanisms of distribution as the gap between those whom the dominant media owners aim to please and those whom they choose to neglect widens.[407] Allowing the marketplace to dictate the nature and function of the Internet has already limited its potential.[408] Poorer populations do not share the resources of wealthy citizens to participate in the media that have been established.[409] Critical research has found time and again that "disadvantaged people are much less likely than privileged ones to use the Internet."[410]

The increased emphasis on financial transactions online has widened the digital divide and intensified the struggle to keep information and consciousness flowing adequately to the underprivileged. "Pay-per call, per view, per bit of information, per keystroke, etc., eliminates the benefits the powerless, poor people and regions enjoyed because of the technical limitations on making every transaction a financial one."[411] In a sense, online services are being "reserved for the wealthiest,"[412] and there is little policy enacted to keep the potentially positive effects of the Internet from disappearing completely.

The drive to sell more subscriptions and reach a highly targeted audience with advertising that caters to their individual tastes will be intense.[413] The cost of services and the targeting of marketing points to a commercial model in which high-value, high-income consumers are the ones marketers seek to serve. Dramatic increases in the price of these advanced services highlight the traditional concerns about commercial interests targeting attractive markets.[414]

Beyond the cost is a lack of education and skills necessary for disconnected citizens to utilize the access they hope to be granted.[415] While "the cost of computing power is decreasing...the standard equipment used on the Internet is growing more complicated every day."[416] This makes it even more difficult for those who have not experienced early incarnations of computer and online technologies to enter the Internet community, as there are virtually no programs or policies directed at aiding these individuals. "Nonparticipants will be left behind," according to Pierre Levy, "and those who have yet to enter the positive cycle of change, including its comprehension and appropriation, will be excluded even more radically than before."[417] The populous will be segregated and the voices and interests of the 'have-nots' will be faintly represented.[418]

Not only is the education more demanding, but access to the resources and networks necessary to command the technology is restricted.[419] Hence, the undereducated cannot gain relevant knowledge, cannot make confident decisions about their own lives, and are crippled when it comes to affecting change in their community. Under these circumstances, "computers further the unequal distribution of power and undermine the very limited democracy that some now enjoy,"[420] as obstacles are added to what is already a treacherous pathway to being heard.

Fears of a widening gap between rich and poor are rising as people express concern about being left behind by the "information revolution," with the 'disconnected' and 'potentially connected' groups expressing the greatest concern.[421] These are people whose needs must be addressed, who must be given the opportunity to connect and to contribute, but who are least able to gain command of the technology. "We browse the Web using patented corporate products that have deliberate biases built into their design,"[422] biases that are slanted towards wealthy consumers and serve no purpose in the pursuit of a just and worthwhile Internet.[423]

While greater equality alone could not cure the Internet, it is a necessary step that would enable communities to be built stronger online, creating a new forum where all voices are able to gain representation.

Demobilizing Citizens

The media goliaths are now in the position to dictate what information is widely available and how rapidly technological change will come about, with relatively no resistance. This has allowed passive consumption of information products to extend to another generation of electronic media, replacing active participation in democratic debate as the primary activity on the Internet.

With the mass media so closely connected to entrenched interests it becomes easy to serve a select few while alienating millions of other citizens. By abusing the power of the technology and misrepresenting its function, companies create difficulties for citizens to identify what is best for themselves and for the nation as a whole. By dominating the production and delivery of information and attempting to pass the Internet's community-building function off as beneficial when in fact it isolates and polarizes people, the major corporations "limit the control one has over the ideas one encounters."[424]

Setting the precedent of consumption over democracy generates a marketplace where profit-maximization is not only glorified, but its debilitating effects are ignored. "The tendency to centralized control, monitoring and information control, and the tendency to treat the products of computer communications systems as marketable commodities"[425] create no impetus for nor imposes any obligation on media owners to serve the public interest. At present, profit maximization overwhelms concern for the common good, a lack of competition disables both resistance and the prospect of advancement, and citizens are under informed as well as misinformed. Because of the commercial control of what is most visible and accessible, "almost no part of the Internet now qualifies as a 'public space' in which free speech would enjoy the strongest protection."[426] The Internet has failed to enhance the citizens' ability "to define themselves and their place in everyday life."[427] Repeating the pattern of television, financial gain tramples citizen sovereignty, as "the media message is unable to exploit the particular context in which the receiver evolves."[428]

The economic relationships that have taken over the mass media have been exacerbated by the Internet, frustrating the hoped for increase in diversity, pluralism and opportunities for entry.[429] "The principal agents promoting the technology are global media conglomerates who are more interested in promoting pay-per-view entertainment than creating a democratic forum in cyberspace where their activities can be scrutinised."[430] This stacks the odds against small groups and individuals, as the bulk of users are directed through corporate portals, which are made attractive by glitzy visuals and distractions. Likewise, "some search engines are commercial ventures in which sites must pay for inclusion in their database,"[431] further deprioritizing small organizations and individuals who could never match large, corporate offerings.

> Under these conditions, citizens who try to operate their own sites for democratic purposes will become increasingly discouraged, since few visitors will be able to find their work and they will be legally barred from using the patented production techniques employed on commercial sites. Thus the Internet will begin to look like the next generation of cable television instead of a decentralized, participatory medium. Most non-profit sites will be as marginal as public-access television stations today.[432]

The result is much more like evolution of the commercial mass media than a media revolution and it has not fundamentally altered the political process yet. The limitations of the Internet reveal the strain that cyberspace, much like television, has put on democracy. Countless twentieth century philosophers and analysts have predicated human responsibility and action as the success model for democracy.

Technological advancements are worthless, harmful even, unless they are translated into human advancements that come directly from institutions that encourage participation and instill confidence in exploration and action. "The existence of a technical infrastructure in no way guarantees that only the most positive virtualities will be actualized."[433] Placing the "burden of social change on technology itself rather than in social institutions…misses an important historical lesson: technologies embody, in their production, distribution and use, existing political and social relationships."[434] As long as commercial interests are founded on unequal distribution of information and resources, the Internet replicates the flaws of previous media revolutions, distracting people from "social problems and collective-action remedies by giving them a false sense of political effectiveness."[435]

"The lesson of media history is that, in an unregulated or lightly regulated regime, what gets transmitted is primarily what is profitable rather than what is in the public interest."[436] We know this because of the shopping mall quality the Internet has taken on. Pretending that the technology will accomplish the goals without active guidance has allowed the Internet to amplify "the passive spectator-democracy of sound-bites and photo-opportunities rather than encouraging real participation."[437] Simply putting more information in people's homes, especially lowest-common denominator information, "is just a continuation of long-term trends that have brought data increasingly within everyone's reach." [438] The message is clear, "Technology is responsible for neither our salvation nor our destruction."[439]

EPILOGUE: WAR COVERAGE

The war in Iraq has triggered a loud, public dispute over the relationship between "embedded" journalists and the military and the role of the media in reporting/supporting the war effort. As a news event, war pushes all the buttons of hyper-commercialized media. It is a gripping, emotional event certain to yield action and compelling images. Embedding journalists maximizes chances that the media can deliver. Yet, it immediately raises some key questions that are prominent in the critique of the media: the loss of objectivity in the close relationship between reporter and subject; the pure passthrough of accounts without any balance; and the discreet, disconnected nature of individual reports.

War reporting moved what had been a simmering debate about mass media in the U.S. from the trade press and an occasional mention on the back pages of the general press to the front page and even the nightly news. Advocates of media reform may be thankful for the new found attention to an important issue, but they should be concerned as well. The issue of war is so politically charged that it may obscure the underlying and long-term media issues. It is difficult to have a constructive dialogue about media reform when any suggestion that we need more objective reporting, balanced commentary, or diverse opinions is painted as giving unpatriotic comfort to the enemy "when our young men and women are in harm's way."[440]

The intensity of the debate over the handling of war reporting can provide an additional, very high profile example of the broader media reform issues if the war coverage is carefully analyzed within a framework that comprehends the fundamental issues that permeate the debate over reform. Having provided that context, this section briefly identifies the issues raised by war coverage.

The electronic media that covered the war reflect the commercial environment that has been created by conscious public policy. The uniformity of coverage has been noted and competing explanations offered, ranging from crass commercialism, excessive concentration, and political opportunism to simple patriotism. While a comprehensive discussion is beyond the immediate focus of this book, two articles that appeared on the front page of the Style section of *The Washington Post* on two consecutive days about a week after the war started serve to frame the war coverage issue.

News American Style

On March 28, 2003, a lengthy article reported on marketing consultant reports commissioned by commercial radio and TV stations about how to cover and comment on the war. The headline tells the story: "For Broadcast Media, Patriotism Pays: Consultants Tell Radio, TV Clients that Protest Coverage Drives Viewers Off."[441] It raises numerous media issues that were at the center of the debate over media reform long before the war in Iraq.

Boosterism for profit.

Now, apparently, is the time for all good radio and TV stations to come to the aid of their country's war.

That is the message pushed by broadcast news consultants, who've been advising news and talk stations across the nation to wave the flag and downplay protests against the war....

Get the following production pieces in the studio NOW.... Patriotic music that makes you cry, salute, get cold chills.... Air the National Anthem at a specified time each day as long as the USA is at war.

The tyranny of the majority reigns on the airwaves, muting debate to protect the bottom line.

Polarizing discussions are shaky ground...

Covering war protests may be harmful to a station's bottom line...

"As a business, you don't want half the population hating you. So you plant your flag in the sand."

Focus group and marketing research dictate that the public is fed happy/soft news that avoids controversy.

In a survey released last week on the eve of war, the firm found that war protests were the topic that tested lowest among 6,400 viewers across the nation... only 14 percent of respondents said TV news wasn't paying enough attention to "anti-war demonstrations and peace activities;" just 13 percent thought that in the event of war the news should pay more attention to dissent...

Some of the orientation reflects opinion polls that show upward of 70 percent of Americans in favor of the war. That means, as one local media executive put it, "almost everyone wants to be seen as pro-military... If one of our guys got on the air and started ranting against the war, it would create unnecessary controversy."

Selective reporting and sourcing shape the agenda.

Among its suggestions for covering the war, the company recently told clients to "dispatch reporters to military bases in the area... Are your local Reserve or Guard units involved? Do they have veterans of the Gulf War still at home..."

It also advised clients to find experts in some 30 categories – including "veterans of Desert Storm," former "G Men," "Military Recruiting Officers" – most of whom would be unlikely to offer harsh criticism.

The line between reporting and advocacy gets blurred and the pretense of objectivity disappears.

In the weeks leading up to the war, Washington talk station WTNT-AM has broadcast an almost unbroken stream of pro-war talk from the likes of G. Gordon Liddy, Laura Ingram, Michael Savage and Don Imus. Another syndicated host heard on WTNT, Glenn Beck, promoted and staged pro-war rallies in various cities, drawing unwelcome attention to his employer, Clear Channel Communications, the nation's largest radio station operator.

The Internet does not necessarily provide diversity.

WTOP-AM/FM, the area's only full-time all-news station has pitched in support of the war effort as well. On its web site, WTOP carries a series of "related links" that include thankthetroops.com; Ways to Help Troops; Sign Up to Thank the Military; National Military Family Association; U.S. Central Command; home pages of the U.S. Army, Marines, Air Force, Navy and Coast Guard and Department of Defense;

the Stars & Stripes military newspaper; and "Email Support to Military." Another box reads "Support Our Troops." Send a greeting, a thank you card, or a donation.

WTOP's Web site offers links to only two antiwar groups; United for Peace and Move ON.

WTOP news director Jim Farley makes a distinction between the station's newscast and its Web site, which he says is "not a news site."

Concentration of ownership has led to homogeneity of views.

"What troubles me… is that the most important part of the system of checks and balances in media coverage has been the diversity of ownership. With increasing concentration of ownership, if one or two big companies are using the same corporate-wide policy, or relying on the same consultants, there aren't effective competitive forces to ensure alternative opinions."

Dominant firms support the official line; diversity of ownership might produce a different mix of news.

"I think there's just political correctness to waving the flag right now… If you were the upstart station in town, you might conceivably come at this from a peacenik angle by going on the air with the body count, by pointing out we haven't got Osama bin Laden or Saddam yet, by saying we should end the madness. But we find it appropriate to wave the flag where I happen to be."

Voices of dissent are excluded.

"The antiwar movement in this country is far bigger than it was during the first few years of the Vietnam War, but you wouldn't know it from the coverage… the media has been completely biased. You don't hear dissenting voices; you see people marching in the streets, but you rarely hear what they have to say in the media."

Covering-All-Sides In Britain

Ironically, on the front page of *The Washington Post* Style section the previous day, another headline told a rather different story: "The 'Beeb' in Their Bonnet: BBC is Taking Flak for its Cover-All-Sides Approach."[442] The contrast could not have been sharper.

A different agenda produces a different slant on the news.

The woman narrating the news is Lyse Doucet, who works for "BBC World," a global broadcast whose tone is so different from that of the

American networks that it sometimes seems to be examining a different war.

The key, BBC News Director Richard Sambrook says from London, is "not having a particular country's agenda or values at the forefront of what we are doing…

The cover-all-sides style, even as British troops are under fire, has brought the BBC a steady fusillade of criticism.

Agenda setting dictates which voices are heard.

A Washington correspondent for the BBC says there has been no shortage of criticism in this country "that the American media has been trying to sell the war. Perhaps the BBC all along has been questioning both sides on whether the war was justified."

Different journalistic traditions result in different approaches to the news.

"British journalism has a culture of being quite critical and quite aggressive in our interviews of politicians and officials…"

American colleagues are "not as tough as the sorts of audiences I have to address would like…" The U.S. reporters who question Defense Secretary Donald Rumsfeld and military leaders are quite knowledgeable,… but "it can look like too cozy an atmosphere."

The stark contrast of the understated British tone makes the American broadcasts seem flag-waving and patriotic. The underlying assumption in these broadcasts seems to be that the U.S. of A. is fighting for a just cause, and the embedded correspondents, while providing unvarnished reports, are openly sympathetic to our fighting men and women.

Sourcing and agenda setting create a different tone.

This attitude permeates the BBC's sober coverage, which does not feature a parade of retired generals or emotional interviews with injured families. On "Breakfast News," a morning show seen only in Britain, anchor Natasha Kaplinsky began a discussion with her "defence correspondent" by saying: "Let's talk about the politicians and how they're manipulating public perceptions."

The audience matters, even for a non-commercial station.

Of course, the BBC is playing to a different constituency from Fox, CNN and MSNBC. Sambrook, whose organization is indirectly funded by the government through licensing fees, points out that a majority of Brits opposed the war before the shooting started.

"If we were to simply take the justification for the war, we would have lost half of our audience."

Cover-all-sides means none are likely to be happy

British member of parliament Alice Mahon said this week that the BBC('s)… "blatant bias does not reflect the concerns of the majority of people in Britain, who still remain unconvinced of the case for war…"

But Times of London Columnist William Rees-Mogg offered the opposite view, calling the BBC "defeatist."

"The Beeb is a mandatory government-run service staffed with the usual people who go into government-run media, i.e. left-wing hacks… How the Beeb ceased to become an objective news source and became a broadcast version of the Nation is one of the great tragedies of modern journalism."

Conclusion

The extensive coverage of homecomings only underscores the issues. They are ideal video events: scheduled, staged, emotional, happy, and perfect photo-ops with exactly the message that the gatekeepers want to convey. The crowds are kept small, we are told, to preserve the intimacy of the event for the friends and family of the returning warriors, except for the intrusion of a few dozen TV cameras.

The full force of media research will be brought to bear on the war coverage, as will the skills of the spinmeisters. The notion that commercial interests were at play seems clear. It is hard to imagine commercial entities foregoing these opportunities or passing up the chance to embed journalists and get the moving pictures they strive for. Whether a less concentrated commercial media sector would have encouraged some to embed but take a more critical view is, at least, debatable. Even if a market could be found for a different point of view, it is not clear whether the military would have tolerated too much of a contrary message. Whether a stronger public broadcasting sector could have followed a course similar to that of the Beeb is an interesting question.

PART III: QUANTITATIVE STUDIES OF MASS MEDIA MARKETS

V. Defining Mass Media Information Markets

Defining the Product and its Uses

A critical step in evaluating the status of the mass media and the impact that a radical change in the rules of media ownership is likely to have is to understand how media are used. During the course of the review of media ownership rules, the Federal Communications Commission invested an immense amount of energy into attempting to prove that there is substitutability between media. This argument is critical to the entire deregulation argument, since it would allow the agency to claim that broadly defined media markets are not concentrated and that owners of media lack influence, since citizens can simply switch sources.

The FCC's effort to define media markets in this way has failed. Its own data shows that there is, at best, only very little substitutability between media, either for viewers as a source of information gathering[443] or advertisers as a source of information dissemination.[444] Both of the major studies of consumer substitution indicate that mass media are more likely to be complements than substitutes. This can be observed at the level of aggregate market data, with consumer usage data, and with consumer opinions about media usage. Because the different media types serve different functions, individuals who consume one media type are stimulated to consume others. For example, hearing a headline on the drive home from work, the consumer is more likely to turn on the news, watch multiple news channels, or peruse the newspaper the next morning to get more details.

There is very clear evidence that different types of media serve different functions. This is particularly important for the two dominant media for news and information, print and broadcast TV. While the advocates of convergence equate all media, the reality is that these are distinct products oriented toward different geographic markets in both the commercial marketplace and the forum for democratic discourse.[445] The dramatic change[446] and increase in intermedia competition[447] that advocates of eliminating restrictions on ownership hypothesize simply do not exist, either as a matter of simple economics or as a matter of diversity in civic discourse.

At the same time, as noted earlier, there is much greater commonality in the production of news for the traditional mass media. If the FCC had looked at the supply-side of the market it would have found that TV and newspaper inputs are substantially the same reporters writing stories.

Once it is recognized that these are distinct products on the demand side, supplied by a common set of inputs on the supply side, the growing concentration within each of the media market segments becomes a source of concern. Each of the market segments is becoming dominated by a small number of large, vertically integrated corporations that pursue profit maximization at the expense of professionalism in journalism and public interest programming. Economies of scale create barriers to entry, particularly in the provision of network facilities. Inadequate rules of fair access have allowed vertically integrated companies to leverage their control over facilities into content markets.

As a result, potentially vigorous competition in content markets has been dampened by much weaker competition in distribution markets. These markets are adjacent to each other, and do not compete. There is some competition or rivalry across media, but newspapers' classified advertising cash cow in no way resembles the high-priced pharmaceutical and auto advertising splashed across national television network prime time programming. These are separate markets that are not yet, and may never be, substitutes for one another.

EMPIRICAL MEASURES OF MARKET STRUCTURE

For the purposes of assessing media markets, after examining basic conditions of production, as in Chapter II, industrial organization analysis focuses on the number and size of firms in the market. Where a small number of large firms dominate a market, the concern is that they can exercise "market power" by raising prices or lowering quality. This causes inefficiency and a transfer of wealth from consumers to producers. Of course, I have argued that analysis of media market structure must also be concerned about performance in terms of democratic discourse. Chapter II and Part II demonstrated that the performance of mass media markets leaves a great deal to be desired.

A clear articulation of the economic approach, which is directly applicable to the debate over media ownership, can be found in the *Merger Guidelines* issued by the Department of Justice and the Federal Trade Commission.

Market power to a seller is the ability profitably to maintain prices above competitive levels for a significant period of time.[*] In some circumstances, a sole seller (a "monopolist") of a product with no good substitutes can maintain a selling price that is above the level that would prevail if the market were competitive. Similarly, in some circumstances, where only a few firms account for most of the sales of a product, those firms can exercise market power, perhaps even approximating the performance of a monopolist, by either explicitly or implicitly coordinating their actions. Circumstances also may permit a single firm, not a monopolist, to exercise market power through unilateral or non-coordinated conduct — conduct the success of which does not rely on the concurrence of other firms in the market or on coordinated responses by those firms. In any case, the result of the exercise of market power is a transfer of wealth from buyers to sellers or a misallocation of resources.[448]

[*] Sellers with market power also may lessen competition on dimensions other than price, such as product quality, service or innovation.

The identification of when a small number of firms can exercise this power is not a precise science. Nevertheless, when the number of significant firms falls into the single digits there is cause for concern, as the following summary of empirical and theoretical findings in the industrial organization literature suggests.

> Where is the line to be drawn between oligopoly and competition? At what number do we draw the line between few and many? In principle, competition applies when the number of competing firms is infinite; at the same time, the textbooks usually say that a market is competitive if the cross effects between firms are negligible. Up to six firms one has oligopoly, and with fifty firms or more of roughly equal size one has competition; however, for sizes in between it may be difficult to say. The answer is not a matter of principle but rather an empirical matter.[449]

As a practical matter, using the Department of Justice *Merger Guidelines* and general economic literature, I apply the following categories to describe media markets (see Table V-1):

Monopoly – 1 dominant firm
Duopoly – 2, relatively equal-sized, firms that dominate the market
Tight oligopoly – 3 to 5 large firms
Moderately concentrated – 6 to 9 firms
Unconcentrated – 10 or more firms
Atomistic competition – 50 firms

The description of markets suggested above is based on theoretical, empirical and practical experience in media markets. In order to assess

TABLE V-1: Describing Market Structures

DEPARTMENT OF JUSTICE MERGER GUIDELINES	TYPE OF MARKET	EQUIVALENTS IN TERMS OF EQUAL SIZED FIRMS	TYPICAL HHI IN MEDIA MARKETS	4-FIRM SHARE
	MONOPOLY	1[a]	5300+	~100
	DUOPOLY	2[b]	3000 - 5000	~100
		5	2000	80
HIGHLY CONCENTRATED	TIGHT OLIGOPOLY		1800 OR MORE	
MODERATELY CONCENTRATED		6	1667	67
UNCONCENTRATED	LOOSE OLIGOPOLY	10	1000	40[c]
	ATOMISTIC COMPETITION	50	200	8[c]

a = Antitrust practice finds monopoly firms with market share in the 65% to 75% range. Thus, HHIs in "monopoly markets can be as low as 4200.

b = Duopolies need not be a perfect 50/50 split. Duopolies with a 60/40 split would have a higher HHI.

c = Value falls as the number of firms increases.

Sources: U.S. Department of Justice, *Horizontal Merger Guidelines*, revised April 8, 1997, for a discussion of the HHI thresholds; William G. Shepherd, *The Economics of Industrial Organization* (Englewood Cliffs, NJ: Prentice Hall, 1985), for a discussion of four firm concentration ratios.

the potential for the exercise of market power resulting from a merger, the Department of Justice analyzes the level of concentration as measured by the Herfindahl-Hirschman Index (HHI).[450] This measure takes the market share of each firm, squares it, sums the result, and multiplies by 10,000.[451] A second method frequently used by economists to quantify market concentration is to calculate the market share of the largest four firms (four firm concentration ratio or CR4).

Under its *Merger Guidelines,* the DOJ considers a market with an HHI of 1000 or less to be unconcentrated. Such a market would have the equivalent of ten equal-sized competitors. In such a market, the four firm concentration ratio would be 40 percent. Any market with a concentration above this level is deemed to be a source of concern. The DOJ considers an HHI of 1800 as the point at which a market is highly concentrated. This level falls between five and six equal-sized competitors. The four firm concentration ratio would be 67 percent.

William Shepherd describes these thresholds in terms of four firm concentration ratios as follows:[452]

> Tight Oligopoly: The leading four firms combined have 60-100 percent of the market; collusion among them is relatively easy.
>
> Loose Oligopoly: The leading four firms combined have 40 percent or less of the market; collusion among them to fix prices is virtually impossible.

Shepherd refers to collusion in his discussion, but it is important to note that it is not the only concern of market power analysis or the *Merger Guidelines.* The DOJ *Guidelines* are oriented toward conditions under which a broad range of types of anticompetitive behaviors are sufficiently likely to occur as to require regulatory action. The *Merger Guidelines* recognize that market power can be exercised with coordinated, or parallel, activities and even unilateral actions in situations where there are small numbers of market players.[453] The area of non-collusive, oligopoly behavior has received a great deal of attention. A variety of models have been developed in which it is demonstrated that small numbers of market participants interacting in the market, especially on a repeated basis, can learn to signal, anticipate, and parallel one another to achieve outcomes that capture a substantial share of the potential monopoly profits.[454] This leads us to identify several other specific types of markets where such behavior is more or less likely.

First, the highly concentrated category can be broken down into two types of markets that are a special source of concern. Although the expression 'monopoly' technically refers to one firm, antitrust practice refers to monopoly power when the market share of a firm is 60 to 70 percent. The CR4 would be close to 100. The HHI can vary, depending on the size of the second firm in the market. A dominant firm with a market share of 65 percent alongside ten small firms would result in an HHI of about 4,300. As a practical matter, in media markets, monopoly situations where the leading firm has over 65 percent of the market share exhibit HHIs of 5,300 or higher. A 'duopoly' refers to a market with only two firms. Two equal-sized firms would be a duopoly with an HHI of 5,000. Duopolies generally fall in the 60/40 percent range, exhibiting HHIs between 3,000 and 5,300. Here, too, the CR4 would be close to 100.

On the other hand, we should not forget that although ten firms constitute an unconcentrated market by DOJ *Guidelines*, that number does not ensure vigorous competition. Generally, a much higher number, perhaps fifty, is associated with vigorous or atomistic competition. With 50 equal size competitors, the HHI would be 200 and the CR4 would be 8.

The *Guidelines* identify the types of mergers that will raise competitive concerns as follows:

> Mergers producing an increase in the HHI of more than 50 points in highly concentrated markets post-merger potentially raise significant competitive concerns... Mergers producing an increase in the HHI of more than 100 points in moderately concentrated markets post-merger potentially raise significant competitive concerns.[455]

The competitive concern is the potential for the exercise of market power. The *Guidelines* define market power as "the ability profitably to maintain prices above competitive levels for a significant period of time [or]...lessen competition on dimensions other than price, such as product quality, service or innovation."[456] While concerns exist in all concentrated markets, the *Guidelines* note that in highly concentrated markets, mergers "are likely to create or enhance market power or facilitate its exercise." To appreciate the nature of these thresholds, a firm with a 15 percent market share that sought to buy another with a two percent market share would violate the 50-point threshold. If the firm being acquired had a market share of just over three percent, it would violate the 100-point threshold.

In order to analyze the level of concentration in a market, one must define the market by deciding which products and which firms are selling in that market. There are two critical decisions – the product definition and the geographic scope of the market.

THE PRODUCT: MEDIA USE FOR NEWS AND INFORMATION

Television and newspapers dominate the news media market. Television provides the announcement function. Newspapers provide

FIGURE V-1: Respondents "Get Most News" from TV And Newspapers

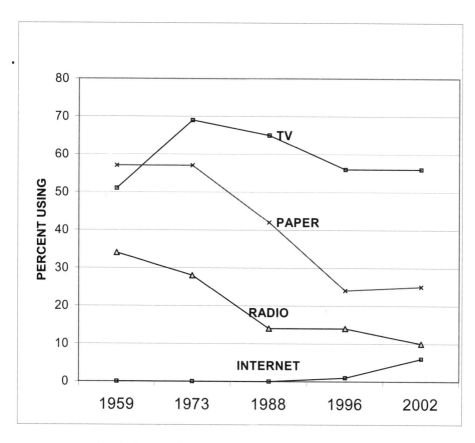

Source: Roper, *America's Watching: 30th Anniversary 1959-1989*; Graber, Doris A., *Processing Politics: Learning from Television in the Internet Age* (Chicago: University of Chicago Press, 2001), p. 3; Nielsen, *Consumer Survey on Media Usage* (Federal Communications Commission, Media Ownership Working Group, September 2002).

in-depth coverage. Other sources of news are dwarfed by these dominant sources.

Approximately 80 percent of respondents to an FCC sponsored survey say they get most of their news and information from TV or newspapers (see Figure V-1). That percentage has been stable since the advent of the Internet. It is even higher for election information.

TABLE V-2: Sources Of News: 2002

(Percent of Respondents)

MEDIUM	LOCAL SOURCE LAST WEEK	NATIONAL SOURCE LAST WEEK	GET MOST NEWS	EXPECT TO USE MORE
TV	85	83	56	27
NEWSPAPER	63	50	23	6
RADIO	35	30	10	7
INTERNET	19	21	6	9

Source: Nielsen, *Consumer Survey on Media Usage* (Federal Communications Commission, Media Ownership Working Group, September 2002).

Responses to the question that asked where people get "most" of their news show the ascendance of TV. By the late 1980s, radio had lost its role. Newspapers suffered a decline in the 1990s. Although the Internet has grown, it still plays a small role compared to TV and newspapers.

When asked about the regular sources of news (as opposed to the place where the respondent gets most news), TV and newspapers still dominate (see Table V-2). This is true for both local and national news.[457] Newspapers play a larger role for local news than national news. Interestingly, when asked about increases in future media use, TV was mentioned far more often than the other sources.

Table V-3 contrasts the responses to two Pew questions dealing with the most important sources of election news with the responses to the FCC question on most important sources. The fact that Pew asked questions specifically about national and local elections is important, since the FCC never asked about the most important sources of local news. The responses to the three questions about most important sources are very close. The FCC's question on any source, rather than most important sources, is quite different from the other three.

The uniqueness of newspapers also stems from the fact that news is their primary function. All of the other mass media combine news and entertainment (see Figure V-2). Of all the media, newspapers are uniquely focused on providing information. In contrast, TV, radio and the Internet combine entertainment and information.

TABLE V-3: QUESTIONS ABOUT IMPORTANCE AND USE OF MEDIA SOURCES FOR LOCAL AND NATIONAL NEWS AND CURRENT AFFAIRS

QUESTION	WEIGHTS			
	TV	Papers	Radio	Internet
PEW QUESTIONS				
How have you been getting most of your[a] news about the presidential election campaign?	60.5	25.5	9.7	4.8
How do you get most of your news about the[b] election campaigns in you state and district?	55.5	27.8	10.9	5.9
FCC QUESTIONS				
What single source do you use most often for[c] local or national news and current affairs?	58.8	24.4	10.5	6.2
What source, if any, have you used in the past[d] 7 days for local news and current affairs?	42.0	31.1	17.5	9.3

a/ Pew Center for the People and the Press, *Sources for Campaign News, Fewer Turn to Broadcast TV and Papers* (Feb. 5, 2000), q. 13.

b/ Pew Center for the People and the Press, *Modest Increase in Internet Use for Campaign 2002* (Jan. 5, 2003), q. 17.

c/ Nielsen Media Research, *Consumer Survey On Media Usage* (Federal Communications Commission, Media Ownership Working Group Study No. 8, September 2002) question no. 10.

d/ Media Ownership Working Group Study No. 8, question no. 1.

Post-September 11 surveys reaffirm this pattern.[458] TV is the primary source for breaking news – what is known in advertising as the announcement function. Radio plays a small role. TV's dominant role persists in the follow-up function while radio drops off. Newspapers take on a larger role in the follow-up function. The Internet does not play such a role. Similar changes are evident on a year-to-year basis. We

FIGURE V-2: Newspapers Are Uniquely Oriented Toward News Gathering

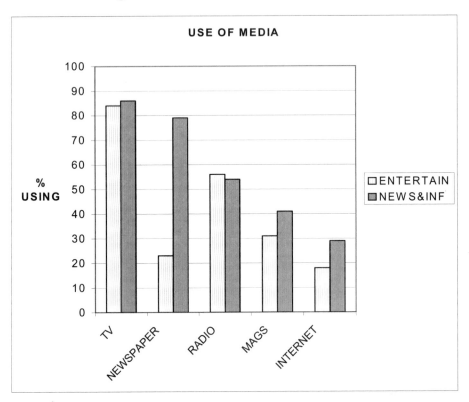

Source: Roper Reports, 01-2, 2001, p. 159.

would expect more interest in news and that is what we find. Newspapers and TV show the largest increase with the Internet slightly surpassing radio.

Cable plays only a small role as a source of local news and information. Only eleven percent of those who rely on cable cite a local cable channel. Few cable operators provide news, and when they do, it frequently replicates one of the broadcast networks. At present, satellite provides no independent local news or information. Indeed, it is struggling just to make all local stations available. While broadcast TV has experienced a decline in news viewing, the primary cause is a shift from watching news over-the-air to watching the same outlets through-the-wire.

A Pew Research Center study makes this point.[459] Between 1993 and 1999, when Internet use became widespread, viewing of network news and network news magazines declined. However, so has viewing of the major non-network (cable) shows like CNN and C-Span. Where did the viewers go? They went to the cable-based offerings of the network stations. In other words, while viewing may be shifting from over-the-air to through-the-wire, according to this data, it is actually becoming more concentrated in the major networks.

Claims that Americans are turning from TV to the Internet for news are not supported by the evidence.[460] The Internet's role as an independent source of news is quite small. The web sites of the main TV outlets and newspapers dominate as sources on the Internet. Even the six percent of respondents who say it is their primary source of news are more likely to say they use the web sites of major TV networks or newspapers than other sites. The Internet should not be counted as an additional local voice.

A survey conducted in mid-2000 sheds further light on this issue. It asked respondents whether they had ever heard of specific online news sources and whether the sources are believable (see Figure V-3). Respondents were much more familiar with the web sites of existing broadcast and newspaper firms and found them much more believable. The use of online media has not substantially changed individual news sources. It is most interesting to note in this context that the Commission's task force study on media substitutability assumed that cable and the Internet are national, not local, sources of news.

A recent study from the UCLA Center for Communications Policy reinforces this point.[461] Respondents report spending about four minutes per day gathering news online. They report about twenty-five minutes per day reading the newspaper. The Pew study shows respondents spent over half an hour a day watching TV news and fifteen minutes a day listening to radio news. In other words, traditional media account for twenty times as much news gathering time as the Internet.

Perhaps the most decisive blow to the claim of an Internet revolution can be seen in responses to questions about where people turned for their main sources of campaign news in presidential elections.[462] TV still overwhelmingly dominates, followed by newspapers, radio and then the Internet. The number of respondents who cite TV and newspapers is

FIGURE V- 3: Web Sites of TV News and Newspapers are Better Known and Believed

(Percent of Respondents)

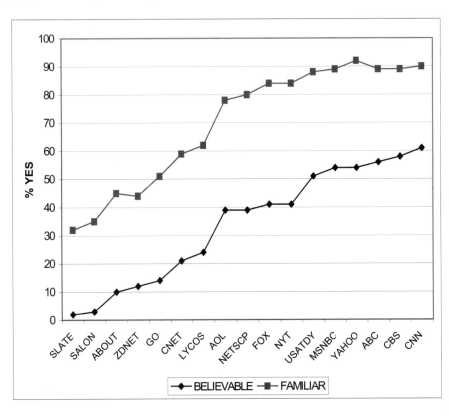

Source: Pew Research Center, "Internet Sapping Broadcast News Audience," June 11, 2000.

over 13 times that of the Internet. This parallels the finding that respondents spend about 15 times as much time gathering news and information on TV and in the newspapers as they do on the Internet.

Figure V-4 shows respondents' total hours of use for each of the major media categorized by the media that was the source of most of their news and information. One-sixteenth of the respondents cited the Internet as their primary source of news. They are the most intensive

FIGURE V-4: Media Usage by Type of Media Used Most Often For News

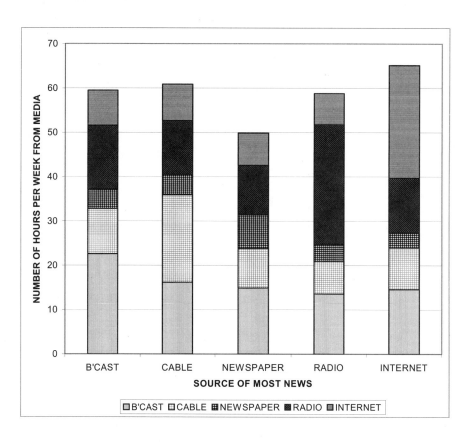

SOURCE: Federal Communications Commission, Study 8, *Consumer Survey on Media Usage*, prepared by Nielsen Media Research, September 2002, Question 7. Multiple responses allowed, percentage of total responses.

users of media, with a very large number of hours devoted to the Internet, compared to the remainder of the population. They are light users of TV.

Radio was cited by one-tenth of the respondents. While their usage of media was about average overall, they were very heavy users of radio and light users of TV.

Newspapers were cited by just under one-quarter of the respondents as their primary source of news. Their total media usage was below average. They had low TV usage but did not have a great deal more newspaper usage than the other groups. Those who cited TV (either broadcast or cable) as their primary source of news had slightly above-average overall use, primarily because they used more TV.

All of the groups who did not cite the Internet as their primary source of news had roughly the same amount of Internet use – between seven and eight hours per week. Similarly, there is relatively little variation across the groups in terms of newspaper usage.

The most detailed substitution analysis commissioned by the FCC involved usage data for markets and individuals. It focused on "the question of whether the changes in the availability or use of some media have brought about changes in the availability or consumers' use of other media, or whether different media serve as substitutes for one another for information consumers."[463] It goes on to claim that "this study examines the extent of substitutability across media."[464]

The study appears to be at best schizophrenic about substitution. On the one hand, it claims a pervasive pattern of substitution[465] and the introduction gives the impression that there is a great deal of substitution. It states that the study "cannot completely answer the question of whether substitution is sufficiently effective that all media should be considered substitutes for news and information purposes."[466] Cautioning us that the substitution is not complete gives the impression that there is a lot of it. That is not the case at all.

In the conclusion, there is more caution. The author states that, at best, in the statistical sense, "there is at least some degree of substitution."[467] At least some is a far cry from complete. The author goes on to introduce a concept of "behavioral neutrality" as a measure of complete substitution stating that "with complete substitution, the civic behavior affected by media consumption will also be unaffected by changes in availability of use of any particular medium."[468] The study cites a variety of evidence that shows that "behavioral neutrality fails."[469] In fact, the study never addresses the extent of substitution in a statistical sense. If there is any substitution, it is minuscule.

Virtually all of the relationships reported based on the macro data fail to demonstrate statistically significant substitutability. Only 19 of the 184 possible relationships are statistically significant by a rigorous standard.

Although the study never analyzes the magnitude of substitutability there are two indications that it is very small. First, cross-media substitution explains virtually none of the variation in media usage. For example, the demographic control variables that are utilized in the analysis explain 12.44 percent of the variance in the number of TV news half hours watched. Adding in the use of the four other media for news and information gathering increases the explained variance to 12.65 percent. In other words, media substitution accounts for less than one-quarter of one percent of the variance in TV media use. Moreover, part of that variance is explained by complementarities (positive relationships) not substitution. In no case did the media variables account for more than 2 percent of the variance in the target (dependent variable) media use.[470]

With little variance explained, one would not expect to find large effects. In economic terms, the cross elasticities of demand are minuscule. For example, in the Internet-TV relationship, for which the study finds the strongest evidence of substitution, I find an elasticity of .02. In other words, if the Internet usage were to double (increase by 100 percent) TV usage would decline by just 2 percent.

To examine the pattern of substitutability/complementarity with Nielsen survey data, I ran correlations and regressions, testing substitutability in a number of subgroups of the population. Simple bivariate correlations and multiple regressions controlling for age and gender were estimated for the following groups of respondents:

All Respondents
Internet Users
Non-Internet Users
TV (broadcast or cable) for most news
Not TV for most news
Broadcast for most news
Cable for most news
Newspaper for most news
Radio for most news
Internet for most news

Not one of the correlations or regression coefficients indicated substitutability. Every correlation and regression indicated complementarity and many were statistically significant.

Another possible approach to the complementarity/substitutability issue is to look at various groups according to their levels of usage. Media junkies might use the media as complements; low volume users might use them as substitutes. To examine this possibility, the relationship between the use of various media was examined in two subgroups. Because the distribution is slightly skewed (the mean is almost one-third higher than the median), I divided the population as follows:

- low use respondents, defined as the 50 percent of respondents whose total use of the media fell below the median, and
- high use respondents, defined as approximately one-third of the respondents whose use fell above the average.

The median use is 45 hours per week; the average use is just under 57 hours per week.

This approach shows a hint of substitution, but just a hint. The complementarities between the media are a lot stronger and larger for the more intensive media users than the substitution effects are among the less intensive users. In neither of the subgroups does substitution between the media explain more than five percent of the variance in usage. In all cases the size of the substitution effects is quite small.

One final observation on substitution should be made. In order to make sense of the statistical results, the FCC's substitution analysis assumes that cable and Internet are non-local media. To the extent that public policy has been primarily concerned about localism and media distribution markets are local, this raises problems for the broad definition of markets. This argument also suggests that one would not expect to find substitution between the cable news sources and the local broadcast sources.

This argument is supported by the Nielsen data. Local broadcast exhibits no significant negative correlation with cable news broadcasts. In fact, it exhibits no significant correlation with any other broadcast sources of news. Once again, I observe positive correlations, suggesting complementarity, with one exception, cable local and CBS, but the size of the coefficient is quite small. The largest coefficients are observed for the national news networks and the cable networks as a separate group, and all are positive. Three of the correlations across broadcast and cable are positive, though small, with the largest being between MSNBC and NBC.

The FCC had just as much difficulty demonstrating substitutability in advertising as it did in usage. The econometric study turned up weak substitutability at best.[471] The theoretical work it commissioned failed to suggest significant substitutability.[472]

GEOGRAPHIC MARKETS

Geographic markets were mentioned in the earlier discussion. The distinction between national and local markets has been made and is quite important for news distribution media, cable TV and the Internet. Defining the local market, which is the focal point of much First Amendment policy, with greater precision is especially important.

Most discussions of TV and newspaper markets use the Designated Marketing Area (DMA) as the geographic market area. This is a very large market area and any analysis based on it will seriously underestimate the level of actual concentration for a number of reasons.

First, on the TV side, use of the DMA overestimates the availability of broadcast stations for many viewers. To the extent that viewers receive their broadcast signals through multi-channel (cable or satellite) distribution, this large market may be appropriate. However, about 15 percent of the population receives broadcast signals over the air. For this group, the DMA is far too large a market definition, since signals do not cover the entire DMA.

Second, many smaller broadcast stations do not enjoy distribution throughout the DMA. While they have a right to request carriage throughout the DMA, it makes little economic sense for them to do so. The local news and advertising from communities that are fifty or a hundred miles away from the dominant central city cannot attract enough attention to make it economically worthwhile, nor should it be expected to. Meeting local needs for information dissemination is an important function that public policy should promote. Basing public policy on the fiction that every TV station is available to every viewer throughout the DMA distorts the reality of the level of concentration in TV markets.

The problem on the newspaper side is even more severe. Newspapers do not have 'must-carry' or retransmission rights throughout the DMA. Newspapers are very geographically focused. They are usually identified with a major central city or county where they achieve dominant circulation. When more than one major city or county falls within a DMA, the perception of the level of concentration is distorted.

To demonstrate this fact, I have examined the newspaper circulation within counties in a number of large DMAs. These DMAs tend to be well below the national average of concentration. However, when I consider circulation in counties, I find that the markets are much more concentrated. In fact, the weighted HHI is on average almost 2000 points higher at the county level.

Figure V-5 shows one example, with a detailed analysis for Los Angeles. This is one of the largest DMAs in the country with many newspapers. Our newspaper data covers about 95 percent of the households. Each individual newspaper dominates a specific county. This is not a "failure" of competition in the traditional sense. Rather, it reflects the nature of the local newspaper business, where a geographic focus is required. Neither local news nor local advertising for large DMAs can be covered in one newspaper, so each paper is significantly specialized in a geographic market.

In spite of these factors, which are likely to lead to an underestimation of concentration in these major media markets, I find that in most DMAs in the country, the number of independently owned major media outlets – TV stations and daily newspapers – is extremely small.

FIGURE V-5: Local Papers Dominate Home Counties

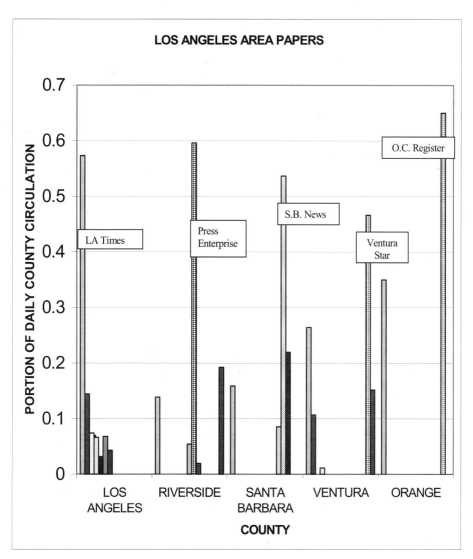

Sources: Eileen Davis Hudson and Mark Fitzgerald, "Capturing Audience Requires a Dragnet," *Editor and Publisher*, October 22, 2001, p. 20. Los Angeles is used as an example because it is the third least concentrated (for newspapers) DMA in the country and the five counties identified above account for 95 percent of the households in the DMA.

VI. ANALYSIS OF MEDIA MARKETS

Although the central concern with media ownership as it affects civic discourse must focus on news and information, the commercial context in which the production of news and information are embedded cannot be ignored. As suggested earlier, those commercial influences impinge on the ability and commitment to gather and disseminate news and information.

This review of the commercial mass media product space shows that the fundamental characteristics of the media market that result in a serious market failure from the point of view of civic discourse are still operative. Mass media revenues are still dominated by advertising. TV dominates the national advertising market. Newspapers and radio still dominate the local advertising market. Substitutability between media remains low. The number of owners is declining, not increasing.

The discussion is divided by media and markets. I discuss broadcast and cable TV distribution media. I discuss programming as national and local content. I also discuss newspapers, radio and the Internet. Each discussion begins with a general description of the business models that apply in the relevant product and geographic markets. In then discuss levels of concentration. Finally, in each case for entities regulated by the FCC, I review major ownership policy decisions over the last two decades that had an impact on the industry.

Based on changes in other ownership rules, it is reasonable to expect that several hundred mergers would quickly take place with implementation of the proposed rules, dramatically reducing the number of major independent voices in these markets. The impact of the three examples discussed below is embedded in the previous discussion of the concentration of media markets. Highlighting the specific impacts of the policy changes reinforces the basic tenet of the behavior of large media corporations: "if you let them, they will merge." Starting from the initial base of highly concentrated markets, eliminating or relaxing ownership limits would have a devastating impact on media concentration.

BROADCAST TELEVISION

Revenues and Output

TV networks still dominate the most valuable viewing time – prime time – and capture the lion's share of national advertising dollars. While there has been an increase in non-prime time cable TV viewing, the big three networks are still "prime time programming juggernauts."[473] The addition of four new broadcast networks, only one of which provides a little news and public interest programming, has not altered the fact that the big three networks still account for the overwhelming majority of high impact news and information shows – 80 or 90 percent. Adding in Fox, which has been built from stations that already did news, the share is well above the 90 percent range.

Network broadcast TV is predominantly national, accounting for almost 60 percent of national advertising revenues; newspapers are local, accounting for 50 percent of local advertising revenues (see Table VI-1). There has been little change in advertising market shares. In 1985, slightly less than one-third of all advertising dollars spent on these media was spent on broadcast. In 2000, broadcast accounted for a little more than one-third of all advertising dollars. In 1985, just over one-half of all advertising dollars was spent on newspapers; in 2000, newspapers accounted for just under one-half. In 1985, radio accounted for one-seventh of advertising; the same was true in 2000.

Network advertising revenue growth has far outstripped population growth or any change in viewing habits. Advertising revenue has grown about 117 percent as compared to adult population/audience, which has grown by about 14 percent. Based on these entertainment/information media, broadcast's share of the total advertising pie has increased from 31 percent to 36 percent since 1985. Reflecting these underlying trends, the FCC found that the financial health of the networks was quite good.[474]

Network TV is primarily a nationally-oriented medium. TV networks dominate the national video product space with original prime time programming. Nevertheless, local advertising revenues and local stations play an important role in the TV market. The tension within the traditional broadcast industry has been fueled by the conflict of economic

TABLE VI-1: Media Industry Advertising Revenue Data

ADVERTISING (Billion $, nominal)

	1985	1993	1996	2001
Broadcast	14.6	28	36	39
Cable	0.7	4	6	15
Radio	6.5	9	12	18
Newspaper	25.2	32	38	44
Internet	0	0	0	6
Total	47	73	92	122

DISTRIBUTION OF ADVERTISING REVENUE WITHIN MEDIA TYPES

	Local	National	Total
Newspapers	84	16	100
Broadcast	32	68	100
Cable	76	24	100
Radio	79	21	100
Internet	0	100	100

Source: U.S. Census Bureau, *Statistical Abstract of the United States: 2001* (U.S. Department of Commerce, 2000), Tables 1125, 1126, 1271.

interests between local stations and national networks. This tension bears directly on the provision of local content, one of the most prominent aspects of policy in electronic media.[475]

One of the changes to which advocates of abandoning ownership limits point is the increase in the number of full power TV stations (Table VI-2). These stations are the dominant suppliers of broadcast television. They have increased from just under 1,000 in 1975 to almost 1,700 in 2000. These numbers include a substantial increase in the number of noncommercial stations.

This positive picture is tempered by two negative developments. Although the number of broadcast TV outlets has grown, the number of news operations at those stations has not. Indeed, the best evidence suggests that it has declined by about 10 percent.[476] In other words, there has been a decline in the number of TV stations that have news operations. By Vernon Stone's reasoning, with virtually every "viable commercial"[477] TV station having a newsroom in 1975, there were about 940 such operations. By 2000, Stone estimates that only 850 had them.

TABLE VI-2: Mass Media Outlets, Ownership And News Operations, 1975-2000

	1975	2000
TELEVISION		
Outlets		
Full Pwr	952	1678
Low Pwr	Na	2396
Owners	543	360
Newsrooms	940	850
Staff/Newsroom		24
DAILY NEWSPAPERS		
Outlets	1756	1422
Owners	863	290
Newsrooms	1756	1422
Staff/Newsroom		62
RADIO		
Outlets	7785	12932
Owners	5100	3800
Newsrooms	~ 6000	4500
Staff/Newsroom		3

Sources: "Notice of Proposed Rulemaking," *In the Matter of Implementation of Section 11 of the Cable Television Consumer Protection and Competition Act of 1992 Implementation of Cable Act Reform Provisions of the Telecommunications Act of 1996 The Commission's Cable Horizontal and Vertical Ownership Limits and Attribution Rules Review of the Commission's Regulations Governing Attribution Of Broadcast and Cable/MDS Interests Review of the Commission's Regulations and Policies Affecting Investment In the Broadcast Industry Reexamination of the Commission's Cross-Interest Policy,* CS Docket No. 98-82, CS Docket No. 96-85, MM Docket No. 92-264, MM Docket No. 94-150, MM Docket No. 92-51, MM Docket No. 87-154, September 13, 2001, p. 6; Vernon Stone, *News Operations at U.S. TV Stations;* U.S. Bureau of the Census, Statistical Abstract of the United States: 2000 Tables 2, 37, 932; *Annual Almanac, Editor and Publisher,* various issues. ; Lisa George, *What's Fit To Print: The Effect Of Ownership Concentration On Product Variety In Daily Newspaper Markets* (2001).

The mixed picture we get by looking at news operations (rather than stations) gets much grimmer when we consider ownership of TV stations. The data show a sharp decline in the number of owners, despite the growth of the number of stations. There are now one-third fewer broadcast owners than there were twenty-five years ago. Local marketing agreements hide even greater diminution of independent news sources.[478]

TABLE VI-3: Concentration Of Local Broadcast Markets

MARKETS COUNT	LOCAL TV MARKETS BY BROADCAST SHARE		LOCAL NEWS BY TV OUTLET	
	NUMBER OF DMAs	PERCENT OF DMAs	NUMBER OF DMAs	PERCENT OF DMAs
MONOPOLY	26	12	18	9
DUOPOLY	56	27	27	13
OTHER HIGHLY CONCENTRATED	112	53	129	62
MODERATELY CONCENTRATED	16	8	33	16
UNCONCENTRATED	0	0	3	1

SOURCE: Owen Bruce, Kent W. Mikkelsen, Allison Ivory, "News and Public Affairs Programming Offered by the Four Top-ranked Versus Lower-Ranked Television Stations," Economic Study A, *Comments of Fox Entertainment Group and Fox Television Stations, Inc., National Broadcasting Company, Inc. and Telemundo Group, Inc., and Viacom,* In the Matter of 2002 Biennial Regulatory Review – Review of the Commission's Broadcast Ownership Rules and Other Rules Adopted Pursuant to Section 202 of the Telecommunications Act of 1996, Cross Ownership of Broadcast Stations and Newspapers, Rules and Policies Concerning Multiple Ownership of Radio Broadcast Stations in Local Markets, Definition of Radio Markets, MB Docket No. 02-277, MM Dockets 02-235, 01=317, 00-244, January 2, 2003; *Television Market Report: 2001* (Washington, D.C.: BIA Financial Network, 2001).

Concentration of Local Markets

In spite of the fact that use of the DMA as the geographic market leads to an underestimation of the level of concentration, we still find that TV markets are highly concentrated (see Table VI-3). Looking at broadcast market shares only, none of the markets is unconcentrated, and only eight percent are moderately concentrated. Over half the markets are tight oligopolies. A quarter of the markets are duopolies.

The broadcast networks have provided data that shows the high level of concentration of local broadcast news.[479] In 70 percent of the markets, original local news is available from only four (or fewer) broadcasters. Even if we include stations that do not produce original local news but air news content produced by someone else, we still find that in 62 percent of the markets there are four or fewer stations airing local news.

Even using a simple voice count approach, which underestimates the concentration of the local market because it treats all broadcasters the same regardless of their market share, virtually every local TV news market in the country is highly concentrated. Nine percent of all local TV news markets are monopolies and thirteen percent are duopolies. Sixty-two percent are tight oligopolies (three to five sources). In other words, over four-fifths (83 percent) of local TV news markets are highly concentrated, tight oligopolies or worse. Only one percent of these markets are "unconcentrated." This means that there are virtually no localities in the U.S. where mergers between two or more local broadcast outlets would not substantially diminish competition in the coverage of local news and informational events.

TV After Relaxation of the Duopoly Rule

To gauge the impact of eliminating the structural limits on TV station ownership, I examined the rate at which mergers took place in TV markets after the introduction of the duopoly rule in September 1999. The duopoly rule allows a station owner to own two stations within one market as long as there remain eight independent TV voices after such a merger. I estimate that mergers became permissible in just under 80 markets since this rule was enacted. Figure VI-1 shows the percentage of markets in which mergers took place. At least one merger took place in over two-thirds of all the markets where they were allowed. In larger markets where five or more mergers were allowed, at least one merger took place in every market (i.e. there are no markets without a merger). In markets where multiple mergers were permitted only about 36 percent of all the possible mergers have taken place. In smaller markets, at least one merger took place in about half the markets where they were allowed.

The media industry claims that duopolies increase the quantity and quality of news, but the evidence does not support this conclusion (see

FIGURE VI-1: Mergers Spurred By The Relaxation Of The Duopoly Rule

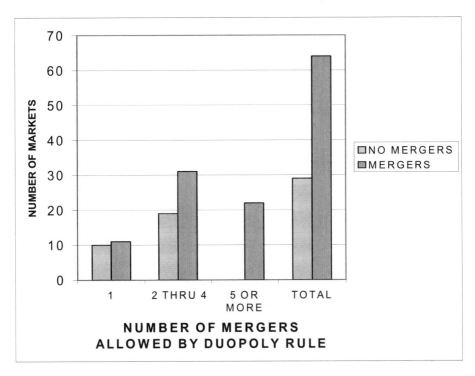

Source: Calculated from *Television Market Report: 2001* (Washington, D.C.: BIA Financial 2001); See Reply Comments of Consumer Federation of America, et al.; *In the Matter of Cross-Ownership of Broadcast Stations and Newspapers; Newspaper-Radio Cross-Ownership Waiver Policy: Order and Notice of Proposed Rulemaking*, MM Docket No. 01-235, 96-197, February 15, 2002.

Table VI-4). Increases in news coverage are equal in duopoly and non-duopoly markets. More importantly, the loss of independent hours of news in duopoly markets exceeds the gain in the total hours of news in those markets. In other words, we get a little more quantity at a severe cost to quality (independent hours of news). Conversely, the ban on duopolies promotes diversity of viewpoints (measured by ownership) without detracting from the quantity of news.

An econometric analysis is consistent with these findings.[480] It finds a small increase in the *probability* that a station will cover news (from 66.5 to 74.5 percent), but no statistically significant differences in the amount

TABLE VI-4: Duopolies Do Not Produce Larger Increases in News Hours

	DUOPOLY[a]/			NON-DUOPOLY[b]/	
	# of Markets	Change in Hours of News	Lost Hours of Independent News	# of Markets	Change in Hours of News
FOX	9	+1.7	-2.5	16	+1.9
NBC	6	+4.4	-12.0	10	+3.9
TOT/ AVG.	15	+2.8	-6.3	26	+2.7

Source: *Comments of Fox Entertainment Group and Fox Television Stations, Inc., National Broadcasting Company, Inc. and Telemundo Group, Inc., and Viacom,* News Programming Exhibit No.1 Fox Entertainment Group Inc. and Fox Television Stations, Inc., News Programming Exhibit No.2 National Broadcasting Company, Inc. and Telemundo Communications Group, Inc.," In the Matter of 2002 Biennial Regulatory Review – Review of the Commission's Broadcast Ownership Rules and Other Rules Adopted Pursuant to Section 202 of the Telecommunications Act of 1996, Cross Ownership of Broadcast Stations and Newspapers, Rules and Policies Concerning Multiple Ownership of Radio Broadcast Stations in Local Markets, Definition of Radio Markets, MB Docket No. 02-277, MM Dockets 02-235, 01-317, 00-244, January 2, 2003.
a/ Viacom data does not provide sufficient detail to conduct the lost hours analysis.
b/ Fox shows much larger gains for non-duopolies when it goes back to its pre-acquisition of stations, which in many cases is a decade or more ago. Use of this data would make non-duopolies appear even more valuable. This analysis uses changes since 11/2000.

of news. Because the networks disregard ownership, the study did not examine the loss of independent news. Also the network-sponsored econometric study cannot address the question of causality. It did not inquire as to whether the duopolists added news after a duopoly was created or merely bought stations that already produced news.

An examination of the detailed data provided by FOX and NBC shows that they did not add news to any stations that did not already carry it and, in one case, they eliminated the news at a duopoly station.[481] Thus, the networks mistakenly ascribed a positive affect to duopolies where none exists. In terms of news carriage, the networks were not able to show a positive effect in the amount of news carried, and completely ignored the negative effect of the loss of an independent news voice.

A similar conclusion emerges from the study prepared for Sinclair by Robert Crandall.[482] Using a lax standard of statistical significance, Crandall concludes that duopolies result in a slight decrease in advertising rates. The decrease is extremely small, just .3 percent. In other words, according to Crandall, prohibiting duopolies (which preserves a valuable independent TV voice) imposes a statistically insignificant and quantitatively minuscule economic cost.

CABLE TV

Revenues and Output

The analysis of TV stations is important because these are important distribution mechanisms and also because these TV stations were historically the source of local programming. One of the most prominent claims of those who argue that dramatic changes have taken place is that the growth in the number of cable networks creates a great deal of diversity. Cable TV systems have become the dominant form of distribution for video programming and they have the capacity to deliver many more channels. These channels need content.

Cable systems operators are the local distribution system for cable, franchised at the local level, although federal preemption has scaled back the role of local franchising authorities. Cable provides local distribution of video content, primarily capturing non-prime time viewing. While total hours watching TV have been almost constant over the past fifteen years, cable's share has grown from fourteen percent to almost 50 percent.

In contrast to network TV, which is funded entirely by advertising, cable is funded primarily by subscription revenues, although national advertising revenues have been growing. Local advertising still plays a small role in cable and cable plays a small role in the local advertising market. Newspapers take in thirteen times as much and radio four times as much local advertising revenue as cable.

Satellite occupies a much narrower product space than cable. It is a high-cost, niche distribution system. Given its cost characteristics, it does not compete with basic cable. Satellite still lacks robust local programming and original prime time programming, thus it is not yet a substitute for network TV or cable. During the 1990s, satellite filled out its niche. It now has about 18 million subscribers compared to cable's almost 70 million. The large channel capacity of Direct Broadcast Satellite (DBS) and high front-end costs dictate the packaging of large numbers of high priced channels and/or long-term contracts. As a result, DBS is a small competitive fringe that is not capable of disciplining cable TV pricing.[483] DBS still costs more than basic cable does, not including the front-end system costs, which undermines its ability to compete on price.[484] Cable makes much more money by increasing prices for basic cable than by trying to compete in the DBS niche.

Concentration of Local Markets

The failure of satellite to discipline cable pricing abuse and the failure of cable to compete with local telephone service are among the greatest disappointments of the 1996 Telecommunications Act. These disappointments tell a great deal about the prospects for cross technology competition. Congress had great hopes for this form of competition. In fact, the only facilities-based competitor for local telephone service actually mentioned by the Act's Conference report was cable TV.[485] Similarly, Congress devoted a whole section to telephone competition for cable through open video systems.[486] Neither of these has proven effective competition. Open video systems are non-existent[487] and the only telephone company that has pursued entry into the cable business as a plain over-builder, Ameritech, was purchased by another telephone company, SBC, which is exiting the cable business.[488]

The failure of competition in multi-channel video is evident in local markets. Approximately 95 percent of the homes passed in the country are served by only one cable company.[489] On average, cable operators have an 85 percent market share for multi-channel video at the local level.[490] In fact, since satellite is concentrated in rural areas where cable is not available, cable's market share in areas where they are both present is higher. The HHI index at the local level is around 7000, indicating an extremely highly concentrated market for multi-channel video service.

The large national cable networks built up over the past couple of decades have been created by buying up small Multiple System Operators (MSOs). There has also been a strong trend toward vertical integration into programming, primarily by purchasing libraries of programs and sports entertainment.

TABLE VI-5: Concentration Of National Multi-Channel Video Subscriber Market

YEAR	4-FIRM	HHI
1984	28	360
1992	48	930
2001		
FCC, without attribution	52	905
with attribution	56*	1101
with attribution + Cablevision	60**	1254
2003		
Post AT&T/Comcast, with attribution	64*	1529
Comcast with attribution + Cablevision	70**	1749

SOURCES AND NOTES: Federal Communications Commission, *In the Matter of Annual Assessment of the Status of Competition in Markets for the Delivery of Video Programming,* First Report, CC Docket No. 94-48, Eighth Report, CC Docket No 00132; Applications and Public Interest Statement In *the Matter of Application for Consent to the Transfer of Control of Licenses Compact Corporation and AT&T Corp. Tansferors to AT&T Comcast Corporation. All* estimates are rounded to the nearest 10.
*AT&T claims 18.8 million subscribers having very recently sold off cablevision stock to get its ownership share to 4.98%.
**AT&T claims of technical compliance with the attribution rules, or its ability to remain in compliance, given how close it has chosen to stay to the limit of non-attribution, have yet to be demonstrated. Cablevision is estimated to have 3 million subscribers.

Cable TV After Deregulation

Cable television was originally conceived as a local medium, to boost penetration of television where broadcast signals were weak and to provide local access. Community Access Television, as it was known in the early years, was franchised and regulated at the local level. The 1984 Cable Act changed that. It preempted most local regulation and short-circuited the power of franchising by rendering the agreements all but permanent.

As a result, the industry is now dominated by a handful of huge national corporations that are vertically integrated into programming. At the national level, cable has undergone a strong trend of increasing concentration since it was deregulated in 1984 (see Table VI-5). In 1984, the national market had the equivalent of approximately 30 equal-sized competitors. With attribution of the systems in which AT&T owns substantial interests, the market now has the equivalent of only five or size competitors.

Lately there has been a strong trend towards regionalizing the local cable companies so that contiguous areas are joined under one company.[491] Given the theme of clustering that has also been struck by the major newspaper chains, the strength of the trend in cable is notable (see Figure VI-2). In 1994 less than five percent of subscribers were in

FIGURE VI-2: The Dramatic Increase in Cable Clusters

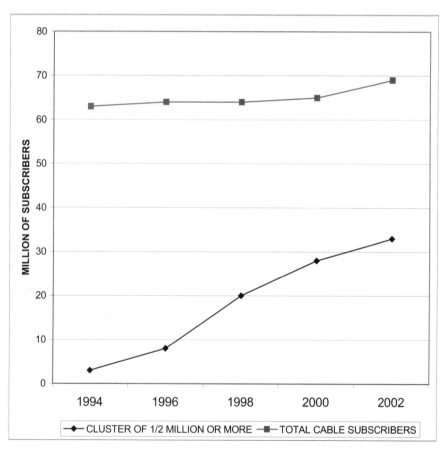

Source: Federal Communications Commission, *In the Matter of Annual Assessment of the Status of Competition in Markets for the Delivery of Video Programming*, Appendix B, various issues.

clusters of half a million subscribers or more. By 2002, almost fifty percent of all cable subscribers were in clusters of that size.

The deregulation of cable prices and the strong trend of concentration in the industry, indicating the failure of head-to-head competition to develop, resulted in a dramatic and continuous increase in cable prices (see Figure VI-3). Since 1996, cable rates have increased by over forty percent, more than two-and-one-half times the rate of inflation.[492] Basic service rates have increased even more rapidly. Advertising and advanced service revenues have been growing even

FIGURE VI-3: Post-Deregulation Trend of Cable Prices

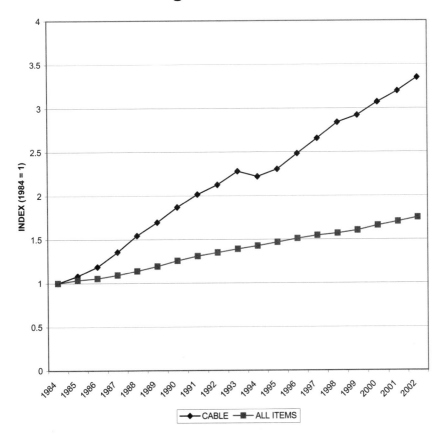

Source: U.S. Bureau of Labor Statistics, *Consumer Price Index*

faster, and total revenue is up almost 60 percent.[493]   On a per subscriber basis, monthly revenues are up over 50 percent. In the longer term, the ability to raise prices at several times the rate of inflation is evident. With the exception of the short period of regulation in 1992-1996, cable prices have been largely unregulated. Whenever they are deregulated, they increase at about 2.5 times the rate of overall inflation.

Not only have prices increased, but the industry has also restructured its revenue stream to maximize the leverage afforded by its market power. It has engaged in bundling, price discrimination, and other anti-consumer behavior (including activities such as efforts to impose negative check-offs and tie-in sales), driving consumers to buy bigger and bigger packages of programs at higher prices. While basic packages were being expanded and bundled to force consumers to pay higher prices, rates for pay services were flat.

PROGRAMMING

National Markets

At one level, the growth of the number of TV channel outlets is impressive. Cable TV networks are measured by their subscriber count (Table VI-6). This is calculated not as the actual number of households that watch a network but as the number of households that take cable service from systems that carry the program. In other words, if a household can pick up the clicker and tune in to a channel that carries a network, that household is counted as a subscriber. This is equivalent to the simple count of the number of over-the-air households that a broadcast station can reach. If an over-the-air signal can reach a household, the network is available.

Using this as the measure of subscribers, I estimate that the total number of subscribers to the 200 largest cable networks and 1500 local TV stations is approximately six billion households. Since there are approximately 106 million TV households, the average number of networks available is over 50 per household. This sounds like a huge number. However, when I examine the viewing and ownership of these networks there is far less change than meets the eye.

Broadcast TV networks are in a different class than the other media in terms of advertising dollars, as described above, because they are in a different category than cable when it comes to capturing audiences. Cable

TABLE VI-6: Dominant Video Program Producers/Distributors

	SUBSCRIBERS		WRITING BUDGET		PROGRAMMING EXPENDITURES	
	$ (Million)	%	$ (Million)	%	$ (Million)	%
FOX/LIBERTY	1250	20.8	236	19.2	3803	8.8
AOL – TW	925	15.4	206	16.8	7627	17.7
CBS/VIACOM	910	15.2	145	11.8	9555	22.1
ABC/DISNEY	705	11.8	132	10.8	6704	15.5
NBC	495	8.3	53	4.4	3418	7.9
Subtotal	4285	71.5	772	63.0	31107	72.0
TOTAL	6000	100.0	1225	100.0	43212	100.0

SOURCES: Federal Communications Commission, *In the Matter of Annual Assessment of the Status of Competition in Markets for the Delivery of Video Programming*, CC Docket No. 00-132, Seventh Report, Tables D-1, D-2, D-3, D-6, D-7; *Television Market Report: 2001* (Washington, D.C.: BIA Financial Network, 2001); Comments of the Writers Guild of America Regarding Harmful Vertical and Horizontal Integration in the Television Industry, Appendix A. Federal Communications Commission, *In the Matter of Implementation of Section 11 of the Cable Television Consumer Protection and Competition Act of 1992 Implementation of Cable Act Reform Provisions of the Telecommunications Act of 1996 The Commission's Cable Horizontal and Vertical Ownership Limits and Attribution Rules Review of the Commission's Regulations Governing Attribution Of Broadcast and Cable/MDS Interests Review of the Commission's Regulations and Policies Affecting Investment In the Broadcast Industry Reexamination of the Commission's Cross-Interest Policy*, CS Docket No. 98-82, CS Docket No. 96-85, MM Docket No. 92-264, MM Docket No. 94-150, MM Docket No. 92-51, MM Docket No. 87-154, January 4, 2002; Bruce M. Owen and Michael G. Baumann, "Economic Study E; Concentration Among National Purchasers of Video Entertainment Programming," *Comments of Fox Entertainment Group and Fox Television Stations, Inc., National Broadcasting Company, Inc. and Telemundo Group, Inc., and Viacom,* In the Matter of 2002 Biennial Regulatory Review – Review of the Commission's Broadcast Ownership Rules and Other Rules Adopted Pursuant to Section 202 of the Telecommunications Act of 1996, Cross Ownership of Broadcast Stations and Newspapers, Rules and Policies Concerning Multiple Ownership of Radio Broadcast Stations in Local Markets, Definition of Radio Markets, MB Docket No. 02-277, MM Dockets 02-235, 01=317, 00-244, January 2, 2003.

TV has only captured a limited amount of prime time viewing, but has captured significant numbers of viewers during non-prime time hours. This is the primary reason that cable's average advertising rates remain low in comparison to broadcast.[494] Non-prime time niche markets do not command significant advertising revenues.

TV ratings and audience market shares show that the networks dominate prime time. The top twenty or so TV shows are all prime time network programs.[495] They fill about three-quarters of the weekly prime time viewing hours (8 pm to 11 pm). The top twenty shows capture between 150 and 225 million household hours of viewing per week. Almost all of these shows are original network programs. A small number of households, 10 to 20 million, might be viewing a network movie. Cable's top products are quite different. Of the top twenty cable network shows, about half are in prime time. They capture 20 to 40 million household hours. About half are re-run movies, not original programming.

Combining news and all of prime time, which is the networks' bread and butter, the big three networks capture about half a billion household hours of weekly viewing. The top three cable networks capture about one-fifth of that and provide virtually no news or public affairs programming.

Of paramount importance for civic discourse policy is the central role that the networks play in the dissemination of news. Television has been the primary source of news for over a decade. On average, each night between 20 and 25 million households tune in to the early evening flagship news shows on the three major networks. In contrast, the four major cable news networks capture about three million viewers over the course of their entire early evening/prime time news offering.

The large number of channels available have not deconcentrated ownership of programming. The top channels are owned by a small number of entities. Of the large number of available channels, almost three-quarters of them serving approximately four billion subscribers, are owned by six corporate entities. The four major TV networks, NBC, CBS, ABC, Fox, and the two dominant cable providers, AOL Time Warner and Liberty, which has carriage arrangements with Comcast and owns 18.5 percent of NewsCorp, completely dominate the tuner. Estimates of the writing budgets of these producers are generally consistent with the subscriber counts. TV programming is a tight oligopoly.

Tom Wolzien, Senior Media Analyst for Bernstein Research, paints the picture vividly—he details the return of the "old programming oligopoly:"

> Last season ABC, CBS and NBC split about 23% [of television ratings].
> . . But if the viewing of all properties owned by the parent companies –
> Disney, NBC, and Viacom – is totaled, those companies now directly

control television sets in over a third of the TV households. Add AOL, Fox and networks likely to see consolidation over the next few years (Discovery, A&E, EW Scripps, etc.), and five companies or fewer would control roughly the same percentage of TV households in prime time as the three net[work]s did 40 years ago. The programming oligopoly appears to be in a process of rebirth.[496]

In addition, the number of independent studios in existence has dwindled dramatically since the mid-1980s. In 1985, there were 25 independent television production studios; there was little drop-off in that number between 1985 and 1992. In 2002, however, only 5 independent television studios remained. In addition, in the ten-year period between 1992 and 2002, the number of prime time television hours per week produced by network studios increased over 200%, whereas the number of prime time television hours per week produced by independent studios decreased 63%.[497]

The ease with which broadcasters blew away the independent programmers should sound a strong cautionary alarm. The alarm can only become louder when we look at the development of programming in the cable market. One simple message comes through: those with rights to distribution systems win.

Of the 26 top cable channels in subscribers' and prime time ratings, all but one of them (the Weather Channel) has ownership interest of either a cable company or a broadcast network. In other words, it appears that you must either own a wire or have transmission rights to be in the top tier of cable networks. Four entities – News Corp./Fox (including cross ownership interests in and from Liberty), AOL Time Warner, ABC/Disney and CBS/Viacom – account for 20 of these channels.

Of the 39 new cable networks created since 1992, only six do not involve ownership by a cable operator or a national TV broadcaster. Sixteen of these networks are partially owned by the top four programmers. Eight involve other cable companies and ten involve other TV broadcasters. Similarly, a recent cable analysis identified eleven networks that have achieved substantial success since the passage of the 1992 Cable Act. Every one of these is affiliated with an entity that has guaranteed carriage on cable systems.[498]

Moreover, each of the dominant programmers has guaranteed access to carriage on cable systems – either by ownership of the wires (cable operators) or by carriage rights conferred by Congress (broadcasters).

· AOL Time Warner owns cable systems reaching approximately eleven million basic cable subscribers, and its cable "footprint" passes twenty-one million homes. It also owns seven local broadcast television stations, five television production studios, and fourteen cable networks, including CNN, CNN/fn, CNN/SI, and CNN Headline News.

· NewsCorp./Fox, which is 20% owned by John Malone's Liberty Media, owns nine cable networks (including Fox News Channel and the Fox Broadcasting Company) and 34 local television stations. Worldwide, NewsCorp.'s cable and satellite programming has approximately 300 million subscribers.

· Disney owns eight television networks, including ABC. These eight networks include Disney's shared ownership of ESPN and other cable networks with Hearst, GE, Comcast, MediaOne, and Liberty Media. Disney also owns ten local television stations and three large television production studios.

· Viacom owns nineteen networks, including CBS and UPN, 35 local broadcast television stations, and five large television production studios.

These five entities have ownership rights in 21 of the top 25 cable networks based on subscribers and prime time ratings. They account for over 60 percent of subscribers to cable networks, rendering this market a tight oligopoly. Other entities with ownership or carriage rights account for four of the five remaining most popular cable networks. The only network in the top 25 without such a connection is the Weather Channel. It certainly provides a great public service, but is hardly a hotbed for development of original programming or civic discourse. Entities with guaranteed access to distribution over cable account for 80 percent of the top networks and about 80 percent of all subscribers' viewing choices on cable systems.

There is certainly more variety available, but whether there is more diversity is debatable, especially when local programming is considered. The dominant cable operators produce a lot of national programming and a few have moved into regional programming, especially sports, but there is little local programming and news. The three major networks have existed for quite some time and the Fox network was cobbled together from existing stations. Many local stations are no longer producing the programming they were fifteen years ago because of changes in Commission rules. For all the immense growth in cable channels and viewing, news is still thoroughly dominated by the networks and network owners.

Although much Communications Act policy focuses on local markets, this discussion of national ownership of programming is relevant for a variety of reasons. The national programmers establish the likely pool from which competitors might be drawn and the barriers to competition that new entrants are likely to face. Dramatic increases in concentration and reductions in the number of potential competitors raise significant concerns. The substantial barrier to entry that the growth of large media conglomerates raises is a separate and reinforcing constraint on competition. To the extent I observe increasing concentration of outlets into fewer hands, it also suggests national groups and chains are expanding.

Concentration of Local Markets

Detailed evidence on viewing shares including all broadcast and cable channels is traditionally treated as proprietary. Recently, total prime time viewing shares for 21 markets were made available.[499] This can be combined with the broadcast network data on ownership and general data on station's affiliations to produce a market structure analysis of individual markets based on market share, or "eyeball" data.

Moving from a market share analysis that includes only broadcast to a market share analysis that includes cable and satellite market shares raises some methodological issues.

The broadcast networks, who have must carry rights and can negotiate for retransmission, have a mixture of broadcast and cable programming. I have attributed all programming (cable, satellite and broadcast) to the parent of the programming network.

In voice count analysis, cable systems have traditionally been counted as one owner. Cable owners control all of the channels on their systems, with the exception of broadcast networks, which have must carry and retransmission rights and a small number of public, educational and governmental (PEG) channels (which do not exist in many communities and have virtually no viewership where they do exist). Because they assert and aggressively defend their rights to choose the programming that gets on their system, all cable systems have been treated as one owner.

A recent *Washington Post* article points to Comcast's blanket refusal to air an anti-war commercial, reminding us of the power of cable operators to control content distributed over the cable platform at critical times of public debate, and affirming that counting the cable owner (or satellite distributor) as, at most, a single voice is the correct approach.[500] Moreover, since there is virtually no competition between cable operators (since they rarely overbuild one another), each cable system is a local monopoly.

Although satellite is beginning to play a meaningful role in the video market, its role in the dissemination of news and information is still very small. Since satellite companies are currently dependent upon broadcasters and the largest cable programming owners for their news and information programming, they do not constitute a significant "voice" in most local markets. In any event, I suggest that satellite video providers — which control the vast majority of programming on their distribution systems, just like cable companies — should be treated, for the purpose of a voice count analysis, as similar to cable.

In the following analysis, which focuses on prime time network market shares, I have not distinguished between cable and satellite. All programs that are not attributed to one of the entities that owns a network are treated as controlled by the cable operators. Given the urban markets, this simplifying assumption would have little impact on the calculation of prime time entertainment HHIs.

AOL Time Warner presents a unique problem for this analysis. It is the number two cable system operator, a broadcast network owner, and one of the largest cable and satellite network program owners. For the purposes of this analysis, I treat it as a separate entity. I subtract its share of cable "eyeball" from the cable total. In communities where AOL Time Warner is the cable operator, this will underestimate market concentration. In communities where it is not the cable operator, the estimate of market structure will be only slightly affected (because AOL Time Warner tends to attract more eyeballs as a cable programmer than a broadcast network owner).

In spite of the growth of cable, prime time viewing remains quite concentrated (see Table VI-7). The twenty-one DMAs for which data is available are quite large, all ranking in the top 60 television markets in the U.S. All twenty-one markets are tight oligopolies as measured by

TABLE VI-7: Measures Of Concentration In Television Prime Time Markets

DMA	DMA Rank Ratio	Four-Firm Concent.	HHI Index	% of Cable Share for Broadcast Owners	% of Broadcasters Who Provide Local News
Minneapolis	13	75	1762	58	64
Tampa	14	69	1432	55	54
Sacramento	19	70	1617	63	70
Pittsburgh	21	77	1798	63	50
St. Louis	22	76	1670	72	44
Baltimore	24	78	1875	52	50
Raleigh	29	73	1732	67	50
Nashville	30	81	1826	54	40
Kansas City	31	71	1641	63	67
Cincinnati	32	76	1723	54	50
Milwaukee	33	73	1776	46	40
Columbus	34	75	1639	55	57
San Antonio	37	61	1188	60	58
Birmingham	39	66	1421	58	50
Norfolk	42	75	1695	61	56
Greensboro	44	69	1606	64	44
Oklahoma City	45	72	1611	61	45
Buffalo	47	70	1530	68	45
Las Vegas	51	68	1495	63	60
Richmond	58	76	1847	67	57
Dayton	60	75	1664	57	40

Owen, Bruce and Michael Baumann and Allison Ivory, "News and Public Affairs Programming Offered by the Four Top-Ranked Versus Lower Ranked Television Stations," Comments of Fox, Economic Study A, *Comments of Fox Entertainment Group and Fox Television Stations, Inc., National Broadcasting Company, Inc. and Telemundo Group, Inc., and Viacom; Comments of Sinclair Broadcasting Corporation Inc,* In the Matter of 2002 Biennial Regulatory Review – Review of the Commission's Broadcast Ownership Rules and Other Rules Adopted Pursuant to Section 202 of the Telecommunications Act of 1996, Cross Ownership of Broadcast Stations and Newspapers, Rules and Policies Concerning Multiple Ownership of Radio Broadcast Stations in Local Markets, Definition of Radio Markets, MB Docket No. 02-277, MM Dockets 02-235, 01=317, 00-244, January 2, 2003.

four-firm concentration ratio. Most are well above the 60 percent market share figure. Measured by the HHI, most markets are moderately concentrated and several are highly concentrated. Most of the moderately concentrated markets are at the higher end of the range. One of the reasons that the growth of cable networks has not de-concentrated the prime time market is that over half of the prime time market share for cable is for channels that are owned by firms that also own national broadcast networks. The phenomenon is simply a migration from over-the-air broadcast to through-the-wire carriage of network-owned programming.

These estimates of concentration for entertainment are certainly lower than estimates of concentration for news and information would be because some broadcasters and many cable operators do not air news. Only about half of the broadcast networks that air entertainment also air local news. If the media companies had provided the Commission more refined data separating news and information from entertainment programming, they would demonstrate that the market for news and information is significantly more concentrated and subject to monopolistic abuse than the entertainment market.

One example is provided in detail: Milwaukee (See Table VI-8). This is the example chosen by the broadcast networks to present detailed analysis.[501] In the Milwaukee market, I attribute all cable market share to AOL Time Warner, since it is the dominant cable provider. The CR4 is 84 percent and the HHI is 2086. This video market is a highly concentrated tight oligopoly. If AOL Time Warner is treated as a separate entity from its programming affiliates, the CR4 is 73 and the HHI is 1726, just below the highly concentrated threshold.

Prime Time Programming After Repeal Of The Fin-Syn Rules

A most instructive example of structural policy that prevented vertical integration from foreclosing access to distribution networks is the financial interest and syndication of programming (Fin-Syn) rules. The intention of the rules was to spread the ownership of programming and prevent the networks from dominating prime time. Judging by what happened after they were repealed, the rules were a potent structural limit. The elimination of these rules resulted in massive consolidation of the media industry.

During the 1980s, when the rules were in effect, prime time, as a market, was not very concentrated (see Table VI-9). Judged both by the HHI and the CR4 the market was unconcentrated. Repeal of the rules resulted in a sharp increase in concentration. The HHI for prime time programming now is well into the moderately concentrated range. The CR4 indicates a tight oligopoly.

The increase in concentration was accompanied by a dramatic shift toward production by the networks. The big three networks went from

TABLE VI-8: Milwaukee Video Market Structure Based On Viewer Shares
(Based on Top Six Entities)

	RATINGS POINTS			MARKET SHARE
	Broadcast Networks	Cable Networks	Total	Percent of Total
ABC/DISNEY	7.65	2.39	10.04	16
CBS/UPN/ VIACOM	11.03	3.11	14.14	22
FOX/Newscorp.	7.89	2.35	10.29	16
NBC	12.14	0	12.14	19
AOL/WB	3.82	3.47	7.29	12 ⎫
				⎬ 27
CABLE MARKET SHARE		9.20	9.20	15 ⎭

Note: Concentration measures, cable as a single owner, CR4 = 84%; HHI = 2086

Sources: Network Ownership = Owen, Bruce and Michael Baumann, "Concentration Among National Purchasers of Video Entertainment Programming," Owen, Bruce and Michael Baumann and Allison Ivory, "News and Public Affairs Programming Offered by the Four Top-Ranked Versus Lower Ranked Television Stations," Comments of Fox, Economic Study A, *Comments of Fox Entertainment Group and Fox Television Stations, Inc., National Broadcasting Company, Inc. and Telemundo Group, Inc., and Viacom, Comments of Sinclair Braodcasting Corporation*, In the Matter of 2002 Biennial Regulatory Review – Review of the Commission's Broadcast Ownership Rules and Other Rules Adopted Pursuant to Section 202 of the Telecommunications Act of 1996, Cross Ownership of Broadcast Stations and Newspapers, Rules and Policies Concerning Multiple Ownership of Radio Broadcast Stations in Local Markets, Definition of Radio Markets, MB Docket No. 02-277, MM Dockets 02-235, 01=317, 00-244, January 2, 2003.

an ownership share of programming of 17 percent in 1989 to 48 percent in 2002 through growth and mergers. Of course, the repeal of the Fin-Sin rules made the mergers "attractive." "New" networks, all of which had been based in major studios, push the network total to 75 percent. Other major studios now account for a very small share of prime time programming. Larger independents, who accounted for 20 to 30 percent under the Fin-Syn rules, now account for less than 10 percent. Smaller producers accounted for about two-fifths of the prime time programming

TABLE VI-9: Concentration Of Prime Time Programming

	HHI	CR4
1970	360	32
1977	571	37
1989	532	35
2002	1356	65

Sources: Mara Epstein, *Program Diversity and the Program Selection Process on Broadcast Network Television* (Federal Communications Commission, Media Bureau Straff Research Paper, No. 5, September 2002); *Prime Time Power and Politics: The Financial Interest and Syndication Rules and Their Impact on the Structure and Practices of the Television Industry* (Ph.D. Dissertation, Department of Culture and Communications, New York University, 2000).

in the 1980s. These producers now account for only one-twentieth of prime time shows.

NEWSPAPERS

Revenues, Output and Owners

Newspapers serve local markets. They capture a very different type of advertising dollar than TV. National advertising accounts for a modest share of radio and newspaper revenues (see Table VI-1, above). Newspapers dominate the local advertising market with classified ads comprising the majority of newspapers' revenues.[502] Radio, newspapers, and magazines are substitutes from an advertiser's perspective. There is some evidence that cable and newspapers are cross elastic for advertisers, which reflects the fact that both are local. Radio and newspapers occupy the non-video local product space.[503] The stability of their market shares indicates that they are not likely to be greatly eroded by new media in the near term.[504]

Newspapers and local TV stations have a complex relationship in the advertising market. Newspapers dominate classified advertising.

Local TV stations have a large local spot advertising market and dominate advertising for local political campaigns. For certain types of products, they have a complementary relationship, with newspapers providing much more detailed product promotion (particularly price). The differences between the media types (newspaper and TV) in newsgathering and analysis, discussed generally in the previous section, apply to the local market.[505]

In the twenty-five years since the adoption of the rule restricting cross-ownership of newspapers and broadcast, daily newspaper operations have declined (see Table VI-2, above). The number of dailies has declined by about nineteen percent. Their circulation has declined by about ten percent.

The shrinkage of outlets in the newspaper market is compounded by the dramatic reduction in the number of owners.[506] I estimate that the number of owners has declined by two-thirds (from 860 to 290). Combining the newspaper and television ownership numbers, as the dominant form of news disseminating media, I find that the number of independent voices has been cut by more than half since the mid-1970s.

Those who argue that the market has changed point to the growth of weekly papers. Although their numbers have declined slightly (three percent), circulation has increased sharply (by 128 percent). Weeklies cannot be compared directly to dailies from the point of view of providing news and information, however. To the extent they provide news, it is not timely. Moreover, their focus tends to be quite different than the daily press. The community-oriented weeklies have a "promotional flavor" and are "strong on neighborhood shopping advertisements but relying heavily on press releases for editorial content."[507] They focus on "lifestyle and consumer issues" and "have not challenged the metropolitan newspaper's news and editorial coverage of major urban and regional issues."[508]

At a minimum, any comparison must recognize the fact that dailies come out every day while weeklies come out every seven days. By this standard, the total number of weekly plus daily newspaper editions printed per week has declined by about three percent and circulation has been constant. Thus, at best, excluding the qualitative difference, no change has occurred.

Newspapers dominate the production of local news content (see Figure VI-4). They are devoted to news, whereas most other media are primarily devoted to entertainment. Newspapers also have large staffs.

On average, daily newspapers probably employ more than half of the reporters in any given city. They produce much more news than television reports. As Downie and Kaiser point out

> Television, like radio, is a relatively inefficient conveyor of information. The text of Cronkite's evening news, after eliminating the commercials, would fill just over half the front page of a full-sized newspaper. A typical network evening news show now mentions just over fifteen or

FIGURE VI-4: News Production Capabilities Across Local Media Outlets

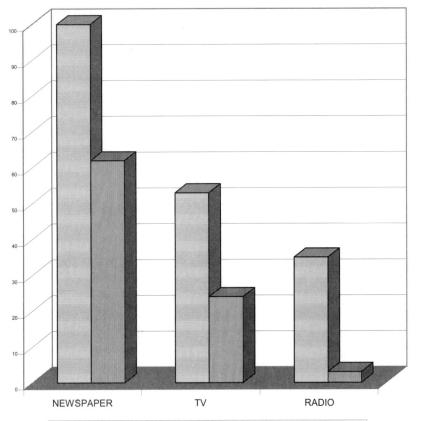

□ % OF OUTLETS DOING NEWS ■ NUMBER OF NEWSROOM STAFF

SOURCES: Vernon Stone, News Operations at U.S. Radio Stations, News Operations at TV Stations; U.S. Bureau of the Census, Statistical Abstract of The United States: 2000 Tables 2, 37, 932; Lisa George, *What's Fit To Print: The Effect Of Ownership Concentration On Product Variety In Daily Newspaper Markets* (2001); *Editor And Publisher, International Yearbook*, Various Issues.

so different subjects, some in a sentence, whereas a good newspaper has scores of different news items every day. A big story on television might get two minutes, or about 400 words. The *Los Angeles Times* coverage of the same big story could easily total 2,000 words.[509]

Concentration of Local Markets

Newspaper markets are even more highly concentrated than TV markets, as summarized in Table VI-10. I have gathered data on sixty-eight large markets to calculate HHIs and analyze the advertising revenues in markets that are comparable to those with newspaper/broadcast TV cross-ownership (23 markets with an average DMA rank of 54).

These markets are even more concentrated as measured by HHIs. Well over half of the markets are monopolies (57 percent). One-fifth are duopolies and the final one-fifth are tight oligopolies.

For the smaller markets, I have counts of media voices but not market shares, but I still find very high levels of concentration. By voice count alone, almost 40 percent are monopolies, a percentage that is four times as large as the voice count percentage for larger markets. By voice count, another 40 percent are duopolies, a percentage that is much larger than the voice count percentage for larger markets.

TABLE VI-10: Newspaper Concentration of Daily Circulation in 68 Large Designated Market Areas

TYPE OF MARKET	Number of Markets	% of Markets
MONOPOLY	39	57
DUOPOLY	12	18
TIGHT OLIGOPOLY	12	18
MODERATELY CONCENTRATED	5	7
UNCONCENTRATED	0	0
TOTAL	68	100

Source: *Editor and Publisher*, various issues

Thus, I believe that well over two-thirds of newspaper markets are monopolies, with another quarter being duopolies, and the final one-tenth are tight oligopolies.

The above DMA-based analysis substantially underestimates the concentration in newspaper markets. It noted that newspapers tend to be very place-specific, providing local news and advertising. They therefore tend to dominate specific areas. When newspaper concentration is measured at the DMA level, Los Angeles is one of the least concentrated DMAs, although still highly concentrated with an HHI of 2400 (the equivalent of four equal-sized competitors). When calculated at the county level, the weighted average HHI is about 2000 points higher (indicating a duopoly).

Gannett also presents evidence on the newspaper market in the Phoenix area[510] with current circulation data for all dailies and weeklies. Using this circulation data, I find that the market is highly concentrated. Gannett's market share is approximately 70 percent. The HHI is 5000. This market falls in the monopoly range.

Cross Ownership and Quality

There are a number of cross-owned newspapers and television entities that were grandfathered when the rule was adopted or waived at a later date. The newspapers claim that they produce superior quality. The evidence presented by the newspaper corporations on cross-ownership has the same weaknesses as the broadcast data and leads to the same incorrect conclusions. There is no time series data provided, so it is hard to ascertain whether the TV stations they own always presented more news, or increased their news after they became cross-owned. More importantly, when I analyze media markets, I find that cross-ownership adds little in quantity, while eliminating an important independent voice.

The media companies also cite an FCC study.[511] However, the FCC's conclusions are not presented as statistically significant (no statistical tests were applied). Moreover, the FCC analysis focuses on the output of stations, rather than the output of markets. I have shown above that when a cross-owned combination dominates a market, other independent stations may move away from the dominant station, reducing news output. The FCC study appears to combine TV stations owned by newspapers that are not in the same market with instances in which the TV station and the newspaper are in the same market.

TABLE VI-11: TELEVISION NEWS AWARDS FOR CROSS-OWNED AND AFFILIATED STATIONS

CROSS OWNERSHIP[a]

	NON-CROSS OWNED	CROSS-OWNED
4 OR MORE AWARDS	12	0
3 AWARDS	8	2
2 AWARDS	14	4
1 AWARD	23	2

OWNED & OPERATED v. AFFILIATED STATIONS
TOP 10 MARKETS[b]

	PERCENT OF STATIONS	PERCENT OF AWARDS
OWNED AND OPERATED STATIONS	70	54
AFFILIATES	30	40

SOURCES:
a/ Spavins, Thomas C., et al., *The Measurement of Local Television News and Public Affairs Programs* (Federal Communication Commission, Media Bureau Staff Research Paper, No. 7, September 2002), Appendices B and C.

b/ "Early Submission of the National Association of Broadcasters and the Network Affiliated Stations Alliance," In the Matter of 2002 Biennial Regulatory Review — Review of the Commissions' Broadcast Ownership Rules and Other Rules Adopted Pursuant to Section 202 of the Telecommunications Act of 1996, Cross Ownership of Broadcast Stations and Newspapers, Rules and Policies Concerning Multiple Ownership of Radio Broadcast Stations in Local Markets, Definition of Radio Markets, MB Docket NO. 02-277; MM Docket Nos. 01-235, 01-317, 00-244, December 9, 2002.

I have identified specific problems with cross-ownership within markets. The evidence does not support the claim to benefits of concentration and cross ownership. The networks contend that the journalistic awards received by cross-owned stations indicate that such stations are "better" than non-cross-owned stations. Looking at a cross-owned situation in the same market, however, it is difficult to conclude that the stations are better or worse (See Table VI-11). I observe many that are better and many that are worse. The inconclusiveness of the award data above is demonstrated by the following observations.

There were nine markets with cross-owned stations in which awards were made. In four markets, the cross-owned stations won all of the awards. They tended to be among the two highest ranked stations. The non-cross-owned stations that won awards in markets where cross-owned stations exist were ranked considerably lower in terms of viewership. On average, they were ranked between third and fourth in their markets, compared to the cross-owned stations that won which were ranked second on average. The five markets where awards were won but the cross-owned station won none were where they tended to be lower ranked. The cross-owned stations that did not win awards were ranked about fourth on average. Generally, the non-cross-owned stations did more with less.

An analysis of the difference between stations that are owned and operated directly by networks compared to stations that are independently owned and only affiliated with the network leads to the same conclusion.[512] This study that controlled for market size showed that the affiliates won more awards. Looking at the quantity of news in markets with cross-owned stations, there is little difference between the stations.

The bold claims that concentration and cross ownership are good for news output is not supported by this data. At best, there is a small difference between stations in newspaper/broadcast combinations and duopolies. Whatever small increases we see in quality and/or quantity come with very large losses in media ownership diversity.

RADIO

Operations

Radio has fallen into a special niche. It serves as background for people as they engage in other activities such as working or driving.[513] This specific function of the radio may derive from the different demands it places on the listener.[514] In this niche, radio is not a primary source of news. Radio is the least often cited of sources of information among the three traditional media.[515]

I have noted the reduction in TV news operations, in spite of the increase in stations. The same thing happened in radio (see Table VI-2, above). While the number of stations has been increasing, the number of newsrooms has been declining.[516] Interestingly, the same policy decisions that have reduced the number of TV stations doing news affected the radio market.

> Most stations dropped news after 1984, when the FCC lifted its requirement that all radio stations must include a certain amount of news and information in the programming schedule.[517]

The small size of newsroom staffs for radio limits their ability to add diversity to civic discourse at the level of information. The concentration of radio ownership into chains has cut back on local reporting.

> Metro Networks alone is – by far – the largest producer of radio news in the country. Although its name is never mentioned on the air, Metro provides newscasts to some one hundred fifty-five stations and seventeen hundred radio stations. Its *average* market penetration is twenty-three affiliates per market. Metro says that it provides news services in sixty-seven of the top seventy-five markets, and that its newscasts are heard by one hundred million people every day. It brags to advertisers that it offers them "the opportunity to reach a broad-based local, regional or national audience, through a single purchase of commercial airtime inventory" by Metro.

> In a large market like Baltimore, which has forty radio stations and twelve TV stations, I believe Metro provides all or most of the news to about twenty-five radio stations – well over half – and two TV stations.

> So much for diversity. There is now, at most, one reporter covering City Hall for all those stations. There is no one to bring a different perspective, to provide the safety valve for a lazy, or even corrupt reporter willing to overlook a story for the wrong reasons.[518]

Radio After the 1996 Act Relaxed Many Restrictions

The consolidation of radio markets in a short period of time after the relaxation of structural limits in the 1996 Act is striking. The radio industry has become concentrated at every level (see Table VI-12).

Even at the national level, where one might think that the existence of a market fragmented into 285 geographic areas and populated by over 10,000 stations would limit the possibility of concentration, I find that the market is moderately concentrated when measured by listeners and revenues. In both cases, the HHI exceeds 1000, the equivalent of ten equal-sized competitors.[519] Just five years earlier, the national HHI was

TABLE VI-12: Concentration In Radio Markets

MARKET DEFINITION	1995/96	2000	2002
NATIONAL			
REVENUE			
HHI	125	1053	1033
CR4			52
LISTENERS			
HHI			1130
CR4			49
FORMATS			
CR4			63
LOCAL			
REVENUE			
HHI	2103	3084	
STATIONS			
CR4			
BY MARKET SIZE			
TOP 10	61		81
TOP 25	64		83
TOP 50	72		86
51-100	83		94
101-285	86		95

Sources: Keith Brown and George Williams, *Consolidation and Advertising Prices in Local Radio Markets* (Federal Communications Commission, Media Bureau Staff Research Paper, September 2002); Peter DiCola and Kristin Thomson, *Radio Deregulation: Has It Served Citizens and Musicians* (Future of Music Coalition, 2002).

125, the equivalent of 80 equal-sized competitors. In a very short period, the national market has gone from being atomistically competitive to a loose oligopoly.

A second view of the national market – product types or formats – also reveals a startling level of concentration. All radio formats have become at least loose oligopolies (four firm concentration ratios greater than 40 percent) and the majority have become tight oligopolies (four firm concentration ratios greater than 60 percent).[520] On a listener-weighted basis, the average format is a tight oligopoly.[521]

However, the radio market is primarily a local market. At that level, the concentration is even greater. The average local market had

FIGURE VI-5: Shift Toward Concentrated Market Types: All Markets

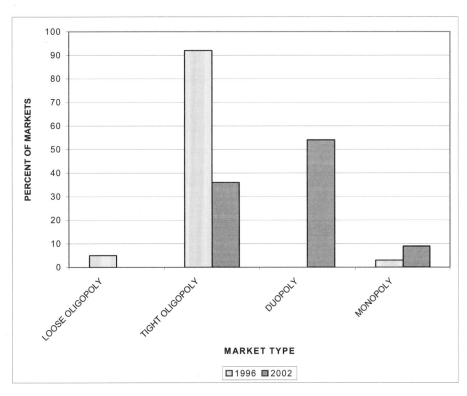

Source: Keith Brown and George Williams, *Consolidation and Advertising Prices in Local Radio Markets* (Federal Communications Commission, Media Bureau Staff Research Paper, September 2002).

the equivalent of five equal-sized competitors in 1995 (HHI of 2103). By 2000, that had increased by almost 1000 points to just over 3000, the equivalent of three equal-sized competitors. The relaxation of the rules allowed the larger markets to become much more concentrated, increasing from the tight oligopoly level to very tight oligopolies.

Figure VI-5 shows this dramatic increase in concentration by assigning markets to the market type categories identified earlier. Even in 1996, most markets were tight oligopolies. However, the merger wave unleashed by the Telecommunications Act of 1996 allowed about half of all markets to become effectively duopolies[522] and almost ten percent of

163

markets to become effective monopolies,[523] while all loose oligopolies were eliminated.[524]

Figure VI-6 shows these market categories for the top 50 markets, where the 1996 Act had the biggest impact. One-sixth of the larger radio markets were loose oligopolies in 1996 and five-sixths were tight oligopolies. None were duopolies. By 2002, the loose oligopolies were eliminated and one-quarter of the markets were duopolies.

FIGURE VI-6: Shift Toward Concentrated Market Types, Top 50 Markets

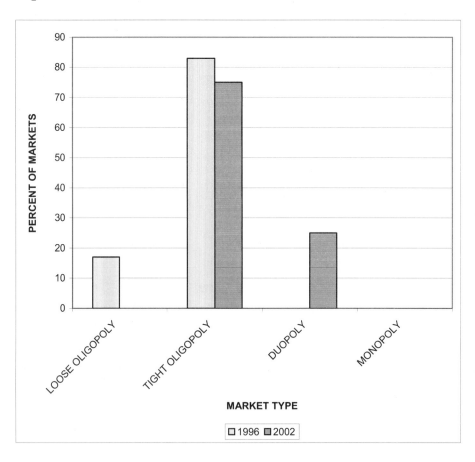

Sources: Keith Brown and George Williams, *Consolidation and Advertising Prices in Local Radio Markets* (Federal Communications Commission, Media Bureau Staff Research Paper, September 2002).

THE INTERNET

Revenues, Output and Owners

In 1985, the Internet was just beginning its commercial phase, accounting for virtually no viewing time or advertising revenue. Fifteen years later, it accounts for only four percent of total viewer time and less than two percent of advertising dollars.

The Internet revolution has provided a wonderful new functionality that allows people to conduct commercial transactions and daily activities in a more efficient manner, but has not yet significantly altered the dynamics of mass media. It provides little if any local content. It appears to occupy a new media space.[525] It provides a national, non-video product.[526] It does not provide independent voices or balance the immense power of traditional mass media to influence public opinion, particularly when public policy has allowed existing media owners to increasingly control the communications infrastructure underlying the Internet and to direct the flow of information on the Internet.

The Internet is starting to look a lot more like cable than broadcast in its revenue model. For example, AOL's bundling is like cable's bundling, adding more and more features that glue in different segments of the market. AOL makes much more in subscription revenue than the entire Internet generates in advertising revenue.[527] This is somewhat greater than the proportion of subscription to advertising on cable.[528] In this subscription model, people pop on and off to meet their short, narrowcast needs, but are not glued to the computer and do not generate a great deal of advertising (or, for the moment, ancillary revenues). It is a personal productivity device particularly well suited to information intensive users.[529] For the vast majority, it is a shopping mall at the fingertips of subscribers, enhancing daily activities. Internet traffic is made up of a few hours of online time per week, spread over a dozen sessions with a minute or so at any given page. The leading advertisers on the Internet are a completely different group than one sees on television.[530]

Given the current state of affairs in which the same few companies own monopoly delivery wires and cable TV stations and dominate the high speed Internet, the prospects that the Internet will be a liberating, democratizing medium seem to be fading. Moreover, given the current state of the dot.bomb revolution, relying on the Internet to discipline powerful media giants is wishful thinking at best.

Concentration

The Internet provides a most instructive lesson for market structure analysis, since, in theory, the number of Internet Service Providers is infinite, yet the market has become concentrated. TV networks and cable companies frequently argue that the number of outlets is all that matters, rather than the market share of the outlets. However, I believe this is the wrong approach, since the distribution of attention is far more concentrated than the number of channels suggests.

For economic analysis, eyeballs are what should be counted, not stations. In other markets, the number of competitors is not the central issue; it is their market share that matters. Recently, Microsoft asserted that there were seven different operating systems in the marketplace with over twenty thousand applications available and at least three different computing environments (handhelds, PCs and the Internet), and therefore Microsoft could not possibly be a monopoly. Even a conservative Appeals Court resoundingly rejected that argument.[531] Market structure analysis must be grounded on actual market shares, not merely the number of participants; the rapidly increasing concentration of the Internet underscores that point. AOL's dominance of subscribership in the U.S. is widely noted (25 million subscribers, putting its market share above 40 percent). Its market share makes it a leading firm in a highly concentrated market.[532] Even more striking is the growth in the concentration of usage.

> Because the number of potential online channels is infinite, some assume that market dominance is an impossibility on the Internet. This is faulty reasoning. Gauging consolidation online simply requires a different measuring stick than it does off-line. Analysis of Media Metrix data over the past three years shows an incontrovertible trend toward online media consolidation.... Between March 1999 and March 2001, the total number of companies controlling 50 percent of user minutes online decreased by nearly two-thirds, from eleven to four.[533]

Because AOL has such a dominant position (over 30 percent of user time), the HHI is about 1200, well above the moderately concentrated threshold. The four firm concentration ratio also falls in the range where concerns about concentration and the abuse of market power begin.

Search engines fall in a similar range. The HHI is at about the level of moderately concentrated (1100). The four firm concentration ratio is at the tight oligopoly level, just under 60 percent.

The Decision to End Common Carriage of Advanced Telecommunications Services

The FCC does not regulate the Internet – the enhanced and information services that are sold to the public. It did, however, regulate the telecommunications services and networks over which those services flow. Starting in 1968 in a series of decisions known as the *Computer Inquiries,* the FCC strove to ensure that the underlying telecommunications network would be open and neutral with respect to data services. The objective was to prevent network owners from leveraging their market power to discriminate against providers of enhanced or information services. Between 1968 and 1996, this approach was remarkably successful, providing a key pillar for the Internet revolution.

With the passage of the Telecommunications Act of 1996 and the advent of high-speed Internet services, the FCC reversed its policy. First by inaction and then by official policy, the FCC allowed cable operators and telephone companies to operate their advanced telecommunications networks as closed, proprietary systems. Unaffiliated Internet Service Providers were quickly squeezed out of the market.

Cable and telephone companies became the dominant providers segmenting the high speed market. Cable has an 80 percent market share in advanced services in the residential market. Telcos have a 98 percent market share in advanced services in the business market.

The results of a five year struggle by AOL to gain access to cable networks provides insight into the problem. Ultimately, AOL signed a three-year contract for access to less than one-half of AT&T's lines under remarkably onerous conditions. They are paying $38 at wholesale for a service that sells for $40 in the cable bundle.

The result has been obvious. In contrast to the commercial dial-up Internet, which witnessed a steady flow of innovations and the growth of a large customer service sector that stimulated the adoption of Internet service by a majority of households, the broadband Internet is wasteland.

The body of potential innovators and customer providers has shrunk (see Figure VI-7). Throughout the history of the commercial narrowband Internet, the number of service providers was never less

167

FIGURE VI-7: Density of Internet Service Providers by Date

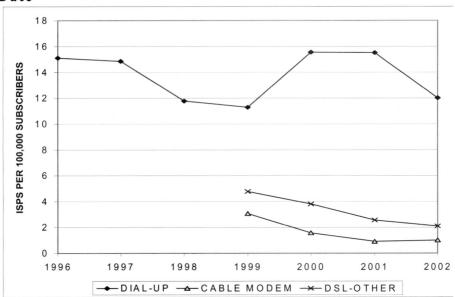

Source: Subscriber counts: Carey, John, "The First Hundred Feet for Households: Consumer Adoption Patterns," in Deborah Hurley and James H. Keller (Eds.), *The First Hundred Feet* (Cambridge: MIT Press, 1999); National Telecommunications Information Administration, *A Nation Online* (U.S. Department of Commerce, 2002). Early ISP counts are discussed in Mark Cooper, *Expanding the Information Age for the 1990s: A Pragmatic Consumer View* (Consumer Federation of America, American Association of Retired Persons, January 11, 1990); see also Janet Abbate, *Inventing the Internet* (Cambridge: MIT Press, 1999 and Matos, F., *Information Service Report* (Washington, D.C.: National Telecommunications Information Administration, August 1988). Since the mid-1990s, annual counts of ISPs have been published in *Boardwatch Magazine*, "North American ISPs," mid year estimates. For high speed ISPs see Federal Communications Commission, *High-Speed Services for Internet Access*," various issue.

than 10 per 100,000 customers. On the high-speed Internet there are now less than 2 ISPs per 100,000 customers. For cable modem service there is less than 1 Internet service provider per 100,000 customers. For DSL service, there are fewer than 2.5 ISPs per 100,000 customers.

Viewed on a market size basis, the impact is even sharper. Whatever you believe about ISPs, they did provide customer care, extend service throughout the country, adapt applications to customer needs, etc. They are like the mechanics and gas stations in the automobile industry. There are simply too few ISPs on the broadband Internet. I also believe they

FIGURE VI-8: HIGH-SPEED INTERNET SUBSCRIBERS

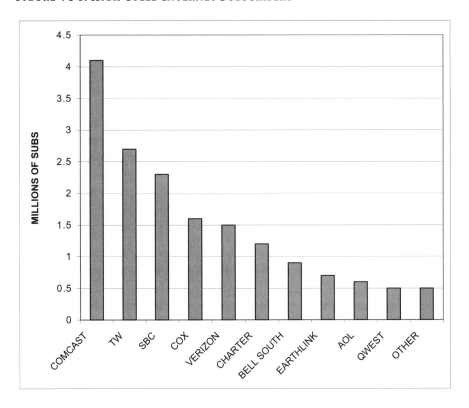

Source: Simon, Bernard, "Some Bet the Future of Broadband Belongs to Regional Bells, Not Cable," *New York Times,* July 21, 200, p. C-1, Federal Communications Commission, *High-Speed Services for Internet Access,*" June 10, 2003.

made a contribution to innovation,which has certainly been lacking on the high-speed Internet.

The problem can be seen on the broadband Internet as well (see Figure VI-8). With both cable and telephone companies seeking to exclude ISPs from competing for subscribers, high-speed Internet has become moderately concentrated.

CONCLUSION

The previous analysis has focused on the total output and number of owners in an absolute sense. I have shown trends of concentration and consolidation on the supply side. These trends become even more pronounced if we look at the availability of media on a per capita (or per household) basis (see Figure VI-9). Describing the availability of electronic voices on a per capita basis gives an indication of the opportunity that an individual will have to be heard and to influence the opinions of his or her fellow citizens through electronic media.

Viewed in this way, I do not find that "media choices have expanded exponentially through technology."[534] The FCC chose ten designated market areas as a representative sample. At best, counting the number of owners, there has been slow growth in the past forty years, but most of that occurred between 1960 and 1980. Looking at the number of owners

FIGURE VI-9: Changes in Broadcast Owners Per Household, 1980-2000

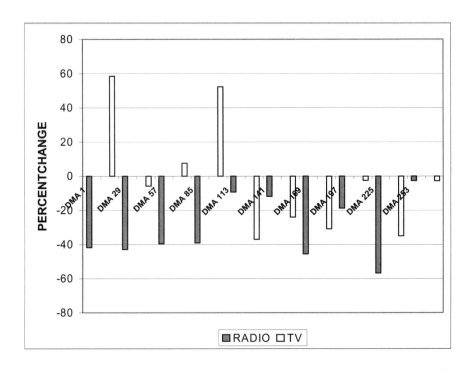

Source: Scott Roberts, Jane Frenette and Dione Stearns, *A Comparison of Media Outlets and Owners for Ten Selected Markets (1960, 1980, 2000)* (Federal Communications Commission, Media Bureau Staff Research Paper, 2002).

per household, there was growth between 1960 and 1980, and then stagnation or decline since 1980. Since 1980, the number of owners per household declined in all ten radio markets and in seven of the ten television markets.

Table VI-13 gives a second general perspective on the same period. It shows the general trend in concentration across the five markets that existed from the early 1980s, as well as the current status of the Internet. It presents the estimates on a population weighted basis, which reflects the fact that many Americans live in large urban markets. Simple, as opposed to weighted, averages would exhibit much higher levels of concentration. The estimates are prepared by directly calculating the

TABLE VI-13: ORDER OF MAGNITUDE TRENDS IN MEDIA MARKET CONCENTRATION (HHI) AUDIENCE SHARES, POPULATION WEIGHTED

MEDIUM/MARKET	Early 1980s	Early 1990s	Early 2000s
BROADCAST TV			
National Prime Time	500	500	1300
Local Stations	3000	2600	2400
MULTICHANNEL VIDEO			
National Subscribers	300	800	1100
Local Subscribers	10000	8800	6800
RADIO			
National Market	100	100	1100
Local Stations	800	1200	2900
NEWSPAPER	3000	3500	3900
INTERNET			
Residential Subscribers			
All			2100
High-Speed			1400
Viewing Time			1200
Search Engines			1100
Local High-Speed Facilities			5300

concentration index of the early 2000s from raw data based on the sources cited throughout this chapter. The early 1990s estimates are based on published sources in the literature. The early 1980s are based on published sources for prime time TV and cable. For local broadcasting, radio and newspapers, the estimates are based on changes in the number of owners. The direction of change and the order of magnitude are the important feature of the table.

While local TV broadcast markets deconcentrated a little, the other markets became more concentrated. All ended the century in at least the moderately concentrated range.

As we have seen, the promise of cable was lost when the industry facility owners were allowed to control the channels and the industry was allowed to go through a simultaneous merger wave, under the theory that one big monopolist is not worse than two little contiguous monopolists. A vigorous cycle of vertical integration into programming was also allowed and more recently clustering has further concentrated the industry. The large increases in concentration in prime time programming and radio flowed directly from public policy decisions in the 1980s and 1990s. The next great hope for deconcentration and democratic discourse, the Internet, has not been up to the task and the growing role of old media and telecommunications giants in that industry does not bode well.

Because greater concentration tends to flow from deregulation of each market, the strategic claim of the advocates of further deregulation and elimination of limits on ownership is to argue that all the different media are part of one big market. Over the past two decades we have allowed a few thousand broadcast licenses and cable TV franchises to fall into the hands of an ever shrinking number of owners. We have missed the opportunity to democratize media ownership modestly by failing to spread the wealth of the powerful broadcast voices to more owners.

Unfortunately for that perspective, the empirical evidence does not support such an assumption. In the past, when the FCC focused on advertising as the measure of the shape of the market, it could not show a great deal of substitution. Now that the nature of use has been subject to scrutiny, we find even less substitutability.

Each of the markets must be analyzed separately and any analytic combination must be done carefully. The next part approaches the public policy problem from this point of view. First it proposes a methodology by which media markets should be analyzed that recognizes the differences between what each of the media produce. It then criticizes the FCC for failing to accept the overwhelming evidence on the nature of media markets.

Part IV: Principles and Practical Approaches for Media Ownership Policy

VII. STRUCTURAL PRINCIPLES FOR MEDIA OWNERSHIP LIMITS

CHECKING CONCENTRATION, CONSOLIDATION AND CONGLOMERATION

This Chapter presents a rigorous, unified framework for media ownership analysis under the Communications Act of 1934. It demonstrates that the current limits on media ownership should not be substantially relaxed. It shows that, consistent with the empirical record, the FCC can adopt a rule based on market structural analysis – which has a long history in the industrial organization literature – that promotes the public interest by limiting mergers. Such a rule should build on economic fundamentals but it must be driven by the First Amendment policy articulated by Congress and endorsed by the courts for the electronic mass media.

This book has shown that legal principles, economic analysis, and decades of empirical evidence do not support the relaxation of structural limits on media ownership and the dramatic increase in concentration that would inevitably follow. The Federal Communications Commission has the ammunition to defend the current rules.

At a practical level, the book answers each of the main questions raised in the court cases and the omnibus media ownership proceeding initiated by the FCC.

For example, in the case of *Sinclair v. Federal Communications Commission*, the D.C. Appeals Court held "that the Commission had failed to demonstrate that its exclusion of non-broadcast media from the eight voices exception 'is necessary in the public interest'."[535] Why didn't the FCC include newspapers and radios in its voice count for the rule that limited the number of markets in which one owner could hold licenses to more than one TV station (the duopoly rule)? The answer it could have given is now clear and supported overwhelmingly by the empirical evidence in the record:

- TV is the dominant source of news and information, while radio, newspapers and the Internet are not good substitutes for TV.
- These other products do not belong in a TV voice count analysis and TV markets are already highly concentrated.
- The limits on TV mergers are well justified.

Similarly, the question posed by the review of the newspaper broadcast cross-ownership ban can be answered with a strong empirical statement. The Commission said it "seeks comments on whether and to what extent we should revise our cross-ownership rule that bars common ownership of a broadcast station and daily newspaper in the same market."

- Newspapers are the second most important source of information and play a unique watchdog role, providing in-depth and investigative reporting.
- All newspaper markets are highly concentrated and virtually all newspaper-TV markets are already concentrated.
- Newspaper-TV combinations should not be allowed in all but a handful of media markets because they would drive media concentration above already unacceptably high levels and allow excessive control over the production of news content in local media markets.

The empirical evidence on radio markets not only confirms that there is a problem, but it underscores the point that antitrust authorities cannot be relied upon to prevent excessive concentration in media markets.

- No additional radio mergers should be allowed because virtually every radio market in the country is highly concentrated.

A HIGH STANDARD IS NECESSARY TO SERVE THE PUBLIC INTEREST

For reasons of both public policy and economic fundamentals, market structure analysis, as the basis for determining merger policy and ownership limits in broadcast media markets, requires a high threshold or standard for competition. Preventing the overall media market from becoming concentrated and submarkets from becoming highly concentrated is a reasonably cautious standard.

The goal of First Amendment policy under the Communications Act is broader than the goal of competition under the antitrust laws. In merger review, the antitrust laws seek to prevent the accumulation of market power while merger review under the Communications Act seeks to promote the public interest. While economic competition is one way of promoting the public interest, the Communications Act and the courts identify several others. Under the Act, the needs of citizens and democracy take precedence.

The competitive concern for antitrust authorities is the potential for the exercise of market power. While concerns exist in all concentrated markets, the *Guidelines* note that in highly concentrated markets, mergers "are likely to create or enhance market power or facilitate its exercise." Although the antitrust authorities frequently allow mergers to go forward after considering other factors, I believe that for media markets these should be firm thresholds. The Sinclair decision notes that in 1995 the Commission had already argued "the merger guidelines of the Justice Department and the Federal Trade Commission might be too low as their purpose lay in defining the point at which antitrust scrutiny is required, and not in encouraging a wide array of voices and viewpoints."[536] Whereas antitrust authorities become concerned about these levels of concentration, Communications Act authorities should be alarmed about concentrated markets like these because of the broader goals of First Amendment policy.

PROMOTING THE PUBLIC INTEREST THROUGH UNCONCENTRATED MEDIA MARKETS

Local Media Markets Should not be Concentrated

The evidentiary record makes it clear that the Commission must proceed cautiously in relaxing limits on media ownership. It shows that the mass media have not experienced an Internet or broadband revolution. The dominant sources of information are still TV and newspapers. Further, there is no simple common "currency" by which TV viewing and newspaper reading can be measured. Different media are used in different ways, have different impacts, and play different roles in civic discourse. The evidence provides strong support to those who feel the analysis of the media under the First Amendment jurisdiction of the Communications Act cannot be reduced to simple economic terms and that the rules should not be relaxed.

At the same time, the record sends a strong warning to those who would rely on economic analysis, especially if different types of media are combined, that great caution is necessary and should be expressed in the form of rigorous market analysis and high competitive standards. Public policy should err in favor of more owners, which translates to greater diversity, to reflect the unique importance and role of media in civic discourse.

Based upon the above legal framework and observations, I propose a two pronged market structure standard that builds on economic fundamentals but is driven by First Amendment jurisprudence. Preventing the overall media market from becoming concentrated and broadcast markets from becoming highly concentrated is a reasonably cautious standard.

The Federal Communications Commission should not tolerate or encourage concentrated media markets. The standard definition of unconcentrated markets, well grounded in economic theory and practice, is a market with the equivalent of ten or more equal-sized producers. Civic discourse demands even more vigilance.

The Commission must approach the market structure analysis in a rigorous manner that reflects the current empirical reality of media markets. Since the *Merger Guidelines* have been a part of market structure policy for two decades, these simple rules are transparent. The data needed to categorize media markets are available.

Furthermore, as a matter of economic fundamentals, caution is needed. Media markets are difficult to define and most data available is limited to very large markets. Concepts like the Designated Market Area (DMA) for TV or the Arbitron rating area for radio create market areas that are generally larger and certainly do not fit precisely with each other or with newspaper markets. Including the Internet or cable in the local market definition, when the FCC's own expert declared these to be national, not local, media, further confounds market analysis.

Given these difficulties in product and geographic market definitions, the FCC should be extremely cautious about thresholds. By combining products that are not good substitutes and do not compete head-to-head in the market, we are likely to overestimate the extent of actual competition. Therefore, based on strict economic grounds, we should be cautious in the thresholds.

Thus, a rule that takes unconcentrated local markets as the minimum standard is justified in both the antitrust and First Amendment contexts (see Figure VII-1).

Broadcast Markets should not be Highly Concentrated or the Source of Excessive Leverage across Sub-Markets

Many TV markets are highly concentrated because they have never had a large number of stations, even though frequencies are available. For these, unconcentrated markets are a goal, but the existence of such

FIGURE VII-1: Media Market Categorization for Merger Review

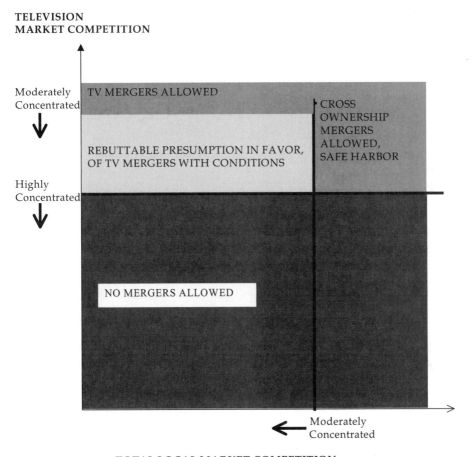

TELEVISION
MARKET COMPETITION

Moderately Concentrated
↓

TV MERGERS ALLOWED

CROSS OWNERSHIP MERGERS ALLOWED, SAFE HARBOR

REBUTTABLE PRESUMPTION IN FAVOR, OF TV MERGERS WITH CONDITIONS

Highly Concentrated
↓

NO MERGERS ALLOWED

← Moderately Concentrated

TOTAL LOCAL MARKET COMPETITION

markets does not mean that where markets are not concentrated, we should abandon that goal or allow mergers to frustrate it. At a minimum, FCC policy should not encourage or allow individual TV broadcast product markets to become highly concentrated.

Excessive market concentration in electronic media cannot be compensated for by cross-media competition. Each product market should be no worse than moderately concentrated. The FCC should not allow horizontal mergers in properly defined TV media markets that are highly concentrated, post-merger. That is, if the merger proposed is in a market that is highly concentrated or would result in a market that is highly concentrated, it should not be allowed.

TV broadcast should not be a source of excessive leverage in the overall media market. The FCC should not allow dominant firms in highly concentrated broadcast markets to merge. The FCC should have a waiver policy to allow horizontal mergers in properly defined media markets that are moderately concentrated (post-merger). The merging parties should be required to show that the merger would promote the public interest. The FCC should require the preservation of functionally separate news and editorial departments in the subsidiaries of the merged entity.

RIGOROUS ANALYSIS OF MEDIA MARKETS

The empirical record does not support the conclusion that the various media products (broadcast video, cable TV, newspaper, radio, Internet) are substitutes. On the contrary, the overwhelming evidence indicates that they are complements. Allowing mergers between them may undermine the ability of each media type to fill the distinct needs that it addresses. Therefore, the Commission must proceed with great caution if it combines media for purposes of market structure analysis. Market structure analysis should recognize the function, reach, and impact of different media products.

Market structure analysis must start with the audience that each media outlet has. Just as market power is grounded in the size of the market an individual firm gains, so too media influence and impact, the ability to be heard, is a function of the audience. It is absurd to ignore the audience of a media outlet in assessing its influence and impact on civic discourse, as it would be absurd to ignore the market share of a firm in assessing its economic market power.

As we have seen, television and newspapers dominate the news media market. Television provides the announcement function. Newspapers provide in-depth coverage. Other sources of news are dwarfed by the two dominant sources. Approximately 80 percent of respondents say they get most of their news and information from TV or newspapers. The percentage of local news is similar, with newspapers playing a role closer to TV. That percentage has been stable since the advent of the Internet. It is even higher for election information. Clearly, market analysis must focus on TV and newspapers. The number of voices could be adjusted to take account of the lesser voices available on radio, the Internet, and other sources.

Much of the FCC's previous analysis has focused on entertainment and advertising markets. The evidence before the Commission now shows that news and information is a distinct product market. Many broadcast stations do not provide news whatsoever. Radio has all but abandoned news. As a consequence, news media markets are much more concentrated than broadcast and video TV markets. National aggregate data suggests that TV news markets are twice as concentrated as TV entertainment markets.

The Commission has considered cable TV as a single additional voice. However, the data before the Commission shows that cable is not an independent source of local news and information. At present, satellite provides no independent local news or information. Indeed, it is struggling just to make all local stations available. The Internet's role as an independent source of news is even smaller. The web sites of the dominant TV outlets and newspapers dominate as sources on the Internet. The Internet should not be counted as an additional local voice.

A RESPONSIBLE APPROACH TO OWNERSHIP LIMITS

I believe the record supports a principled approach to market structure analysis and a much higher standard. The high standards described above for merger policy under the Communications Act can be summarized in two principles.

- No mergers between TV stations and newspapers should be allowed if the overall media market in a locality is or would become concentrated as a result of the merger.
- No mergers involving TV stations should be allowed if the TV market in a locality is or would become highly concentrated as a result of the merger.

Counting Voices in a Total Media Market

The courts have suggested that the FCC adopt a consistent methodology for voice counts for all of the rules. The empirical evidence supports the proposition that each of the media constitutes a separate product. Rules about mergers within those markets can be written in terms of the number of voices within the individual product and geographic markets, as long as a consistent methodology and analytic framework is utilized across all markets.

However, the cross-ownership rule poses more of a challenge. The case can be made that TV and newspapers play such important and unique roles in civic discourse that they should be kept separate. This book has suggested that if the two are to be allowed to combine, a cautious market structure approach should be taken.

The rules must reflect the reality of the marketplace and should promote unconcentrated markets, with all voices being counted. The following formula is consistent with the record before the Commission.

Voice Count = [(Broadcast + Newspaper)/.8]-jointly owned voices

The important role of newspapers and the closeness of usage in local markets lead us to equate TV and newspapers. Market share data must be used as the basis for voice counts and can be readily translated into voice count equivalents. As an example, consider the following calculation, which is actually close to the national average.

A broadcast HHI of 2000 converts to the equivalent of five equal-sized voices (10,000/2000). Newspaper HHIs would be similarly converted to equal-sized voice equivalents (e.g., an HHI of 5000 converts to two equal-sized voice equivalents). Thus, treating TV and newspapers equally, we start with seven major voices.

As a first approximation, the Commission could assume the major TV and newspaper voices represent 80 percent of the market (based on the survey evidence). To continue the previous example, the TV plus newspaper voice count of seven voice equivalents represents 80 percent of the market. Therefore, we can divide that voice count by .8 to adjust for the lesser voices. This increases the voice count to 8.75 (7/.8=8.75).

This is a generous estimate of the voice count for three reasons. First, in many markets there is at least some cross-ownership of radio stations by newspapers and TV broadcasters. This should be taken into account by increasing the adjustment factor. In the above example, the adjustment was .8, based on .1 for radio and .1 for Internet and other. If the radio holdings of broadcasters and newspapers have a market share of 40 percent of the radio market, then the adjustment for radio would be decreased to .06. The voice count would be 8.33 (7/.84=8.33). Second, as noted above, the typical geographic market definitions used are too broad.

Third, the Internet and other categories do not represent independent sources of local news.

In spite of the generous voice count, the number of markets that are not concentrated is small. Figure VII-2 shows the estimation of market voices based on this approach. There are about one dozen that are unconcentrated. A large number fall into the moderately concentrated region.

FIGURE VII-2: Total Media Voices

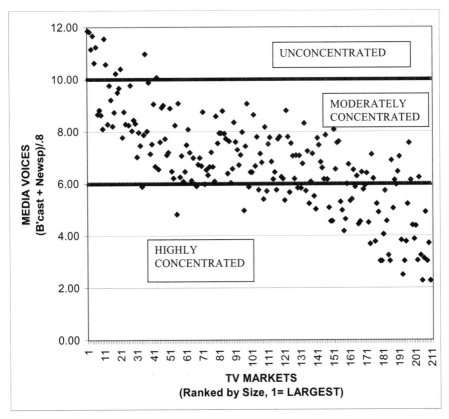

SOURCE: Market profiles from *Editor and Publisher* and *Media Week*, various issues; "Initial Comments of the Newspaper Association of America," and "Initial Comments of Hearst Argyle," Exhibit 1, Selected Media "Voices" by Designated Market Areas, *In the Matter of Cross-Ownership of Broadcast Stations and Newspapers; Newspaper-Radio Cross-Ownership Waiver Policy: Order and Notice of Proposed Rulemaking*, MM Docket No. 01-235, 96-197, Table 3. Year 2000 newspaper circulation for 68 markets. Missing data estimated by regression of DMA size.

185

Reasonable Adjustments to Counting of Voices

Existing cross-ownership and duopoly situations should be taken into account in the final market-wide voice count. For example, the television HHI would attribute viewers of both stations in a duopoly to the parent firm. Similarly, where a newspaper is cross-owned with a television station, both the TV and newspaper audience should be attributed to one owner.

An exception for very small outlets (a diminimus exception) should be allowed to promote civic discourse. Relatively small newspaper or television outlets (less than five percent market share) should be exempted from the above rules. To the extent that larger media outlets seek to obtain cross technology partners, this should be allowed as it can increase the availability of important voices.

Similarly, the Commission should keep the traditional failing firm exception. Under the principle that it is better to keep a media voice that is bankrupt in the market through a merger than to lose it, failing firms have been allowed to merge, even where such a merger would not otherwise be approved.

The empirical estimate of market structure analysis can be altered if empirical evidence indicates changes are justified. The above principles are well supported in the record before the Commission. They are based on data that can be reviewed and updated on a regular basis, as required by the Telecommunications Act of 1996. The biennial review process affords the Commission the opportunity to systematically and routinely examine the assumptions used in constructing the market thresholds and media weights.

ESTABLISHING THRESHOLDS AND MARKET SCREENS

Having counted voices, it is important to keep in mind that thresholds and market screens apply to the post-merger market. That is, if we establish a rule that total local media markets should not be allowed to become concentrated through mergers, it means that the total number of voices should not be less than ten after the merger. This means that scrutiny must start when the number of voices reaches eleven, since a merger could lower the voice count below the threshold. Similarly, in the case of specific product markets, if we adopt a policy that prevents markets from becoming highly concentrated, we would not want fewer than six voices and we would begin scrutinizing mergers when the voice count reached seven.

The adoption of this approach would make a small number of cross-ownership mergers possible (see Figure VII-3). Based on the unconcentrated total market requirement, about a dozen markets would be candidates. Factoring in the requirement that TV markets not be highly concentrated, the number of markets in which cross-ownership mergers would be allowed would fall to fewer than half a dozen.

FIGURE VII-3: Two-Pronged Market Standard for Cross-Ownership

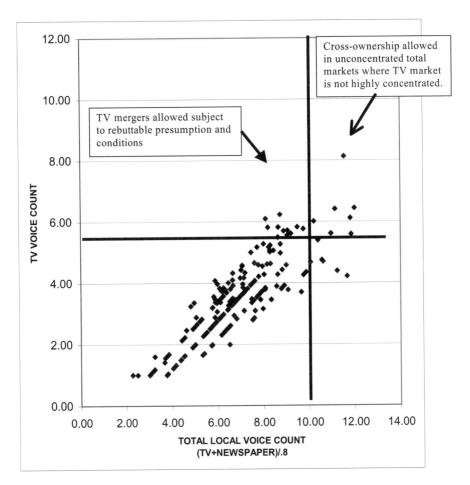

SOURCE: Calculated by Author, see Figure VII-2.

The market share based approach would have an impact on the number of markets in which TV mergers would be allowed. There are just over two dozen such markets. Almost all of these are markets in which duopoly mergers would be allowed today. There are just over another two dozen markets that pass the current voice count test, but would fail the market share based test.

The above analysis is based on market shares for entertainment. Market shares for news are not readily available to the public (although they are routinely collected for proprietary purposes). However, a simple count of local stations that program news is available. If the FCC were to count only those broadcast stations that produce news, the results would be similar to the results based on the entertainment market share based approach, as Figure VII-4 shows. The reason is that the stations with smaller audiences do not contribute much to the HHI. They are also the stations that are least likely to provide news.

If the unconcentrated total market thresholds/moderately concentrated thresholds are applied to the simple news voice count markets, where both important newspapers and TV stations are counted on a simple basis (not market share based), the number of markets where cross-ownership mergers would be allowed is similar to the market share based analysis, although somewhat different markets could witness mergers (see Table VII-1). They would be allowed in about 10 markets. Applying the simple voice count approach to TV markets, I conclude that mergers should be allowed in about 20 markets.

FIGURE VII-4: Simple News v. Market-Share Voice Counts

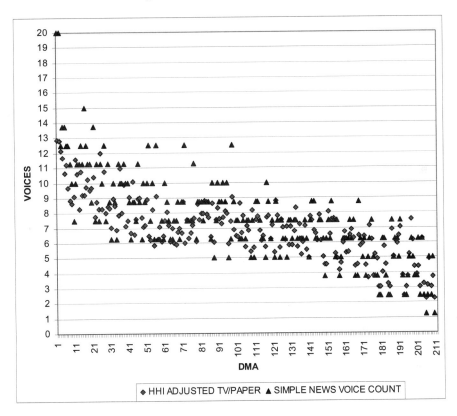

Source: Newspaper voice count, "Initial Comments of the Hearst," In the Matter of Cross-Ownership of Broadcast Stations and Newspapers; Newspaper-Radio Cross-Ownership Waiver Policy: Order and Notice of Proposed Rulemaking, MM Docket No. 01-235, 96-197. Television voice count, Bruce Owen, Michael Baumann and Allison Ivory, "News and Public Affairs Programming Offered by the Four Top-Ranked Versus Lower Ranked Television Stations," Comments of Fox, Economic Study A. Comments of Fox Entertainment Group and Fox Television Stations, Inc., National Broadcasting Company, Inc. and Telemundo Group, Inc., and Viacom, In the Matter of 2002 Biennial Regulatory Review – Review of the Commission's Broadcast Ownership Rules and Other Rules Adopted Pursuant to Section 202 of the Telecommunications Act of 1996, Cross Ownership of Broadcast Stations and Newspapers, Rules and Policies Concerning Multiple Ownership of Radio Broadcast Stations in Local Markets, Definition of Radio Markets, MB Docket No. 02-277, MM Dockets 02-235, 01=317, 00-244, January 2, 2003; HHI adjusted voice count, see Figure VII-2.

TABLE VII-1: Markets Eligible for Cross-Ownership Mergers
(Cities Surpassing Threshold on Two or More Screens)

DMA	CROSS-OWNERSHIP MERGERS				DUOPOLY MERGERS	
	Total Local Market Unconcentrated		TV Market Not Highly Concentrated		TV Market Not Highly Concentrated	
	Market Share	Simple News	Market Share	Simple News	Market Share	Simple News
New York	x	x		x		x
Los Angeles	x	x	x	x	x	x
Chicago	x		x		x	x
Philadelphia	x	x		x		x
San Francisco	x	x		x		x
Houston	x			x	x	x
Miami		x		x		x
Denver	x			x	x	x
Orlando	x	x				x
San Diego	x			x		x
Phoenix					x	x
Boston						x
Dallas						x
Minneapolis						x
Tampa						x
Sacramento						x
Hartford						x
Grand Rapids						x
Fresno						x
El Paso						x

VIII. HOCUS POCUS WITH THE FCC's DIVERSITY INDEX: MAKING MARKET POWER DISAPPEAR

UNLEASHING A MERGER WAVE

In its final order, the FCC created a Diversity Index that applies neither the rigorous analysis nor the high First Amendment standards articulated in the previous chapter. The FCC's Diversity Index plays the central role in determining where to allow newspaper-broadcast cross-ownership mergers to take place.[537] In a lengthy discussion, the FCC describes how it used the index to identify markets that would be "at risk" from excessive loss of diversity if such a merger were to take place.[538]

The FCC abandoned a principled analysis of media market structure in favor of political deals; hence the media ownership proceedings lost any hint of intellectual or public policy integrity. The fundamental principles of market structure analysis that the FCC violated were critical to the creation of the "Diversity Index." In order to eliminate or dramatically relax the limits on newspaper-TV cross-ownership and TV station ownership, the FCC accepted concentrated media markets defined loosely in terms of products and broadly in terms of geographic scope as acceptable First Amendment policy. It ignored audience size (market shares), actual patterns of media use, and the dramatic difference between entertainment and the dissemination of news and information. This is inconsistent with the Communications Act and the recent court remands of ownership rules.

In short, the FCC is

- looking at the wrong product (entertainment),
- analyzing the wrong market (national news),
- doing the market structure analysis incorrectly (not considering market shares and attaching incorrect weights to media types), and
- choosing a dangerously low standard.

The result will be to allow markets to become extremely concentrated. The FCC proposal guts the public interest standard for media ownership under the Communications Act. **The impact on media market structure will be devastating. The FCC has declared a free fire zone for media mergers.**

191

Under the old rules,

- no TV-newspaper mergers were allowed, except where a firm was failing;
- TV duopolies were allowed in about 60 markets that covered about two-thirds of the national population;
- Every merger was subject to a rigorous public interest review.

Under the new rules,

- TV-newspaper mergers will be allowed in approximately 180 markets, in which about 98 percent of the population lives.
- TV duopolies and even triopolies will be allowed in over 160 markets covering 95 percent of the population.
- Triopolies would be allowed in markets in which 23 percent of the population resides.
- There will be absolutely no public interest review of mergers.

The order is completely unbalanced, favoring the private interest of media owners at the expense of the public interest.

- The order gives the broadcast industry the right to seek a waiver and show that a merger is in the public interest outside of the free-fire zone. However, the public has no right to challenge mergers and show that they are not in the public interest inside the free-fire zone.
- The FCC's analysis also appears to be applying logically inconsistent approaches across media markets, an analytic flaw that was particularly offensive to the D.C. Circuit Court. Every inconsistency favors more mergers.

The Diversity Index is a grotesque distortion of the market structure analysis routinely conducted by economists and produces results that are absurd on their face. As a result, the FCC's new rules would allow the overwhelming majority of media markets in America to become extremely concentrated. In Washington, the magician claims that media markets are competitive, but the reality across America would be media giants dominating local markets.

ILLOGICAL RESULTS

In this Chapter I explain how the FCC missed the mark with the Diversity Index, examining in detail four of the markets the FCC used as examples. The following are some of the results that the FCC's Diversity Index produces:

♦ In the New York City area, Shop at Home Incorporated TV, the Dutchess Community College TV and Multicultural Radio Broadcasting Inc. (with three radio stations) all have more weight than the New York Times.

♦ Again in New York, Univision TV has more weight than ABC Inc., NBC/GE, Viacom or News Corp., even when Viacom's and News Corp.'s radio stations and newspapers are included. Univision is three times as important as the New York Times.

♦ In Birmingham, AL, the most important news source is the Internet delivered by telephone companies.

♦ In Altoona, PA the Fox affiliate, Peak Media, has twice the weight of the NBC and CBS affiliates, even though each of the latter has over four times the audience.

♦ In Charlottesville, VA, Virginia educational television has more weight than the Daily Progress, the only daily newspaper in town.

I also examine the impact of the numerous flaws in the Diversity Index on the analysis and policy recommendations for a set of Designated Market Areas (DMAs) that include many state capitols. These are extremely important local markets for purposes of civic discourse. I find a pervasive pattern of illogical and unrealistic results. Among the most notable I find the following for mid-sized markets.

♦ In the Tallahassee DMA, the Thomasville Tribune with average daily circulation just under 10,000 is given equal weight with the Tallahassee Democrat, with more than 50,000 daily circulation, and twice as much weight as the local CBS affiliate, which has over 50,000 viewers a day and 59 percent of the TV market.

♦ In the Lexington KY DMA, the Corbin Times Tribune, with average daily circulation of 5,000, is equal to the Lexington Herald Leader with average daily circulation of 115,000 and given 1.3 times as much weight as the CBS duopoly, with an average of 66,000 viewers. A top four TV station with 29,000 daily viewers cannot merge with a top four TV station with 17,000 daily viewers, but a TV duopoly with 66,000 average daily viewers can merge with a newspaper with 115,000 readers.

To leave no doubt about the distortion in market analysis that results from the FCC's Diversity Index, I apply it to the facts of the Microsoft case. In that case, both the District Court and the D.C. Circuit Court of

Appeals found that Microsoft had monopoly power in the PC operating system market under antitrust laws.[539] Yet, under the FCC Diversity Index, the computer market would not even be considered moderately concentrated. In other words, the FCC's sleight of hand makes the monopoly disappear.

If the Diversity Index "informed" the judgment of the Commissioners who voted for it, then they were misinformed about the reality of American media markets.[540]

The Commission arrived at these absurd results by making a series of faulty assumptions using a number of factually incorrect conclusions. Above all, the FCC has decided to ignore the audience of the individual outlets that will actually merge and swap. In other words, the FCC's Diversity Index never considers the actual market share of these media outlets.

The FCC attempts to put a façade of market structure analysis on the Diversity Index by assessing the importance of each medium, rather than each firm. That is, while it treats all TV stations equally, no matter how many people view them, it did assign different weight to TV as a medium than newspapers, radio or the Internet.   All TV stations are treated equally because they use the same technology to broadcast.[541]

To the extent that cross-media analysis is necessary to determine what different types of media are included and how much they should count, a weighting scheme may have made sense. However, the FCC got the weighting completely wrong. It underweights TV and daily newspapers and vastly overweights weekly newspapers, radio and the Internet, giving them more than twice the weight they deserve. In fact, its own experts and analysis, not to mention the evidentiary record, demonstrated that the Internet should not even be included as a local news source.

CONTRADICTORY ASSUMPTIONS IN CONSTRUCTING THE DIVERSITY INDEX

Market shares play the central role in market structure analysis.[542] The FCC decision to abandon this fundamental tenet of sound economic analysis has no basis in the professional literature. Its efforts to justify this radical break with common practices are feeble at best and flat out wrong at worst. It is also inconsistent with much of the analysis in the order.

The most blatant contradiction underlying the Diversity Index occurs within the discussion of the cross ownership rule. The FCC justifies getting rid of the ban on cross ownership on the basis of a discussion of the market share and "influence" of the various media. Yet, when it comes to writing the new rule, it declares that market share and influence do not matter.

In a paragraph labeled *Benefits of Common-Ownership* the FCC claims that cross ownership yields diversity benefits, stating the following:

> A recent study, for example, determined that, on average "grandfathered" newspaper-owned television stations, during earlier news day parts, led the market and delivered 43% more audience share than the second ranked station in the market and 193% more audience than the third ranked station in the market.[543]

In a paragraph labeled *Harm to Diversity Caused by the Rule*, the Commission claims that the newspaper cross-ownership ban harmed diversity. It again made direct reference to market shares:

> Newspapers and local over-the-air television broadcasters alike have suffered audience declines in recent years. In the broadcast area, commenters have reported declines in the ratings of existing outlets as more media enter the marketplace. For example, the number of television stations in the Miami-Ft. Lauderdale and the adjacent West Palm Beach markets has increased from 10 to 25 from 1975 to 2000. As more stations have begun to program local news, however, the ratings for individual stations have dropped. Broadcast groups owned by GE, Disney, Gannett, Hearst-Argyle and Belo have lost 10 to 15% of their aggregate audience in the past five years. Local over-the-air broadcast TV's share of total television advertising dollars, which includes the new broadcast networks, new cable networks and syndication providers, has fallen from 56% in 1975 to 44% in 2000. E.W. Scripps Company argues that consolidation among established media outlets and the proliferation of new media outlets since 1975 requires broadcasters and newspapers to grow, consolidate, and achieve critical scale in their local markets to survive and effectively serve the public.[544]

It is not the number of stations that matters most, but the loss of market share or audience that is the driving force in the argument.

> Given the decline in newspaper readership and broadcast viewership/ listenership, both newspaper and broadcast outlets may find that the efficiencies to be realized from common ownership will have a positive impact on their ability to provide news and coverage of local issues. We must consider the impact of our rules on the strength of media outlets, particularly those that are primary sources of local news and

information, as well as on the number of independently owned outlets.[545]

How does one measure the strength of media outlets, but by their audience size?

The FCC goes on to assert that "Given the growth in available media outlets, the influence of any single viewpoint source is sharply attenuated."[546] How does one measure the influence of an outlet, but by its audience size? The FCC presents no measure of influence or evidence of its "sharp attenuation" other than market share and audience data.

Having relied extensively on market shares in declaring that the blanket prohibition on cross-media mergers cannot be sustained, the FCC then refuses to incorporate the audience of outlets into the Diversity Index. Instead, the FCC assumes, contrary to fact, that all outlets within each medium are equal in size.

> We have chosen the availability measure, which is implemented by counting the number of independent outlets available for a particular medium and assuming that all outlets within a medium have equal market shares.[547]

This counterfactual assumption is what opens the door to the absurd results. The FCC assumes, incorrectly, that each TV station has the same strength and influence as every other TV station in the market. It assumes that each newspaper has the same strength and influence as every other newspaper in the market. It assumes that each radio station has the same influence and strength as every other radio station in the market.

INCONSISTENCIES IN THE COUNTING OF OUTLETS

The equal market shares assumption conflicts with another set of analyses in the order. In the discussion of both the television and radio ownership limits, the Commission presents an extensive discussion of coverage or reach of the outlets. This discussion leads to important decisions in both cases.

The FCC presents an extensive analysis of the coverage or reach of TV and radio stations, but presents no such analysis of newspapers. Worse still, it concludes that signals that cannot be easily received for purposes of the TV ownership limits should be discounted. It concludes that radio signals must be analyzed in small markets because of their limited strength for purposes of the radio ownership limits. However, it ignores or forgets these conclusions when it comes to the cross-ownership rules. In other words, voices that cannot easily be heard and therefore are not counted for the purposes of one set of rules suddenly can be heard and are then counted for the purposes of another set of rules. The only consistency in the FCC's analysis in this instance is that it gives the largest media companies exactly what they wanted in both cases.

For example, the Commission concludes that the weaker signal and therefore lesser coverage of UHF stations require them to be discounted.

> [B]ecause our assumption regarding DMA-wide carriage is not universally true, and in recognition of the signal propagation limitations of UHF signals, we adopt herein a waiver standard that will permit common ownership of stations where a waiver applicant can show that the stations have no Grade B overlap and that the stations are not carried by any MVPD to the same geographic area...

> As discussed in our national television ownership rule section, UHF stations reach fewer households than VHF stations because of UHF stations' weaker broadcast signals. Reduced audience reach diminishes UHF stations' impact on diversity and competition in local markets. Accordingly, we will consider whether one or both stations sought to be merged are UHF stations.[548]

It also concludes that the smaller Arbitron areas are more appropriate for the radio analysis.

> We understand that geographic areas are less accurate than contours in measuring the signal reach of individual stations. But radio stations serve people, not land; and while radio signals may overlap over uninhabited land or even water' people in the United States tend to be clustered around specific population centers. The fact that radio signals are not congruent with geographic boundaries does not undermine the logic of relying on geographic areas to define radio markets.

> As explained below, we will rely on the Arbitron Metro Survey Area (Arbitron Metro) as the presumptive market. We also establish a methodology for counting the number of radio stations that participate in a radio market. We initiate below a new rule making proceeding to define radio markets for areas of the country not located in an Arbitron Metro, and we adopt a modified contour-overlap approach to ensure the orderly processing of radio station applications pending completion of that rule making proceeding.[549]

In the cross-ownership rule, the FCC engages in no such analysis. It does not analyze the coverage of newspapers and it forgets about its coverage analysis for TV and radio.[550] UHF stations are not discounted and all radio stations are assumed to cover the entire DMA.

Our cable television signal carriage rules generally permit a television broadcast station within a DMA to obtain cable carriage throughout the DMA, and our DBS signal carriage rules generally ensure that all television stations within a DMA are treated the same with respect to satellite retransmission. For this reason, we assume that all television broadcast stations in a DMA are available throughout the DMA. As explained above, each broadcast television station receives an equal share of the broadcast television weight.

We combine the television stations in each DMA with the radio stations in the Arbitron radio metro with which the DMA is paired. There are 287 Arbitron radio metros in the country. Each one is smaller than the DMA within which it lies. Arbitron radio metros do not cover the entire country. More sparsely populated areas are not included in radio metros; approximately one-half of radio stations are not in a metro market. As explained below in the cross-media limits section of this *Order*, we use the Diversity Index to help us identify markets that are "at risk" for excessive concentration in the "viewpoint diversity market." Once those markets have been identified, and cross-media limits imposed, the actual implementation of the cross-media diversity limits will not require information on a local radio market, only on the television market (DMA) within which the radio stations are located that are part of a proposed merger5[51]

It is blatantly contradictory to assume that a signal that does not reach a viewer/listener for purposes of competition analysis and media specific ownership rules somehow magically reaches them for purposes of the diversity analysis under the cross-ownership rule.

CONTRADICTIONS IN THE ECONOMIC ANALYSIS

The FCC tries to justify abandoning market shares with an economic argument. The audience shares of the dominant mass media do not matter, we are told, because entry into the market is easy and the production of news can be expanded at little marginal cost. This claim is simply wrong, contradicted by the evidence before the Commission and even by the Commission's own words.

The Order states that "This point has particular force when dealing with competition in the marketplace of ideas because media outlets can rapidly expand their distribution of content (including local news and current affairs) at very low marginal cost." Yet, in the discussion of the need to relax the duopoly rule, the Commission reaches the exact opposite conclusion, stating, "Moreover, rising news production costs and other factors may cause broadcasters to turn to less costly programming options."[552]

A look at the empirical facts about trends in the industry before the Commission reinforces this view. There has been almost no entry into the business of publishing daily newspapers, the mainstay of print journalism, in decades. The record shows that the number of papers and owners has been shrinking, not expanding.[553] Entry into the TV business has taken place. The number of full power stations has increased. However, the FCC acknowledges that the important public policy goal is to encourage entry by new owners, since owners control the electronic voices of the outlets. The number of owners has declined sharply. Moreover, the number of stations providing news has declined slightly or at best been flat. The claim that ownership entry is easy at the level of long-term competition (i.e. sinking new capital into the market) is not supported by the record.

The FCC might claim that it is addressing the marginal cost of expanding news production for stations already doing news, which it deems to be low. At least for these stations the marginal cost of expanding output, although not low, would not involve starting a whole news department. If this were the argument on which the FCC was relying, it should have counted only broadcast stations that currently provide news in its index and not those stations that do not. It did not make this distinction. As shown in the previous chapter,[554] market structure analysis based on a news voice count yields a result similar to market structure analysis based on market shares because the stations with small market shares do not contribute much to the total Hirshman Herfindahl Index, which is the FCC's preferred measure of concentration) are also less likely to do news.

However, the actual language used by the FCC to describe the cost of news production will not allow it to get away with this sleight of hand. There is no doubt that the difficulty and expense of news production stems from its variable costs, not its fixed costs.

> The study finds that although equipment prices are dropping rapidly, rising demand for qualified personnel is increasing the amount stations must spend on salary and benefits. Smith Geiger concludes that a start up news operation would not "break even" until year 13 in a small market and year 14 in a mid-sized market. The study concludes that in this climate, if a local station were to cease news operations, "it is difficult to imagine another entity stepping in to take its place." Smith Geiger notes that although news operations earn a profit, they require

the parent company or station to carry a significant cost load and deal with other intangibles such as personnel management, liability, and community goodwill. Smith Geiger concludes that this may lead local stations to exit the local news business in favor of lower cost alternatives, such as acquired programming, which it estimates will earn a higher profit in both small and mid-sized markets. Smith Geiger ultimately concludes that "the continuing profitability of a local television news operation is now highly uncertain." Many commenters agree. NAB submitted an additional study which compares the average cost of producing news by affiliates of "Big Four" networks (*i.e.*, ABC, CBS, Fox, and NBC) in markets of various sizes. These data show that the average news expense of affiliate stations has increased by as much as 104% between 1993 and 2001.[555]

The FCC's economic analysis is also inconsistent in its discussion of substitutability. The FCC claims that patterns of usage also support the decision not to rely on market shares.[556] It does so on the basis of claims about substitution between media. This claim is contradicted by its own data and analysis in other parts of the Order.

In each of the competition analyses the evidence on competition in advertising media markets indicates that they are separate products. In contrast, the FCC claims that the evidence on the use of media for diversity purposes in the marketplace of ideas indicates they are one large market. The econometric evidence in the record supports the opposite conclusion. Substitutability between media for advertising purposes, although not great, is much larger than the substitutability of the media for usage purposes.[557]

INCONSISTENCIES ACROSS POLICY ANALYSES

The failure to conduct a rational market structure analysis for purposes of the cross ownership rule draws the FCC into a broad range of contradictions with the other rules at the level of policy. Based on sound market structure analysis of the local and national television markets, the FCC concludes that the dominant firms – the top four local stations and the four major national networks – should not be allowed to merge with each other. The FCC identifies a host of dangers in such mergers and little potential public interest benefit from them.

According to the FCC, such mergers would increase economic market power.

> To the contrary, such mergers are likely to create or enhance market power or to facilitate its exercise...

So, for example, if Fox merged with GE and Disney merged with Viacom, the HHI would increase by almost 767 points. Then, if these two companies merged with each other, the HHI would increase by 2,246 points. Either of these changes in the HHI would be scrutinized under DOJ Merger Guidelines. Since these networks own television stations, the change in the HHI would actually be higher than in these examples. [558]

Dominant firm mergers create dominant firms that are much larger than their nearest rivals.

Moreover, in local markets, there is a general separation between the audience shares of the top four-ranked stations and the audience shares of other stations in the market….

Thus, although the audience share rank of the top four-ranked stations is subject to change and the top four sometimes swap positions with each other, a cushion of audience share percentage points separates the top four and the remaining stations, providing some stability among the top four-ranked firms in the market. Nationally, the Big Four networks each garner a season to date prime time audience share of between ten and 13 percent, while the fifth and sixth ranked networks each earn a four percent share While there is variation in audience shares within local markets, these national audience statistics are generally reflected in the local market station rankings. The gap between the fourth-ranked national network and the fifth-ranked national network represents a 60% drop in audience share (from a ten share to a four share), a significant break point upon which we base our rule…

The recent growth of cable and DBS does not alter our conclusion. Despite that growth, the top-four networks continue to provide the greatest reach of any medium of mass communications. The top-four networks attract much larger prime-time audiences in relation to advertisement-supported cable networks. Broadcasting's percentage share of advertising revenue continues to exceed its percentage share of viewing. Moreover, despite a decrease in audience share, the top-four networks continue to command increases in advertising rates, a further testament to the strength of broadcasting television as an advertising medium. [559]

These huge firms can distort the market for inputs available to other distributors of content.

The vertically integrated networks would limit competitors' access to programming by denying remaining networks access to the production output of the merged network. In addition the merged firm can raise the price paid by those competitors for programming created and produced by the merged network's program production assets.

A top-four network merger would give rise to competitive concerns that the merged firm would restrict the consumption of programming by using its market power to limit competitors' access to sources of programming. In addition, the merged network could use its market power to control the price it pays for programming or to raise competitors' costs of acquiring programming. In concentrated markets, viewers have access to fewer programming choices if the number of national, independent purchasers of programming decreases due to limited access to programming and higher programming costs. [560]

The firms combining in such a merger are likely to have a diminished incentive to compete.

Permitting combinations among the top four would reduce incentives to improve programming that appeals to mass audiences. The strongest rival to a top four-ranked station is another top four-ranked station... When formerly strong rivals merge, they have incentives to coordinate their programming to minimize competition between the merged stations. Such mergers harm viewers...

There we conclude that Big Four networks continue to comprise a "strategic group" within the national television advertising market. That is due largely to those networks' continued ability to attract mass audiences. It is this network programming that explains a significant portion of continued market leadership of the top four local stations in virtually all local markets. Thus the continued need for the Dual Network rule to protect competition at the network level also supports our decision to separate ownership of local stations carrying the programming of Big Four networks...

The top-four networks compete largely among themselves for advertisers that seek to reach large, national, mass audiences – a significant portion of the national advertising market that provides the top-four networks with a significant portion of their profits. We therefore conclude that a merger of two or more of the top-four networks would substantially lessen competition in the national advertising market, especially within the strategic group, with the concomitant harm to viewers described above.[561]

Furthermore, there is likely to be little public interest benefit from dominant firm mergers because the merging parties are likely to be healthy and already engaged in the production of news and information products.

In contrast, no commenter discussed the efficiencies and public interest benefits associated with a merger between two financially strong stations. Nothing in the record indicates that such mergers will produce efficiencies that translate into benefits for the viewing public.

One reason that combinations involving top four-ranked stations are less likely to yield public interest benefits such as new or expanded local news programming is that such stations generally are already originating local news.

As noted in the national TV ownership rule section, we conclude that affiliates play an important role in assuring that the needs and tastes of local viewers are served. Elimination of the dual network rule would harm localism by providing the top-four networks with increased economic leverage over their affiliates, thereby diminishing the ability of the affiliates to serve their communities.[562]

Each and every one of these reasons given to ban mergers between dominant entities in TV markets is a valid reason to ban a merger between dominant TV stations and dominant newspapers in the local media market. A merger between a dominant TV station and a dominant newspaper results in an entity that dwarfs its nearest competitors in terms of control of news production.[563] The dominant firm would control a large percentage of the reporters in the market. It would also have a sufficiently large cross-media presence to diminish the antagonism between print and video media, thereby reducing competition. It would have a diminished incentive to compete (especially across media types) and an increased incentive to withhold product. It can leverage its market power in cross promotion. The public interest benefit is likely to be small because these are the most profitable entities in their local market and not likely to add product that promotes the public interest. Indeed, the synergies sought are likely to diminish the total resources available for news production.

Bogus Legal Arguments Against Sensible Market Structure Analysis

The FCC offers two general legal arguments as to why it cannot or should not use market shares in its construction of a Diversity Index. These simply do not withstand scrutiny.

The FCC declares that basing the Diversity Index on market shares or audiences would run afoul of constitutional prohibitions on content regulation.

> If we were to adopt a usage measure designed to reflect our concern with local news and current affairs, we would need information on viewing/listening/reading of local news and current affairs material. To implement this procedure, it would be necessary first to determine which programming constituted news and current affairs. We believe that this type of content analysis would present both legal/Constitutional and data collection problems.[564]

The claim is completely unfounded and contradicted by extensive analysis conducted throughout the Order.

First, the FCC recognizes its constitutional authority to deal with types of programs in the case of children's programming.[565] In that instance, Congress is prescribing a quantity of programming to be aired. If such a policy passes constitutional muster, then merely counting the quantity of programming stations choose to add is no threat to the First Amendment.

Moreover, the FCC declares at the beginning of the Order that news and information should be the focus of its analysis.[566] In the cross ownership discussion it cites studies of local news and information shows that it claims demonstrate that removing the ban will promote the public interest.[567] In the discussion of the duopoly rule it presents extensive discussions of the quality and content of local news and information programming.[568] The FCC does a lengthy analysis of merger impacts based on the simple question of whether a station does or does not originate local news shows. [569]

The extent of the analysis of local news programming in which the FCC engages for purposes of the duopoly rule shows at least one simple distinction that would be a non-infringing implementation. In justifying the ban on mergers between top four stations in a market, the FCC relies on the fact that 85% of the top four firms originate local news.[570] In contrast, only 19% of the remainder of the stations broadcast news. It concludes that banning top four mergers and allowing other mergers has a high probability of promoting the public interest since this reduces the chances of "losing" an independent source of news.

When it comes to the definitions of the Diversity Index, however, it suddenly and incorrectly claims that it cannot identify local news programming without straying into content regulation, which is frowned upon by First Amendment jurisprudence. How can it discover at the end of the Order that all this analysis, upon which it relied in determining the local impact of various media ownership rules, is suddenly constitutionally suspect for establishing a new set of rules?

The FCC also claims it can, or should, ignore the size of the audience because the purpose of diversity policy is only to prevent the complete suppression of ideas. If an idea can get out into the public through any means of mass communications, diversity has been served, in the FCC view.

> The decision of whether to do weighting turns on whether our focus is on the availability of outlets as a measure of potential voices or whether it is on usage (*i.e.*, which outlets are currently being used by consumers for news and information). We have chosen the availability measure, which is implemented by counting the number of independent outlets available for a particular medium and assuming that all outlets within a medium have equal shares. In the context of evaluating viewpoint diversity, this approach reflects a measure of the likelihood that some particular viewpoint might be censored or foreclosed, *i.e.*, blocked from transmission to the public.[571]

I disagree with this view of the public policy purpose of the Communications Act. The FCC has given up all pretense of ensuring a broad opportunity for ideas to circulate and will allow owners of the electronic media outlets to amass huge audiences by buying dominant newspapers and leading TV stations.

> Nor is it particularly troubling that media properties do not always, or even frequently, avail themselves to others who may hold contrary opinions. Nothing requires them to do so, nor is it necessarily healthy for public debate to pretend as though all ideas are of equal value entitled to equal airing. The media are not common carriers of speech.

> The cited First Amendment policy was first established by the Supreme Court in Associated Press v. United States, 326 U.S. 1, 20 (1945), and has been consistently reaffirmed since then.[572]

The FCC has abandoned the principle that First Amendment policy should promote "the widest possible dissemination of information from diverse and antagonistic sources." In its place, it adopts the position that preventing the complete suppression of an idea is all that democracy needs to thrive.

Given the prominent role that market shares play in the analysis of industrial organization, the clear First Amendment jurisprudence that rejects the FCC's extraordinarily narrow vision of diversity, and the weak and contradictory economic arguments within the Order, the FCC has clearly erred in its decision to ignore audience size.

MEDIA WEIGHTS

Asking the Wrong Questions Produces the Wrong Answers

As noted, the FCC can insist that if it is to offer a coherent analytic framework, it must combine outlets and audiences of different media types in some manner. It must find a way to weight the various media. Unfortunately, the FCC got the media weights wrong. The agency fails to ask the proper questions on its survey instrument and chose not to conduct a second survey.[573] It then combines questions that distort the weights. It cites other surveys to support some of its analytic conclusions, but does not notice that those same surveys contradicted its much more important assumptions and choices.

The FCC asked respondents "What single source do you use most often for local and national news and current affairs?"[574] This question gets directly at the relative importance of the news sources. Unfortunately, the FCC did not ask the question about local news only.

The FCC fell back on a much weaker question for local news: "What source, if any, have you used in the past 7 days often for local news and current affairs?"[575] This was an open question in which respondents were allowed multiple responses. Sources they mention here clearly came to their minds. One might infer that what they recall reflects the importance of the sources to them.

Unfortunately, the FCC did not accept these responses. It then followed up with a prompted question directed only at those who did not mention a source.[576] The FCC asked those people who failed to mention a source whether they had used it. The FCC then combined the answers to the two questions, giving them equal weight. This approach was certain to overweight the less prevalent sources by asking many more people about those sources a second time with a prompted question.

In the course of justifying its decision not to include magazines in the final weighting, the FCC cites Pew Center studies in support of this decision.[577] The Pew studies also had a great deal of useful information about all sources of news and information, but the FCC chose to ignore it.

Table VIII-1 translates the responses to four questions (two from Pew and two from the FCC) into weights according to the methodology used by the FCC. It contrasts the results to the Diversity Index weightings.

The two Pew questions on campaign sources and the FCC question on most important sources of news all yield very similar results. The TV weight is in the range of 55 – 60, almost twice the weight given it by the FCC. The newspaper weight is in the range of 24 to 28, equal to the FCC weight. The radio weight is in the range of 10 to 11, less than half the weight given it by the FCC. The Internet is in the range of 5 – 6, less than half the weight given it by the FCC.

The Pew question on where people get most news for local elections is particularly important: " How do you get most of your news about the election campaigns in your state and district?" I use it as the basis for the weights in our comparative analysis.

The FCC's failure to ask the proper questions about the importance of local news sources also undermines its ability to set the weights for daily newspapers compared to weekly newspapers. Relying on the question about any source of local news, the FCC establishes a ratio of 2.5 to 1 between dailies and weeklies. The problem here should be evident. Asking people whether they had referred to a source any time in the past seven days and then giving equal weight to dailies and weeklies misses the obvious point that weeklies come out once a week and dailies come out five, six or seven times. Many people get as many as seven dailies to one weekly.

If we divide the weekly responses by 7, we conclude that dailies should be weighted 11.5 times weeklies. Interestingly, when the FCC asked about the most often used source, dailies were mentioned 12.2 times as often as weeklies. For purposes of comparison with the FCC diversity weights, within the newspaper category, I set dailies at 92 percent and weeklies at 8 percent, an 11.5 to 1 ratio, (rather than the 70.3% and 29.7% weights used by the FCC).

Moreover, the FCC analysis only looks at the demand side of the market. Newspapers play a much larger role on the supply side. They employ many more reporters and newsroom staff and produce many more and much longer news stories than TV or radio. This further supports the view that the FCC has overweighted radio.

Table VIII-1: Weights Based On Various Questions About Importance And Use Of Media Sources For Local And National News And Current Affairs

QUESTION	WEIGHTS			
	TV	Papers	Radio	Internet
FCC Diversity Index[a]	33.8	28.8	24.8	12.5
PEW QUESTIONS				
How have you been getting most of your[b] news about the presidential election campaign?	60.5	25.5	9.7	4.8
How do you get most of your news about[c] the election campaigns in your state and district?	55.5	27.8	10.9	5.9
FCC QUESTIONS				
What single source do you use most often[d] for local or national news and current affairs.	58.8	24.4	10.5	6.2
What source, if any, have you used in the[e] past 7 days for local news and current affairs?	42.0	31.1	17.5	9.3

a/ Federal Communications Commission, "Report and Order," In the Matter of 2002 Biennial Regulatory Review – Review of the Commission's Broadcast Ownership Rules and Other Rules Adopted Pursuant to Section 202 of the Telecommunications Act of 1996, Cross Ownership of Broadcast Stations and Newspapers, Rules and Policies Concerning Multiple Ownership of Radio Broadcast Stations in Local Markets, Definition of Radio Markets, MB Docket No. 02-277, MM Dockets 02-235, 01=317, 00-244, July 2, 2003, at para. 415.

b/ Pew Center for the People and the Press, *Sources for Campaign News, Fewer Turn to Broadcast TV and Papers* (Feb. 5, 2000), q. 13.

c/ Pew Center for the People and the Press, *Modest Increase in Internet Use for Campaign 2002* (Jan. 5, 2003), q. 17.

d/ Nielsen Media Research, *Consumer Survey On Media Usage* (Federal Communications Commission, Media Ownership Working Group Study No. 8, September 2002) question no. 10.

e/ Media Ownership Working Group Study No. 8, question no. 1.

TABLE VIII-2: MEDIA WEIGHTS

MEDIA	FCC DIVERSITY INDEX	CFA W/INTERNET	CFA W/O INTERNET
TV	33.8	55.5	58.8
Radio	24.8	10.9	11.5
Dailies	20.2	25.6	27.6
Weeklies	8.6	2.2	2.4
Internet	12.5	5.9	0

Reasonable Weights for Combining Media in Market Structure Analysis

Table VIII-2 summarizes a reasonable set of weights for the media. Television and daily newspapers should be given much more weight than the FCC gave them. Radio, weeklies and the Internet should be given less importance. Indeed, the only task force report that addressed the Internet in any detail assumed that it was a national source, not a local source. My earlier analysis strongly supports that view. The FCC has no justification for including it in the Diversity Index, which is a measure of local sources. Therefore, Table VIII-2 also includes a scenario that is based on TV, newspapers and radio only.

The analysis in the next section also includes a scenario based on a count of TV stations that originate local news, rather than TV entertainment market shares.

MEDIA MARKET STRUCTURE

Detailed Analysis of the FCC Examples

Table VIII-3 presents the results of my analysis of the distortion introduced into the proposed rule by the flaws in the Diversity Index.

TABLE VIII-3: MEDIA MARKET CONCENTRATION RATIOS (HHI)

AREA	FCC DI	INDIVIDUAL ASSUMPTIONS			COMBINED CHANGE		
		Use Aud. Shares	Reweight Radio/ Internet	Internet is national	Reweight & Use Audience	Reweight & Use Internet Audience is national	Reweight & Use Internet is national TV News Voice Count
New York	373	361	906	438	965	1055	725
Birmingham	591	796	852	803	871	951	961
Altoona	960	1384	1231	1413	1781	1987	1676
Charlottesville	1358	2420	2045	2077	3823	4256	4256

Taken together, these flaws result in a gross distortion in the assessment of the state of diversity and competition in media markets.

Even in the largest markets in the country, the FCC should not be pursuing a policy of blanket approval of mergers. For New York City, instead of an HHI of 373, a reasonable approach would produce an HHI of 1055 if the HHI is computed as it should be, taking market share into account. In other words, instead of depicting New York City as having the equivalent of 27 equal-sized competitors, it should be seen as having about 10 when market share is considered. This is moderately concentrated and just at the level where antitrust authorities become concerned about mergers.

The differences in the larger markets, when one uses proper methods by accounting for market share, are informative. New York is more concentrated than Birmingham when market shares are considered because of the high level of cross-ownership in New York. In New York, eight of the largest owners are in two of the three media. In Birmingham, there is not one cross-ownership situation. There are also four times as many noncommercial TV stations in New York, but one and one quarter times as many commercial TV stations. The FCC's approach tends to underweight cross-ownership by the largest players in the market and overweight small and non-commercial outlets. These stations are much less likely to do local news. Even if the FCC were to rely on a count of TV stations doing news, the picture it would get would be very different.

Thus, the FCC's conclusion about the health and diversity of local media markets is entirely a function of its faulty assumptions and analytically incorrect approach to market structure analysis.

For Charlottesville, VA, the smallest TV market considered, the distortion is even more troubling. Instead of an HHI of 1358, about halfway up the moderately concentrated zone, the HHI should be over 4200. Instead of painting a picture of a market with the equivalent of over seven equal-sized competitors, the proper picture is just over three.

Irrational Outcomes in Other Markets

The FCC's sample cities do not tell the entire story. While the FCC bases its rule on a DMA analysis, the examples are city-by-city and not properly defined.[42] To flesh out the illogical results of the Diversity Index, I examine state capitol DMAs. These are critically important DMAs for the purposes of civic discourse. As Table VIII-4 shows, I identify four types of anomalies that result from the FCC approach.

- The within-media anomalies for newspapers are the result of the failure to consider the audience.
- The within-media anomalies for TV are the result of the failure to consider the audience and coverage of stations.
- The between-media anomalies result from multiple failures – audience, coverage and weighting.
- The merger anomalies result from the failure to apply the dominant firm analysis to cross-media mergers.

The FCC analysis consistently and repeatedly equates media outlets that are of vastly different strength and influence, both within media types and across media. It precludes dominant firm mergers in the TV market that appear to be substantially less threatening to diversity in civic discourse than the cross-media mergers it would allow.

TABLE VIII-4: IRRATIONAL CONCLUSIONS RESULTING FROM UNREALISTIC ASSUMPTIONS AND INCOMPLETE ANALYSIS: STATE CAPITOL DMAs

DEFINITIONS:

DMA of State Capitol; (RANK of DMA)
1. Smallest newspaper compared to largest newspaper; anomaly results from failure to consider markets share. Circulation is total weekly divided by 7.
2. Smallest commercial, largest non-commercial TV station compared to largest commercial TV station; anomaly results from failure to consider market shares and coverage. TV stations are measured by average day part share, 9:00 AM to Midnight
3. Weight of smallest newspaper compared to largest TV station: anomaly results from failure to consider market share, coverage and weights. Average daily circulation compared to TV viewership measured as households based on average commercial day-part share multiplied by households using television
4. Smallest TV-TV merger disallowed compared to largest TV-newspaper merger allowed; anomaly results from failure to apply dominant firm analysis to cross media mergers. The station is the top in viewership. Newspaper is average daily circulation.

EXAMPLES:

ALBANY NY DMA (55)
1. Register Star with ,7,000 avg. daily circulation is equal to the Time Union with 100,000 avg. daily circulation
2. ABC with less than 1% TV market share and WMHT PBS with 2% TV market share are equal to NBC with 3% TV market share
3. Register Star 7,000 avg. daily circulation is equal to 57% of NBC with 55,000 avg. daily viewers
4. TV station with 37,000 a vg. daily viewers cannot merge with a TV station with 17,000 avg. daily viewers, but a TV station with 55,000 avg. daily viewers can merge with a newspaper with 100,000 readers

ANNAPOLIS MD IN BALTIMORE DMA (24)
1. Cecil Whig with 10,000 avg. daily circulation is equal to the Baltimore Sun with 325,000 avg. daily circulation
2. ABC with 13% TV market share and MD PBS with 3% TV market share are equal to NBC with 28% TV market share
3. Cecil Whig with 10,000 avg. daily circulation is equal to 133% of NBC with 150,000 avg. daily viewers
4. TV station with a 71,000 daily viewers cannot merge with a TV station with 54,000 daily viewers, but a TV station with 150,000 viewers can merge with a newspaper with 325,000 readers.

AUGUSTA ME IN PORTLAND ME DMA (76)
1. Berlin Daily with 6,000 avg. daily circulation is equal to the Portland Press Herald, with avg.84,000 daily circulation
2. Fox with 1% TV market share and Maine PBS with 3% TV market share are equal to NBC with 41% TV market share
3. Berlin Daily with 6,000 avg. daily circulation is equal to 95% of NBC with 48,000 avg. daily viewer
4. TV station with 21,000 avg. daily viewers cannot merge with a TV station with 6,000 avg. daily viewers, but a TV station with 48,000 avg. daily viewers can merge with a newspaper with 84,000 avg. daily readers

BOISE ID (124)
1. The Argus Observer with 6,000 avg. daily circulation is equal to the Idaho Statesman with 70,000 avg. daily circulation
2. UPN with 9% TV market share and KAID PBS with 4% TV market share are equal to NBC with 43% TV market share
3. Argus Observer with 6,000 avg. daily circulation is equal to 150% of NBC with 28,000 avg. daily viewers
4. TV station with 11,000 avg. daily viewers cannot merge with a TV station with 9,000 avg. daily viewers, but a TV station with 28,000 avg. daily viewers can merge with a newspaper with 70,000 avg. daily readers

BOSTON MA /CONCORD NH (6)
1. Athol Daily News with 4,000 avg. daily circulation is equal to commonly owned Boston Globe/ Worcester Telegram with 605,000 avg. daily circulation of 605,000
2. Pax with 1% TV market share and WGBH PBS with 3% TV market share are equal to NBC with 25% TV market share
3. Athol Daily with 4,000 avg. daily circulation is equal to 50% of NBC with 235,000 avg. daily viewers
4. TV station with 192,000 avg. daily viewers cannot merge with a TV station with 142,000 avg. daily viewers, but a TV station with 235,000 avg. daily viewers can merge with newspaper with 605,000 avg. daily readers.

DENVER CO (18)
1. Steamboat Today with 8,000 avg. daily circulation is equal to the Denver Post with 420,000 avg. daily circulation
2. An independent TV station with less than 1% TV market share and KRMA PBS with 2% TV market share are equal to NBC with 26% TV market share
3. Steamboat Today with 8,000 avg. daily circulation is equal to 50% of NBC with 150,000 avg. daily viewers
4. TV station with 100,000 avg. daily viewers cannot merge with a TV station with 88,000 avg. daily viewers, but a TV station with 152,000 avg. daily viewers can merge with a newspaper with 420,000avg. readers.

INDIANAPOLIS IN (25)
1. Call Ledger with 3,000 avg. daily circulation is equal to the commonly owned Indianapolis Star/Muncie Star Press with 300,000 avg. daily circulation
2. UPN with 7% TV market share and WFYI PBS with 3% TV market share are equal to CBS with 28% TV market share
3. Call Ledger with 3,000 avg. daily circulation of is equal to 45% of CBS with 128,000 avg. daily viewers
4. TV station with 64,000 avg. daily viewers cannot merge with a TV station with 32,000 avg. daily viewers, but a TV station with128,000 avg. daily viewers can merge with a newspaper with 300,000 avg. daily readers

LEXINGTON KY (65)
1. Corbin Times Tribune with 5,000 avg. daily circulation is equal to the Lexington Herald Leaser with 115,000 avg. daily circulation
2. Pax with less than 1% TV market share and WKLE PBS with less than 1% TV market share are equal to co-owned CBS stations with 42% TV market share
3. Times Tribune with avg. daily circulation of 5,000 is equal to 130% of co-owned CBS stations with 66,000 avg. daily viewer
4. TV station with 29,000 avg. daily viewers cannot merge with a TV station with 17,000 avg. daily viewers, but a TV duopoly with 66,000 avg. daily viewers can merge with a newspaper with 115,000avg. daily readers

NASHVILLE TN (65)
1. Paris Post with5,000 avg. daily circulation is equal to the Tennessean with 200,000 avg. daily circulation
2. PAX with less than 1% TV market share and WNPT PBS with 3% TV market share are equal to co-owned Sinclair stations with 36% TV market share
3. The Paris Post with 5,500 avg. daily circulation is equal to 100% of Sinclair stations with avg. daily viewers of 150,000
4. TV station with 80,000 avg. daily viewers cannot merge with a TV station with 47,000 avg. daily viewers, but a TV duopoly with 150,000 avg. daily viewers can merge with a newspaper with 200,000 avg. daily readers

PROVIDENCE RI (48)
1. Westerly Sun with 10,000 avg. daily circulation is equal to the Providence Journal with 175,000 avg. daily circulation
2. Paxson with 1% TV market share and RI PBS with 1% TV market share are equal to NBC with 41% TV market share
3. Westerly Sun with 10,000 avg. daily circulation is equal to 69% of ABC with110,000 avg. daily viewers
4. TV station with 35,000 avg. daily viewers cannot merge with a TV station with 24,000 avg. daily viewers, but a TV station with 110,000 avg. daily viewers can merge with a newspaper with 175,000 avg. daily readers

TALLAHASSEE FL (107)
1. Thomasville Tribune with 10,000 avg. daily circulation is equal to the Tallahassee Democrat with 50,000 avg. daily circulation
2. UPN with less than 1% TV market share and WFSU PBS with less than 1% TV market share are equal to CBS with 59% TV market share
3. Thomasville Tribune with 10,000 avg. daily circulation of 10,000 is equal to 204% of CBS with 50,000 avg. daily viewers
4. TV station with 12,000 avg. daily viewers cannot merge with a TV station with 10,000 avg. daily viewers, but a TV station with 50,000 avg. daily viewers can merge with a newspaper with 50,000avg. daily readers

TOPEKA KS (138)
1. The Council Grove Republican with 1,5000 avg. daily circulation is equal to the Topeka Capital Journal with 55,000 avg. daily circulation
2. An independent with less than 1% TV market share and KTWU PBS with 3% TV market share are equal to CBS with 46% TV market share
3. The Council Grove Republican with 1,500 avg. daily circulation is equal to 55% of CBS with 24,000 avg. daily viewers
4. TV station with 7,000 avg. dialy viewers cannot merge with a TV station with 3,000 avg. daily viewers, but a TV station with 24,000 avg. daily viewers can merge with a newspaper with 55,000 avg. daily readers

TRENTON NJ/WILMINGTON DE IN PHILADELPHIA PA DMA (6)
1. Phoenixville Phoenix with 15,000 avg. daily circulation is equal to the Philadelphia Inquirer/Daily News, with 405,000 avg. daily circulation
2. Paxson with 1% TV market share and WHYY PBS with 3% TV market share are equal to ABC with 26% TV market share
3. Phoenix with 15,000 avg. daily circulation is equal to 60% of ABC with 395,000 avg. daily viewers
4. TV station with 275,000 avg. daily viewers cannot merge with a TV station with 200,000 avg. daily viewers, but a TV station with 395,000 avg. daily viewers can merge a with newspaper with 405,000 avg. daily readers.

SETTING HIGH STANDARDS

Allowing Concentrated Media Markets Under the Diversity Index

Measuring the concentration of markets is only part of the job for a policymaker. The FCC must also decide which mergers are to be allowed or disallowed given the structure of markets. How much of an increase in concentration and loss of competition and diversity should be tolerated. The Department of Justice and the Federal Trade Commission have issued *Merger Guidelines.* Under these *Guidelines,* mergers that would increase the HHI by 100 points in a market that is moderately concentrated after the merger are a source of concern. Mergers that increase the HHI by more than 50 points in a market that is highly concentrated after the merger are a source of concern.

I believe that because of the importance of mass media in democratic debate and civic discourse, the Communications Act warrants higher standards. At a minimum, the economic standards of the antitrust laws should be an absolute floor as the goal for Communications Act policy.

Unfortunately, the FCC has gone in exactly the opposite direction (see Table VIII-5). Even using it faulty Diversity Index, In over half the scenarios for broadcast-newspaper mergers, the FCC has offered blanket approval to mergers that would violate the *Merger Guidelines* by a substantial margin. All of the market/merger scenarios underlined in bold in Table VIII-5 violate the threshold of a 100-point increase in the HHI.

Consider Birmingham, AL, as an example. Birmingham ranks in the top quintile of both the TV and radio markets. Thus, it is well above the national average. Birmingham would be allowed to go from the equivalent of just over 10 equal-sized firms to the equivalent of just under six. A string of newspaper-TV mergers and TV-TV mergers under the FCC blanket approval policy could raise the HHI by almost 900 points.[579] This would render the total media market well up into the moderately concentrated range. Over 400 points of the increase comes from the newspaper-TV mergers. The largest entity in the market would control over half the reporters in the market.

TABLE VIII-5 : FCC BLANKET APPROVAL OF MERGERS THAT VIOLATE THE *MERGER GUIDELINES* (HIGHLIGHTED VIOLATE)

BASE CASE   **AVERAGE CHANGE IN DIVERSITY INDEX RESULTING FROM MERGERS**

TV Stations In Market	Average Diversity Index	Newspaper and Television	Newspaper, TV, and ½ Radio	Newspaper and TV Duopoly	Newspaper, Radio, and TV Duopoly
4	928	242	408	----	----
5	911	223	393	376	846
6	889	200	340	357	688
7	753	121	247	242	533
8	885	152	314	308	734
9	705	86	207	172	473
10	635	51	119	101	292
15	595	48	145	97	302
20	612	40	128	80	350

Source: Federal Communications Commission, "Report and Order," In the Matter of 2002 Biennial Regulatory Review – Review of the Commission's Broadcast Ownership Rules and Other Rules Adopted Pursuant to Section 202 of the Telecommunications Act of 1996, Cross Ownership of Broadcast Stations and Newspapers, Rules and Policies Concerning Multiple Ownership of Radio Broadcast Stations in Local Markets, Definition of Radio Markets, MB Docket No. 02-277, MM Dockets 02-235, 01-317, 00-244 July 2, 2003, Appendix D.

Allowing Local Media Monopolies

The results in Table VIII-5 are based on the Diversity Index, which severely underestimates the extent of concentration in media markets. In order to appreciate the impact of this radical deregulation of media, I have examined the impact of the newspaper-TV cross ownership change based on real world facts.

While the FCC focuses its analysis on TV, I believe it is necessary to examine both the TV and the newspaper sides of the market to appreciate how troubling the potential mergers are. The FCC has set its rules in terms of the number of TV stations. Looking at the problem from the point of view of the number of newspapers, I find that the FCC would approve mergers that fracture the *Merger Guidelines*. The discussion of Birmingham gives an indication of the problem.

Of the 168 markets where the FCC would inappropriately allow mergers, about one-quarter, over 45, are one-newspaper towns. That is, the second newspaper has a market share of less than five percent.

Another 72 are two newspaper towns. Thus, approximately two-thirds of these markets would have one or two newspaper-TV combinations. Table VIII-6 shows the markets at greatest risk, where the TV market is already highly concentrated and there is little newspaper competition. In these markets, a merger between the dominant paper and the dominant TV stations creates an entity that towers over the local media environment.

Moreover, even in multiple newspaper towns, most markets are dominated by a single paper. We have data on seventeen of the fifty-five two-paper towns in which the FCC would inappropriately allow mergers. This sample of markets is representative of all two-paper towns, with an average DMA ranking of thirty-eight compared to thirty-nine for all two-paper cities. We find that the number one newspaper has a market share of 80 percent compared to fifteen percent for the number two newspaper.

This very lax rule holds the prospect of having many markets dominated by a single newspaper-TV combination, with few TV stations and no prospect of an equal combination being formed in the market. In a typical one-paper city, the local media giant would have a 90 percent share of the newspaper circulation, one-third of the TV audience, and one-third of the radio audience. No second entity could come close to matching this media power. The thirty-six markets include over 20 million households, or one-fifth of the country. There are some very large cities on the list, like Atlanta, Baltimore and New Orleans, as well as small cities.

Two-newspaper markets would be somewhat less concentrated, but the FCC would still allow excessively high levels of concentration that would not support vigorous competition. In the typical two-paper town, the dominant firm would have two-thirds of the newspaper market and one-third of the TV and radio markets. The second firm would be a paper with only one-fifth of the circulation. These cities include approximately 38 million households, or about one-quarter of the national population. This pre-merger market would fall just below the highly concentrated threshold. The merger would raise the HHI by about 1000 points. This is over nine times the level that triggers antitrust concerns.

The problems that these mergers pose are obviously not close calls. Even if the number two TV station (which typically has a market share of 24 percent) in either of these types of markets were to combine with the dominant newspaper, the increase in concentration would far exceed the threshold that triggers concern. In fact, even if the fourth largest station, which typically has a market share of ten percent, were to combine with

TABLE VIII-6: MOST CONCENTRATED NEWS MARKETS FOR TO CROSS-OWNERSHIP UNDER THE FCC DRAFT ORDER

One or Two Paper Markets Where TV News Market is Highly Concentrated

Albany, GA

Amarillo, TX

Atlanta, GA

Augusta, GA

Austin, TX

Baton Rouge, LA

Beaumont-Port Arthur, TX

Bluefield-Beckley-Oak Hill, WV

Boise, ID

Buffalo, NY

Charleston, SC

Chattanooga, TN

Chico-Redding, CA

Colorado Springs-Pueblo, CO

Columbus, GA

Columbus, OH

Columbus-Tupelo-West Point, MS

Dayton, OH

Des Moines-Ames, IA

Duluth, MN-Superior, WI

Evansville, IN

Fargo-Valley City, ND

Flint-Saginaw-Bay City, MI

Ft. Smith-Fayetteville-Springdale-Rogers, AR

Green Bay-Appleton, WI

Greenville-New Bern-Washington, NC

Harlingen-Weslaco-McAllen-Brownsville, TX

Jackson, MS

Joplin, MO-Pittsburg, KS

Knoxville, TN

La Crosse-Eau Claire, WI

Lafayette, LA

Lansing, MI

Lincoln-Hastings-Kearney, NE

Little Rock-Pine Bluff, AR

Louisville, KY

Macon, GA

Monroe, LA-El Dorado, AR

Montgomery, AL

Nashville, TN

New Orleans, LA

Norfolk-Portsmouth-Newport News, VA

Omaha, NE

Pittsburgh, PA

Portland-Auburn, ME

Reno, NV

Richmond-Petersburg, VA

Roanoke-Lynchburg, VA

Rochester, NY

Rockford, IL

Savannah, GA

Shreveport, LA

Sioux City, IA

Springfield, MO

St. Louis, MO

Syracuse, NY

Tallahassee, FL-Thomasville, GA

Terre Haute, IN

Toledo, OH

Traverse City-Cadillac, MI

Tucson, AZ

Tyler-Longview, TX

Wausau-Rhinelander, WI

West Palm Beach-Ft. Pierce, FL

Wheeling, WV-Steubenville, OH

Wichita-Hutchinson, KS

Wilmington, NC

the leading newspaper, the resulting increase in concentration would far exceed the antitrust threshold. This supports the observation that it is inconsistent to preclude mergers between the top four TV outlets under the duopoly rule but not between top four TV stations and newspapers for the cross ownership rule.

There -re another dozen markets that are extremely concentrated from the TV side, which would result in a very small number of integrated news producers. These markets raise the total population of markets at severe risk to about 70 million households. .

The FCC would approve mergers that fracture the *Merger Guidelines* (see Table VIII-7). In one-paper cities, the pre-merger market is highly concentrated and the merger with a top rated TV station would raise the HHI by approximately 1100 points. Recall that the antitrust authorities believe mergers that raise the HHI by 50 points in a market such as this "are likely to create or enhance market power or facilitate its exercise."

TABLE VIII- 7: INCREASE IN HHI CAUSED BY LEADING PAPER-TV STATION MERGERS (Based on TV Entertainment HHI and Newspaper Circulation HHI)

		LEADING PAPER	
		ONE-PAPER CITY (90% Circulation Share)	TWO-PAPER CITY (80% Circulation Share)
TV STATION			
RANK	MARKET SHARE		
1	30	1115	1000
2	24	821	723
4	10	290	252
Merger Guideline Threshold	na	50	100

220

One entity would thoroughly dominate the media landscape in these markets, accounting for over one-half of the local market. The increase in concentration is over twenty times the level that triggers antitrust concerns. Even mergers with the fourth ranked firms would far exceed the threshold. Much the same is true of the two-paper markets.

DIVERSITY INDEX HOCUS POCUS: AN APPLICATION TO THE PERSONAL COMPUTER MARKET

To underscore the FCC's extreme departure from established analytic practice, I work a similar example using the facts and findings of the Microsoft case to show how completely at odds the FCC Diversity Index is with standard market analysis. The District Court found and the Appeals Court upheld that Microsoft has monopoly power based on its market share. As the Appeals Court summarized the facts:

> Having thus properly defined the relevant market, the District Court found that Windows accounts for a greater than 95% market share... The Court also found that even if Mac OS were included, Microsoft share would exceed 80%.[580]

Note that the Appeals Court felt the Intel-PC market should be kept separate from the Mac market for purposes of antitrust analysis, but it accepted the District Court conclusion that Microsoft's market share was huge even in the more broadly defined personal computer market.

For the purpose of this analysis, I consider the case of operating systems in the broad computer market that includes both PCs and Macs. In other words, the computer market is made up of two very different types or "mediums" for operating systems, PCs and Macs. They are similar in some respects, but quite different in others, like newspapers and TV. At the time, Apple accounted for 17 percent of the personal computer market, while Intel-PCs accounted for 83%. The PC market was deemed to have six operating systems in addition to Windows: Linux, OS/2, BEos, Solaris, Unix, and DR-DOS. Windows has a 95 percent market share in the PC-based segment of the computer market. Apple has a 100 percent market share in the Mac segment of the market.

Because the FCC methodology does not consider the market share of the individual firm operating systems, Apple's weight is .17, since it has 100 percent of the Mac share. Microsoft's weight is only .12, since it is one of six firms in the PC segment of the computer market. Instead of an HHI of 6700, the FCC approach yields an HHI that would be just below 1300, which is in the middle of the moderately concentrated range.

The distortion does not stop there. Just as the FCC has done with respect to local news sources, Microsoft tried to cram all manner of devices into the definition of the computer market, but the court refused to allow this. Microsoft wanted to include handheld devices, information appliances, and web sites in the definition of the operating system market. The Appeals Court supported the decision of the District Court to reject these arguments, offering the following observation in the case of information devices:

> In particular, the District Court found that because information appliances fall far short of performing all of the functions of a PC, most consumers will buy them only as a supplement to their PCs.[581]

TV and radio stations that do not broadcast news certainly fall far short of performing all of the functions of TV stations that broadcast news. TV stations that do not do news should not be included in that market. Other outlets that do not provide local news also should not be included and the weights need to be realistic if they are included. The large role that the FCC attributes to radio and the Internet further distorts the analysis, just as it would have distorted the picture of the personal computer market.

Because the court refused to consider this unjustified expansion of the market definition to include non-computers, I cannot present a precise estimate of how this would affect the analysis of the facts in the Microsoft case. This takes us to the question of how the weights were chosen, the topic of a separate discussion. For purposes of comparison, I treat the other appliances like the Internet in the FCC analysis. I reduce the market share of the PC operating systems by attributing a weight for appliances equal to the Internet in the FCC analysis of media markets. The HHI drops to less than 800, well below the moderately concentrated threshold.

Figure VIII-1 shows the distorted picture that the FCC's Diversity Index would paint of the computer operating system market. This methodology paints the computer operating system market as unconcentrated. Windows becomes the third most important competitor, behind Mac and the dominant alternative appliance.

In essence, the FCC has adopted the Microsoft approach to market structure analysis that the District or Appeals Court rejected on a 7-0 vote. This is the same court that will review the new FCC ownership rules.

FigureVIII-1: Making The Microsoft Monopoly Disappear

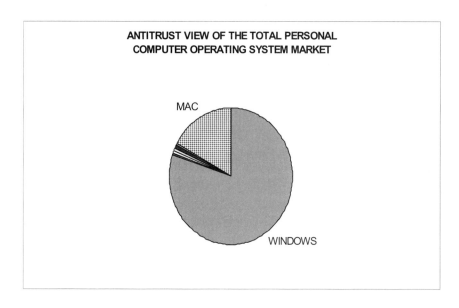

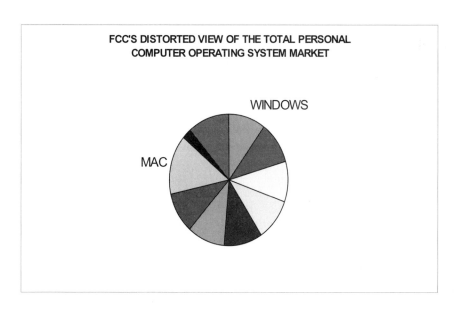

CONCLUSION

I conclude that the "empirical gap"[582] to which the D.C. Appeals Court referred in the Sinclair decision has been closed, just not in the way Chairman Powell or his predecessor, Mark Fowler, would have liked. The hard data and evidence on the record does not support their narrow economic view of the role of the media in democracy or the rules the FCC has proposed. A set of rules that limits merger activity to a small number of markets is well justified on the basis of the empirical data, statutory language and Supreme Court jurisprudence.

If the empirical record shows anything, it shows that over the past two decades lax antitrust enforcement and a narrowing view of First Amendment policy by federal agencies have allowed media markets to become far too concentrated. A vibrant forum for democratic discourse demands many more media voices, especially if the focus is on freedom of speech, not freedom of listening.

Advocates of elimination of the limits on ownership harp on the fact that there are more listening/viewing choices than ever. More is not the issue; enough is the question. Listening/viewing is not the central concern; speech is the focal point.

Three networks were certainly not enough; but eight (or four broadcast news stations) are not enough either, not when the average designated market area has almost two million people. By these standards, electronic voices, particularly the right to speak with a TV license, are scarce indeed.

The claim that the Internet levels the playing field between Joe Six Pack and the major media owners should not be taken as an excuse to allow greater concentration of broadcast voices. It is absurd on its face, but even if it were true, it would easily support the proposition that current holders of broadcast licenses should not mind if they are prevented from acquiring any more licenses. After all, if they want more distribution, they can use the Internet. Why should anyone hold two licenses, when 99.999% of those who might want a license in their local area cannot have *one?*

Indeed, we might carry the argument one step farther. The networks should be given a reasonable time period to migrate their distribution to the Internet and give the spectrum back to the people, who own it. As suggested in the introduction, it could then be used to empower millions of people to find an electronic voice through unlicensed use of the spectrum. The networks would protest, of course. The reason is simple – the TV broadcast spectrum to which they hold exclusive licenses has immensely greater reach and power than the Internet addresses they can easily obtain.

Hundreds of national entertainment channels controlled by a handful of companies may produce variety for consumers as viewers, although even that claim is subject to question. But, they certainly do not create an abundance of opportunity for citizens to be speakers. And, they do not provide the diversity of information necessary for citizens to make informed decisions about the increasingly complex and demanding set of local, national and international issues confronting the nation.

Endnotes

[1] The ongoing proceedings include Federal Communications Commission, *Cross-Ownership of Broadcast Stations and Newspapers, MM Docket No. 01-235; Newspaper/Radio Cross Ownership Waiver Policy*, MM No. 98-82; *Rules and Policies Concerning Multiple Ownership of Radio Broadcast Stations in Local Markets*, MM Docket No. 01-317. The proceedings were initiated in Federal Communications Commission, *Notice of Proposed Rule Making*, In the Matter of 2002 Biennial Regulatory Review – Review of the Commission's Broadcast Ownership Rules and Other Rules Adopted Pursuant to Section 202 of the Telecommunications Act of 1996, Cross Ownership of Broadcast Stations and Newspapers, Rules and Policies Concerning Multiple Ownership of Radio Broadcast Stations in Local Markets, Definition of Radio Markets, MB Docket No. 02-277, MM Dockets 02-235, 01=317, 00-244, September 23, 2002, p. 28 (hereafter, Initial Notice). Limits on the ownership of cable systems are also being reviewed in Federal Communications Commission, *In the Matter of Implementation of Section 1 of the Cable Television Consumer Protection and Competition Act of 199; Implementation of Cable Act Reform Provisions of the Telecommunications Act of 1996; The Commission's Cable Horizontal Ownership Limits and Arbitration Rules, Review of the Commission's Regulation and Policies Affecting Investment in the Broadcast Industry, Reexamination of the Commission's Cross-Interest Policy*, CS Dockets No. 98-82 and 96-85, MM dockets Nos. 92-264, 94-150, 92-51, 87-154 (hereafter, Cable Notice).

[2] Chairman Powell used the expression in describing the digital convergence (See "Law in the Internet Age," D.C. Bar Association Computer and Telecommunications Law Section and the Federal Communications Bar Association, September 29, 1999). The revolution and its implications for the media are woven through his "Broadband Migration" speeches (see "The Great Digital Broadband Migration," Progress and Freedom Foundation, December 8, 2000; "Digital Broadband Migration: Part II," Press Conference, October 31, 2001).

[3] *Fox Television Stations, Inc. v. FCC*, 280 F.3d 1027 (hereafter Fox v. FCC); *Sinclair Broadcasting, Inc. v. FCC*, 284 F.3d 148 (D.C. Circ. 2002) (hereafter Sinclair v. FCC).

[4] Telecommunications Act of 1996, Pub. LA. No. 104-104, 110 Stat. 56 (1996), 202(h).

[5] While attributing an agenda to the Chairman of the FCC by the press is to be expected, the Chairman's biases were so blatant that even one of the Appeals Court judges remarked on the futility of sending rules back to an agency that was so hostile to them (see Judge Sentelle, Concurring and Dissenting in Part," *Sinclair Broadcast Group, Inc. v. Federal Communications Commission*, April 2, 2002).

[6] February 24, 2002.

[7] Labaton, Steve, "Give and Take, FCC Aims to Redraw Media Map," *New York Times*, May 11, 2003, concludes with a typical quote that points to media developments that are in the future.

[8] Powell, Michael K., "The Public Interest Standard: A New Regulator's Search for Enlightenment," 17th Annual Legal Forum on Communications Law, American Bar Association, April 5, 1998. The difference between simple economics under the antitrust law and civic discourse under the Communications Act is woven into the fabric of the statutes. Under the antitrust laws, mergers may be "prohibited if their effect may be substantially to lessen competition or to tend to create a monopoly," or "if they constitute a contract, combination…, or conspiracy in restraint of trade," or "constitute an unfair method of competition" (U.S. Department of Justice and the Federal Trade Commission, *Horizontal Merger Guidelines*, 1997 [hereafter Horizontal Merger Guidelines], section 0). The standard under the Communications Act is higher, reflecting the special role of communications and mass media in our democracy. The Federal Communications Commission is charged to transfer cable, broadcast and telecommunications licenses only upon a "finding by the Commission that the public interest, convenience and necessity will be served." (USC, 47, 310 (b)).

[9] Associated Press v. United States, 326 U.S. 1, 20 (1945) (hereafter Associated Press).

[10] Federal Communications Commission, "Report and Order," In the Matter of 2002 Biennial Regulatory Review – Review of the Commission's Broadcast Ownership Rules and Other Rules Adopted Pursuant to Section 202 of the Telecommunications Act of 1996, Cross Ownership of Broadcast Stations and Newspapers, Rules and Policies Concerning Multiple Ownership of Radio Broadcast Stations in Local Markets, Definition of Radio Markets, MB Docket No. 02-277, MM Dockets 02-235, 01=317, 00-244 (hereafter, Order), July 2, 2003, at para. 353, 420,

[11] Copps, Michael J., "Statement of Commissioner Michael J. Copps, Dissenting," *Federal Communications Commission,* June 2, 2003, p. 2.

[12] For example, Bagdikian, Ben, *The Media Monopoly* (Boston: Beacon Press, 2000), which described the concentration of media, was first published in 1983 and Esslin, Martin, *The Age of Television* (New Brunswick: Transaction, 2002), which raised concerns about the impact of television on civic and political functions, was first published in 1982.

[13] Goodman, James, "Statement of James Goodman," presented at *Media Monopoly: Should the FCC Permit the Consolidation of Media Ownership*, New America Foundation, May 9, 2003; Labaton.

[14] Powell, The Public Interest.

[15] Baker, C. Edwin, *Media, Markets and Democracy* (Cambridge: Cambridge University Press, 2001) [hereafter Media Markets), p. 3; Sunstein, Cass,

Republic.com (Princeton: Princeton University Press, 2001), cites this quote in the front matter of the book.

[16] Fox v. FCC, pp. 12-13.

[17] Fox v. FCC, pp. 12-13.

[18] Fox v. FCC, pp. 12-13.

[19] Associated Press.

[20] Sunstein, Republic, p. 40.

[21] Associated Press, p. 17.

[22] Red Lion Broadcasting v. FCC, 395 US 367 (1969); FCC v. National Citizens Committee for Broadcasting, 436 U.S. 775 (1978), Sinclair Broadcasting.

[23] *Turner Broadcasting System, Inc. v. FCC*, 512 U.S. 622, 638-39 (1994) (hereafter *Turner I*); *Time Warner Entertainment Co., L.P. v. FCC*, 240 F.3d 1126 (D.C. Cir. 2001) (hereafter *Time Warner III*).

[24] Sunstein, Republic, p. 106.

[25] Id, p. 122, concludes a chapter entitled Citizens as follows:

"My central claim here has been that the citizens of a democratic polity may legitimately seek a communications market that departs from consumer choices, in favor of a system that promote goals associated with both freedom and democracy. Measures that promote these goals might be favored by a large majority of citizens, even if, in their capacity as consumers, they would choose a different course. Consumers are not citizens and it is a large error to conflate the two. One reason for the disparity is that the process of democratic choice often elicits people's aspirations."

[26] Id., p. 31, elaborates on the forum concept as follows:

"[T]he public forum doctrine promotes three important goals. First, it ensures that speakers can have access to a wide array of people... What is important is that speakers are allowed to press concerns that might otherwise be ignored by their fellow citizens.

"On the speakers' side, the public forum doctrine thus *creates a right of general access to heterogeneous citizens*. On the listeners' side, the public forum creates not exactly a right, but an opportunity, if perhaps an unwelcome one: *shared exposure to diverse speakers with diverse views and complaints...*

"Second, the public forum doctrine allows speakers not only to have general access to heterogeneous people, but also to specific people and specific institutions with whom they have a complaint... The public forum ensures that you can make your views heard by legislators, simply by protesting in front of the state legislature itself...

"Third, the public forum doctrine increases the likelihood that people will be exposed to a wide variety of people and views."

[27] Id., p. 45, elaborates on the fundamental difference as follows:

"Consumer sovereignty means that individual consumers are permitted to choose as they wish, subject to the constraints provided by the prices system, and also by their current holdings and requirements…

The idea of political sovereignty stands on different foundations. It does not take individual tastes as fixed or given. It prices democratic self-government, understood as a requirement of 'government by discussion,' accompanied by reason giving in the public domain."

[28] Krotoszynski, Ronald J., Jr. and A. Richard M. Blaiklock, "Enhancing the Spectrum: Media Power, Democracy, and the Marketplace of Ideas, *University of Illinois Law Review*, 2000, p. 860:

"It is not possible to offer up a specific formula to determine how many media outlets are sufficient to safeguard meaningful democratic deliberations. Even so, the consequences associated with the absence of a sufficient number of independently owned media outlets are sufficiently unappealing to justify rules incorporating a healthy margin of safety."

[29] Id., p. 814.

[30] Id, pp. 833-834:

"This linkage between media power and political power gives rise to a compelling need to check media power to avoid disruption of the electoral process. Just as unchecked political power presents an unacceptable threat to liberty, so, too, unchecked media power requires structural controls to maintain a viable marketplace of ideas. To the extent that the Commission's diversity policies have as their objective dividing and checking media power, those policies serve a critical function. Critics of the Commission's policies who advocate sole reliance on market forces to protect diversity have simply failed to consider the importance of maintaining structural diversity among the electronic media as a means of enhancing democracy."

[31] Id., pp. 872…873-874.

[32] 274 U.S. 357 (1927).

[33] Sunstein, Republic, p. 110, argues that "[T]he right of free speech is itself best seen as part of the project of helping to produce an engaged, self-governing citizenry."

[34] Sunstein, Republic, pp. 46-47.

[35] *National Broadcasting Co., Inc. et al. v. United States, et. al.*, 319 U.S. 190 (1943] 70.

[36] 436 U.S. 775 (1978), 95.

[37] 395 U.S. 388 (1969).

[38] Sinclair v. FCC, p. 15.

[39] Sunstein, Republic, p. 115

[40] Id., p. 40.

[41] Id., Republic, p. 108.

[42] Davidson, Paul, "FCC Could Alter Rules Affecting TV, Telephone, Airwaves," *USA Today*, February 6, 2002.

[43] Goodman, Media Monopoly, points to his decision not to air *Married by America*, which he maintains offends his local community's values by denigrating women and devaluing the institutions of marriage, and to strip network commercials from World Series advertising, which he felt were too violent or had too much explicit sexual content to be aired in the midst of family programming like the World Series.

[44] Ching, Frank, "Misreading Hong Kong," *Foreign Affairs*, May 1997.

[45] Anon, "Comcast Rejects Antiwar TV Spots," *Washington Post*, January 29, 2003, p. A7.

[46] Fiss, Owen, "Essays Commemorating the One Hundredth Anniversary of the Harvard Law Review: Why the State?" *Harvard Law Review* 100, 1987.

[47] Krotoszynski and Blaiklock, p. 868.

[48] Associated Press.

[49] Krotoszynski and Blaiklock, p. 867.

[50] Baker, Media, Markets, pp. 297-307; Baker, C. Edwin, "Giving Up on Democracy: The Legal Regulation of Media Ownership," Attachment C, *Comments of Consumers Union, Consumer Federation of America, Civil Rights Forum, Center for Digital Democracy, Leadership Conference on Civil Rights and Media Access Project,* (before the Federal Communications Commission, *In the Matter of Cross Ownership of Broadcast Station and Newspaper/Radio Cross-Ownership Waiver Policy*, MM Docket No. 01-235, 96-197, December 3, 2001) [hereafter, Democracy].

[51] Krotoszynski and Blaiklock, p. 868.

[52] Baker, Media Markets, p. 120.

[53] Associated Press, 52 F. Supp. p. 372.

[54] Stucke, Maurice E. and Allen P. Grunes, "Antitrust and the Forum for Democratic Discourse," *Antitrust Law Journal*, 69, pp. 282-283.

[55] Id., p. 273.

[56] Krotoszynski and Blaiklock, pp. 832...876:

"The owners of a television or radio station possess a unique ability to influence the direction of public affairs through selective coverage of contemporary events and candidates for public office…

"As noted earlier, television plays a unique role in contemporary American society. Accordingly, concentration of media ownership that encompass television stations represent a tangible threat to the marketplace of ideas than other kinds of concentration of media power. Under this reasoning, it might be acceptable to permit multiple ownership of some media assets within a single marker and not permit multiples or cross-ownership of other media assets."

[57] Sunstein, Republic, p. 35.

[58] Sunstein, Republic, p. 184.

[59] Stucke and Grunes:

"Nor did the majority of the justices jump through the typical hoops of defining a relevant market, determining market share and the restraints' impact on price and examining issue of entry or expansion by the other news wire services. Rather the majority was satisfied that AP was sufficiently large to impact the forum for democratic discourse, in that it was "a vast, intricately reticulated, organization, the largest of its kind, gathering news from all over the world, the chief single source of news for the American press, universally agreed to be of prime consequence."

[60] Sunstein, Republic, pp. 201-202.

[61] Lessig, Lawrence, *Code and Other Laws of Cyberspace* (New York: Basic Books, 1999), Chapter 9, calls this translation.

[62] U.S. Bureau of the Census, *Statistical Abstract of the United States: 2001* (U.S. Department of Commerce, 2001), Table 1, 647, 1258, 1259, 1297; *Statistical Abstract of the United States: 1986*, p. 406, 407.

[63] Sullivan, Lawrence, "Economics and More Humanistic Disciplines: What are the Sources of Wisdom for Antitrust," *University of Pennsylvania Law Review*, 1977, p. 125:

"Americans continue to value institutions the scale and workings of which they can comprehend. Many continue to value the decentralization of decision making power and responsibility. Many favor structures in which power in one locus may be checked by power in another."

[64] Sunstein, Republic, pp. 185-190.

[65] Although Lessig, Code, extols the virtues of the Internet, noting that "When the Constitution speaks of the rights of the 'press,' the architecture it has in mind is the architecture of the Internet," he is also profoundly pessimistic about the prospects for maintaining that architecture in the face of commercialization:

"Now we are changing that architecture. We are enabling commerce in a way we did not before; we are contemplating the regulation of encryption; we are

232

facilitating identity and content control. We are remaking the values of the Net, and the question is: Can we commit ourselves to neutrality in this reconstruction of the architecture of the Net?

"I do not think that we can. Or should. Or will. We can no more stand neutral on the question of whether the Net should enable centralized control of speech than Americans could stand neutral on the question of slavery in 1861. We should understand that we are part of a worldwide political battle; that we have views about what rights should be guaranteed to all humans, regardless of their nationality; and we should be ready to press these views in this new political space opened up by the Net. (p. 200)

"The decision then is not about choosing between efficiency and something else, but about which values should be efficiently pursued. To preserve the values we want, we must act against what cyberspace otherwise will become. The invisible hand, in other words, will produce a different world, and we should choose whether this world is one we want." (p. 209)

[66] Owen, Bruce M., "Statement on Media Ownership Rules," Attachment to *Comments of Fox Entertainment Group and Fox Television Stations, Inc., National Broadcasting Company, Inc. and Telemundo Group, Inc., and Viacom,* In the Matter of 2002 Biennial Regulatory Review – Review of the Commission's Broadcast Ownership Rules and Other Rules Adopted Pursuant to Section 202 of the Telecommunications Act of 1996, Cross Ownership of Broadcast Stations and Newspapers, Rules and Policies Concerning Multiple Ownership of Radio Broadcast Stations in Local Markets, Definition of Radio Markets, MB Docket No. 02-277, MM Dockets 02-235, 01=317, 00-244, January 2, 2003, p. 5.

[67] Owen, Statement, p. 10.

[68] Owen, Statement, p. 9.

[69] *Comments of Fox Entertainment Group and Fox Television Stations, Inc., National Broadcasting Company, Inc. and Telemundo Group, Inc., and Viacom,* In the Matter of 2002 Biennial Regulatory Review – Review of the Commission's Broadcast Ownership Rules and Other Rules Adopted Pursuant to Section 202 of the Telecommunications Act of 1996, Cross Ownership of Broadcast Stations and Newspapers, Rules and Policies Concerning Multiple Ownership of Radio Broadcast Stations in Local Markets, Definition of Radio Markets, MB Docket No. 02-277, MM Dockets 02-235, 01-317, 00-244, January 2, 2003 (hereafter Fox, et al.), pp. 59-63; *Comments of Sinclair,* In the Matter of 2002 Biennial Regulatory Review – Review of the Commission's Broadcast Ownership Rules and Other Rules Adopted Pursuant to Section 202 of the Telecommunications Act of 1996, Cross Ownership of Broadcast Stations and Newspapers, Rules and Policies Concerning Multiple Ownership of Radio Broadcast Stations in Local Markets, Definition of Radio Markets, MB Docket No. 02-277, MM Dockets 02-235, 01-317, 00-244, January 2, 2003, pp. 31-33 {hereafter Sinclair); *Comments of Media General,* In the Matter of 2002 Biennial Regulatory Review – Review of the Commission's Broadcast Ownership Rules and Other Rules Adopted Pursuant to Section 202 of

the Telecommunications Act of 1996, Cross Ownership of Broadcast Stations and Newspapers, Rules and Policies Concerning Multiple Ownership of Radio Broadcast Stations in Local Markets, Definition of Radio Markets, MB Docket No. 02-277, MM Dockets 02-235, 01-317, 00-244, January 2, 2003 (hereafter Media General), p. 4; *Comments of Hearst,* In the Matter of 2002 Biennial Regulatory Review – Review of the Commission's Broadcast Ownership Rules and Other Rules Adopted Pursuant to Section 202 of the Telecommunications Act of 1996, Cross Ownership of Broadcast Stations and Newspapers, Rules and Policies Concerning Multiple Ownership of Radio Broadcast Stations in Local Markets, Definition of Radio Markets, MB Docket No. 02-277, MM Dockets 02-235, 01-317, 00-244, January 2, 2003, p. 3; *Comments of Clear Channel,* In the Matter of 2002 Biennial Regulatory Review – Review of the Commission's Broadcast Ownership Rules and Other Rules Adopted Pursuant to Section 202 of the Telecommunications Act of 1996, Cross Ownership of Broadcast Stations and Newspapers, Rules and Policies Concerning Multiple Ownership of Radio Broadcast Stations in Local Markets, Definition of Radio Markets, MB Docket No. 02-277, MM Dockets 02-235, 01-317, 00-244, January 2, 2003 (hereafter Clear Channel), pp. 5-6.

[70] Owen, Bruce and Kent W. Mikkelsen, "Counting Outlets and Owners in Milwaukee: An Illustrative Example, Economic Study F: Attachment to Fox," et al., Table F-8.

[71] Owen, Statement, p. 10.

[72] Owen, Statement, p. 1.

[73] Owen, Statement, p. 6.

[74] Owen, Statement, p. 11.

[75] Owen, Statement, p. 10; Fox et al., pp. 27, 47, 49, 57, 58, 64; Sinclair, pp. 18-20, 46; Gannet, p. 18; Belo, In the Matter of 2002 Biennial Regulatory Review – Review of the Commission's Broadcast Ownership Rules and Other Rules Adopted Pursuant to Section 202 of the Telecommunications Act of 1996, Cross Ownership of Broadcast Stations and Newspapers, Rules and Policies Concerning Multiple Ownership of Radio Broadcast Stations in Local Markets, Definition of Radio Markets, MB Docket No. 02-277, MM Dockets 02-235, 01-317, 00-244, January 2, 2003, p. 25; Media General, p. 4; Clear Channel, p. 8.

[76] Owen and Mikkelsen.

[77] Chairman Powell has expressed his doubts about the ability of the public to understand the issues (Jurkowitz, Mark, "FCC Chairman: Consolidation Hasn't Inhibited Variety, Fairness," *Boston Globe*, April 17, 2002):

"The Citizen Kane anxiety… could be genuine in some instances. But it is very difficult to discern what exactly are these viewpoints that are eking through that we're worried about… I think to the average consumer this is too sublime a concept for a lot of them to get agitated by."

Kenneth Ferree, head of the Media Ownership Task Force appointed by the Chairman dismissed the idea of holding public hearings with the claim that they would be "an exercise in foot stomping," (Labaton, Stephen, "A Lone Voice for Regulation at the F.C.C." *New York Times*, September 30, 2002). Another aide to Chairman Powell argued that "What the head of the PTA in Kansas City has to say about the issue isn't going to add anything that's not already in the record" (Boliek, Brooks, "FCC's Copps to Conduct Hearings," *Hollywood Reporter*, November 22, 2002).

[78] McConnell, Bill, "Deregulation Foes Plan to Fight On," *Broadcasting and Cable*, June 2, 2003.

[79] Referred to by Senator Olympia Snowe, Senate Commerce Committee, May 13, 2003, and Commissioner Jonathan Adelstein, "Big Macs and Big Media: The Decision to Supersize," Media *Institute*, May 20, 2003.

[80] *Seattle Post Intelligenser, PI-Daily Poll*, May 2003.

[81] Digital Media Forum, *Survey Findings on Media Mergers and Internet Open Access*, September 13, 2000. Consumer Federation of America, *Media Policy Goals Survey*, September 2002; Consumer Federation of America and Center for Digital Democracy, *Mergers and Deregulation on the Information Superhighway: The Public Takes a Dim View: Results of a National Opinion Poll*, September 1995; Project on Media Ownership, People for Better TV, *Findings of a National Survey*, Lake Snell Perry & Associates, May 1999.

[82] Scherer, F. Michael and David Ross, *Industrial Market Structure and Economic Performance* (New York: Houghton Mifflin Company, 1990), p. 18:

"We begin with the political arguments, not merely because they are sufficiently transparent to be treated briefly, but also because when all is said and done, they, and not the economists' abstruse models, have tipped the balance of social consensus toward competition."

[83] Id., p. 18.

[84] Id., p. 18.

[85] Lessig, Code, pp. 166-167:

"Relative anonymity, decentralized distribution, multiple points of access, no necessary tie to geography, no simple system to identify content, tools of encryption – all these features and consequences of the Internet protocol make it difficult to control speech in cyberspace. The architecture of cyberspace is the real protector of speech there; it is the real "First Amendment in cyberspace," and this First Amendment is no local ordinance…

"The architecture of the Internet, as it is right now, is perhaps the most important model of free speech since the founding. This model has implications far beyond e-mail and web pages."

[86] Lessig, Code, p. 183.

[87] Cooper, Mark, "Antitrust as Consumer Protection: Lessons from the Microsoft Case," *Hastings Law Journal,* 52, 2001.

[88] Berry, Steven T. and Joel Waldfogel, "Public Radio in the United States: Does it Correct Market Failure or Cannibalize Commercial Stations?," *Journal of Public Economics,* 71, 1999, point out free entry may not accomplish the economic goals set out for it either. There is evidence of the anticompetitive behaviors expected to be associated with reductions in competition, such as price increases and excess profits. Wirth, M. O., "The Effects of Market Structure on Television News Pricing," *Journal of Broadcasting,* 1984; Simon, J., W. J. Primeaux and E. Rice, "The Price Effects of Monopoly Ownership in Newspapers," *Antitrust Bulletin,* 1986; Rubinovitz, R., *Market Power and Price Increases for Basic Cable Service Since Deregulation,* (Economic Analysis Regulatory Group, Department of Justice, August 6, 1991); Bates, B. J., "Station Trafficking in Radio: The Impact of Deregulation," *Journal of Broadcasting and Electronic Media,* 1993.

[89] Ray, W. B., *FCC: The Ups and Downs of Radio-TV Regulation* (Iowa: Iowa State University Press, 1990); Hopkins, Wat W., "The Supreme Court Defines the Forum for Democratic Discourse," *Journalism and Mass Communications Quarterly,* Spring 1996; Firestone, C.M. and J. M. Schement, *Toward an Information Bill of Rights and Responsibilities* (Washington, DC: Aspen Institute, 1995); Brown, Duncan H., "The Academy's Response to the Call for a Marketplace Approach to Broadcast Regulation," *Critical Studies in Mass Communications,* 11: 1994, 254; Benkler, Yochai, "Free as the Air," *New York University Law Review,* 74, 1999.

[90] Baker, Democracy, p. 42.

[91] Waldfogel, Joel, *Who Benefits Whom in Local Television Markets?* (Philadelphia: The Wharton School, November 2001) (hereafter Waldfogel, Television), p. 1. Other papers in the series of studies of "preference externalities" were made a part of the record in conjunction with Joel *Waldfogel's* appearance at the FCC Roundtable, including, *Preference Externalities: An Empirical Study of Who Benefits Whom in Differentiated Product Markets,* NBER Working Paper 7391 (Cambridge, MA: National Bureau of Economic Research, 1999); with Peter Siegelman, *Race and Radio: Preference Externalities, Minority Ownership and the Provision of Programming to Minorities,* Advances in Applied Microeconomics, 10, 2001; with Felix Oberholzer-Gee, *Electoral Acceleration: The Effect of Minority Population on Minority Voter Turnout,* NBER Working Paper 8252 (Cambridge, MA: National Bureau of Economic Research, 2001); with Lisa George, *Who Benefits Whom in Daily Newspaper Markets?,* NBER Working Paper 7944 (Cambridge, MA: National Bureau of Economic Research, 2000); as well as the statement *Comments on Consolidation and Localism,* Federal Communications Commission, Roundtable on Media Ownership (October 29, 2001) [hereafter, Localism); with Felix Oberholzer-Gee, *Tiebout Acceleration: Political Participation in Heterogeneous Jurisdictions* (NBER, 2001) (hereafter Participation).

[92] Baker, Democracy, p. 43.

[93] Waldfogel, Television, p. 1.

[94] Sunstein, Republic, discusses the implications for democracy, pp. 108-109.

[95] Baker, Democracy; Baker, C. Edwin, *Advertising and a Democratic Press* (Princeton: Princeton University Press, 1994). Krotoszynski and Blaiklock, p. 831:

"The larger the audience the station generates, the higher the station's potential advertising revenues. Broadcasters, therefore, attempt to find and air programming that will appeal to the largest possible audience. In doing so, broadcasters necessarily air programming that is likely to appeal to most people within the potential audience – that is they air programming that appeals to the majority culture's viewpoint."

[96] Waldfogel, Preference Externalities, p. 27.

[97] Waldfogel, Preference Externalities, pp. 27-30.

[98] Waldfogel, Television, p. 3; Baker, Democracy, p. 80.

[99] Oberholzer-Gee and Waldfogel, Participation, pp. 36-37.

[100] Baker, Democracy, pp. 43-44:

"Monopolistic competition theory applies to media goods. They... characteristically manifest the 'public good' attribute of having declining average costs over the relevant range of their supply curves due to a significant portion of the product's cost being its 'first copy cost,' with additional copies having a low to zero cost. There are a number of important attributes of monopolistic competition that are relevant for policy analysis and that distinguish it from the standard model of so-called pure competition, the standard model that underwrites the belief that a properly working market leads inexorably to the best result (given the market's givens of existing market expressed preferences and the existing distribution of wealth). The first feature to note here is that in monopolistic competition often products prevail that do not have close, certainly not identical, substitutes. Second, this non-substitutability of the prevailing monopolistic product will allow reaping of potentially significant monopoly profits."

[101] Krostoszynski and Blaiklock, pp. 832...833:

"The owners of a television or radio station possess a unique ability to influence the direction of public affairs through selective coverage of contemporary events and candidates for public office....

"To be sure, concentrations of political power present a more direct kind of threat to democracy than do concentrations of media power. That said, it is possible to use media power as a means of channeling, if not controlling the flow of political power. The owners of a television or radio station have a unique opportunity to influence the outcomes of electoral contests – both by reporting on candidates favorably and unfavorably and through benign (or malign) neglect. Media exposure is like oxygen to candidates for political office, particularly at the federal level. If a television station pretends that a candidate does not exist, her chances of election are considerably reduced."

[102] Baker, Democracy, p. 43. Krotoszynski and Blaiklock, p. 875, put it as follows: "There is simply no reason to believe that someone like Ted Turner or Rupert Murdock will consistently seek to maximize economic returns rather than use media power to influence political events in ways he deems desirable."

[103] Baker, Democracy, p. 73.

[104] Krotoszynski and Blaiklock, p. 867: "Employees are unlikely to criticize their employers, and this truism holds true for the fourth Estate."

[105] Siegelman and Waldfogel, p. 23.

[106] Id., p. 25.

[107] Baker, Democracy, p. 47.

[108] Id., pp. 67-68.

[109] Baker, Media Markets, pp. 96-97:

"Thus, from the perspective of providing people what they want, media markets are subject to the following criticisms. They provide much too much "bad" quality content – bad meaning content that has negative externalities. Media markets also may produce a wasteful abundance of content responding to mainstream taste. Otherwise, the main problem is underproduction. Markets predictably provide inadequate amounts and inadequate diversity of media content. Especially inadequate is their production of "quality" content – quality meaning content that has positive externalities. Production of civically, educationally, and maybe culturally significant content preferred by the poor is predictably inadequate. Smaller groups will often be served inadequately, either in relation to democracy's commitment to equally value their preferences or due to the consequences of monopolistic competition."

[110] Baker, Democracy, p. 16.

[111] Rifkin, Jeremy, *The Age of Access* (New York: J.P. Tarcher, 2000).

[112] Krotoszynski and Blaiklock, p. 866:

"The Commission historically has placed a high value on local control of broadcasting on the theory that local control would result in the provision of programming that better meets the needs of the community of license…

"A quick perusal of cable programming practices demonstrates the veracity of the proposition. With the exception of PEG channels and leased-access channels, cable programming presents very little programming responsive to the needs, wants, and desires of local communities. If you want the prized hog competition at the state fair covered live, you need a local media presence. Elections for city, county and even state officers might go uncovered if left to the networks or national cable news channels. Although alternative sources of information exist, including the Internet and local newspapers, most Americans continue to rely upon local and network television for their news programming.

With respect to local news, local broadcasters are effectively the only game in town."

[113] Waldfogel, Television, p. 13; Waldfogel, Localism, p. 9.

[114] Krotoszynski and Blaiklock, pp. 871...875-876:

"The Commission's efforts to preserve localism as a feature of the broadcast media will be effectively thwarted if large, corporate entities are permitted to amass large station holdings and use central programming techniques to achieve economies of scale and scope...

"Common ownership of media outlets is not conducive to competition in news and other local content programming. Consolidated news department, like consolidated marketing departments, are a common feature of multiple station groups. Divided control of media outlets within a community creates a healthy competition among news and programming sources."

[115] Baker, Democracy, p. 64.

[116] Id., p. 64:

"Consider the merger of two entities that supply local news within one community – possibly the newspaper and radio station... Presumably the merged entity would still have an incentive to engage in at least a profit-maximizing amount of investigative journalism. But how much is that? The amount spent in the pre-merger situation may have reflected merely an amount that the media entity's audience wanted and would pay for (either directly or indirectly through being "sold" to advertisers). Alternatively, the pre-merger profit maximizing level for each independent entity may have reflected a competitive need to compare adequately to a product offered by its competitor. In this second scenario, competition may have induced increased but still inefficiently small expenditures on investigative journalism.

"Given the first scenario, if the provision of investigative journalism and exposes was satisfying an audience demand, there would be little necessity for the two media entities to supply different sets of exposes to the two audiences. Presumably the merged enterprise could share the results of its investigative journalism, now supplying to each entity's respective audience (customers) only the amount previously supplied by the larger of two investigative units... What is from the perspective of the merged entity a profitable 'synergy' is from the perspective of the community an inefficient loss of positive externalities."

[117] Sunstein, Cass, "Television and the Public Interest," *California Law Review*, 8, 2002, p. 517.

[118] As the works of Benkler and others have shown, the public good quality of information production goes well beyond the realm of the media and civic discourse and is especially critical to a period that is called an information age. See Benkler, Yochai, "Intellectual Property and the Organization of Information Production," *International Review of Law and Economics*, 22, 2002; "Coase's Penguin,

or Linux and the Nature of the Firm," *Yale Law Journal*, 112, 2002; "The Battle Over the Institutional Ecosystem in the Digital Environment," *Communications of the ACM*, 44:2, 2001; "From Consumers to Users: Shifting the Deeper Structure of Regulation Toward Sustainable Commons and User Access," *Federal Communications Law Journal*, 56, 2000. Lawrence Lessig's analysis of the impact of communications structures on innovation is another body of work that focuses on the nexus between choices about economic/institutional structures, public goods, and political action (see *Code and The Future of Ideas: The Fate of the Commons in a Connected World* (New York: Random House, 2001)). The narrow focus here on media and civic discourse reflects the nature of this proceeding and in no way is intended to belittle the broader public goods concerns.

[119] Sunstein, Television, p. 517, citing Frank, Robert H. and Phillip J. Cook, *The Winner Take All Society* (1999), p. 191, as well as Bourdieu, Pierre, *On Television* (New York: The New Press, 1998), and Baker, C. Edwin, "Giving the Audience What it Wants," *Ohio State Law Journal* 58, 1997.

[120] Netanal, Neil, *Is the Commercial Mass Media Necessary, or Even Desirable, for Liberal Democracy*, TPRC Conference on Information, Communications, and Internet Policy, October 2001, pp. 20-24.

[121] Krotoszynski and Blaiklock, pp. 867-868:

"Accordingly as fewer and fewer entities control more and more broadcast outlets, the incentive to expose disinformation or to correct for under coverage of a particular story decreases. If Ted Turner enjoyed a media monopoly, would CNN and *Time* have fallen upon their swords so quickly in the aftermath of the Operation Tailwind story scandal? It seems highly unlikely. The pervasive, negative attention brought to bear on CNN's and *Time's* conduct in reporting this story forced Time Warner to take aggressive corrective action....

"The project of outlet diversity bears a clear relationship to the project of maintaining a viable, participatory democracy. To the extent that the ownership rules and policies divide and subdivide media ownership, it does the public a service. Moreover, this service is independent of antitrust concerns regarding price fixing or undue market power. The commission's pursuit of diversity in the context of media regulation relates to fostering accountability to the public."

[122] Shah, Rajiv, J. Jay and P. Kesan, *The Role of Institutions in the Design of Communications Technologies*, Telecommunications Policy Research Conference, Conference on Information, Communications, and Internet Policy, October 2001.

[123] Baker, Media Markets, p. 120.

[124] Rifkin, The Age of Access, pp. 7-9.

[125] Layton, Charles, "What do Readers Really Want?", *American Journalism Review*, March 1999, reprinted in Roberts, Gene and Thomas Kunkel, *Breach of Faith: A Crisis of Coverage in the Age of Corporate Newspapering* (Fayetteville: University of Arkansas Press, 2002); McConnell, Bill and Susanne Ault, "Fox TV's Strategy: Two by Two, Duopolies are Key to the Company's Goal of Becoming a

Major Local Presence," *Broadcasting and Cable,* July 30, 2001; Trigoboff, Dan, "Chri-Craft, Fox Moves In: The Duopoly Marriage in Three Markets Comes with Some Consolidation," *Broadcasting and Cable,* August 6, 2001; Trigoboff, Dan, "Rios Heads KCOP News," *Broadcasting and Cable,* October 14, 2002; Beam, Randall A., "What it Means to Be a Market-Oriented Newspaper," *Newspaper Research Journal,* 16, 1995; "Size of Corporate Parent Drives Market Orientation," *Newspaper Research Journal,* 23, 2002; Vane, Sharyn, "Taking Care of Business," *American Journalism Review,* March 2002; *The Business of News, the News About Business,* Neiman Reports, Summer 1999.

[126] Levin, H. J., "Program Duplication, Diversity, and Effective Viewer Choices: Some Empirical Findings," *American Economic Review,* 1971; Lacy, Stephen, "A Model of Demand for News: Impact of Competition on Newspaper Content," *Journalism Quarterly,* 1989; Johnson, T. J. and W. Wanta, "Newspaper Circulation and Message Diversity in an Urban Market," *Mass Communications Review,* 1993; Davie, W. R. and J. S. Lee, "Television News Technology: Do More Sources Mean Less Diversity," *Journal of Broadcasting and Electronic Media,* 1993, p. 455; Wanta, W. and T. J. Johnson, "Content Changes in the St. Louis Post-Dispatch During Different Market Situations," *Journal of Media Economics,* 1994; Coulson, D. C., "Impact of Ownership on Newspaper Quality," *Journalism Quarterly,* 1994; Coulson, D. C. and Anne Hansen, "The Louisville Courier-Journal's News Content After Purchase by Gannett," *Journalism and Mass Communications Quarterly,* 1995; Iosifides, Petros, "Diversity versus Concentration in the Deregulated Mass Media," *Journalism and Mass Communications Quarterly,* Spring 1999; Lacy, Stephen and Todd F. Simon, "Competition in the Newspaper Industry," in Stephen Lacy and Todd F. Simon, [eds] *The Economics and Regulation of United States Newspapers* (Norwood, NJ: Ablex, 1993).

[127] Soloski, John, "Economics and Management: The Real Influence of Newspaper Groups," *Newspaper Research Journal,* 1, 1979; Bennet, W. Lance, *News: The Politics of Illusion* (New York: Longmans, 1988); Busterna, J. C., "Television Ownership Effects on Programming and Idea Diversity: Baseline Data," *Journal of Media Economics,* 1988; Edwards, E. S. and N. Chomsky, *Manufacturing Consent* (New York: Pantheon, 1988); Glasser, Theodore, L. David, S. Allen and S. Elizabeth Banks, "The Influence of Chain Ownership on News Play: A Case Study," *Journalism Quarterly,* 66, 1989; Katz, J., "Memo to Local News Directors," *Columbia Journalism Review,* 1990; McManus, J., "Local News: Not a Pretty Picture," *Columbia Journalism Review,* 1990; Price, Monroe E., "Public Broadcasting and the Crisis of Corporate Governance," *Cardozo Arts & Entertainment,* 17, 1999.

[128] Just, Marion, Rosalind Levine and Kathleen Regan, "News for Sale: Half of Stations Report Sponsor Pressure on News Decision," *Columbia Journalism Review-Project for Excellence in Journalism,* November/December 2001, p. 2.

[129] Strupp, Joe, "Three Point Play," *Editor and Publisher,* August 21, 2000, p. 23; Moses, Lucia, "TV or not TV? Few Newspapers are Camera Shy, But Sometimes Two Into One Just Doesn't Go," *Editor and Cable,* August 21, 2000, p. 22;

Roberts, Gene, Thomas Kunkel, and Charles Clayton (eds.), *Leaving Readers Behind* (Fayetteville: University of Arkansas Press, 2001), 10.

[130] Belo, pp. 8-9; Karr, Albert, "Television News Tunes Out Airwaves Auction Battle," *Wall Street Journal*, May 1, 1996, p. B1.

[131] See Quincy Illinois Visitors Guide, 2001 edition; McConnell, Bill, "The National Acquirers: Whether Better for News or Fatter Profits, Media Companies Want in on TV/Newspaper Cross-Ownership," *Broadcasting and Cable*, December 10, 2001.

[132] Kunkel, Thomas and Gene Roberts, *"The Age of Corporate Newspapering; Leaving Readers Behind," American Journalism Review*, May 2001. On coverage of the 1996 Telecommunications Act see Gilens, Martin and Craig Hertzman, "Corporate Ownership and News Bias: Newspaper Coverage of the 1996 Telecommunications Act," Paper delivered at the Annual Meeting of the American Political Science Association, August 1997, p. 8.

[133] Davis, Charles and Stephanie Craft, "New Media Synergy: Emergence of Institutional Conflict of Interest," *Journal of Mass Media Ethics*, 15, 2000, pp. 222-223.

[134] The story "broke" in the *Washington Post* with the publication of a segment of Bob Woodward's *Bush At War* (New York: Simon and Schuster, 2002), p. 207, which Ailes disputed (see Grove, Lloyd, "The Reliable Source," *Washington Post*, November 19, 2002). The incident reinforced the perception of Fox News as "The Most Biased Name in News: Fox Channel's Extraordinary Right-wing Tilt." Ackerman, Seth, *The Most Biased Name in News* (FAIR, August 2002), a bias that is embodied in the "format, guests, expertise, topic and in-house analysts." *Cable News Wars: Interviews* (PBS, Online Newshour, March 2002), p. 2.

[135] Goldberg, Bernard, *Bias* (Washington, DC: Regnery, 2002), p. 190.

[136] Goldberg, p. 222, citing "On Media Bias, Network Stars Are Rather Clueless," *Wall Street Journal*, May 24, 2001.

[137] Anon, "The Fox News Presidential Advisor," November 21, 2002, *Washington Post*, p. A36.

[138] Klugman, Paul, "In Media Res," *New York Times*, November 29, 2002, p. A39.

[139] Kelly, Michael, "Left Everlasting," *The Washington Post*, December 11, 2002, p. A33.

[140] Kelly, Michael, "Left Everlasting (Cont'd)," *The Washington Post*, December 18, 2002, p. A35.

[141] Lichter, S. Robert, "Depends on How You Define 'Bias'," *The Washington Post*, December 18, 2002, A19.

[142] Kahn, Kim Fridkin and Patrick J. Kenny, "The Slant of News: How Editorial Endorsements Influence Campaign Coverage and Citizens' Views of Candidates," *American Political Science Review*, 96, 2002, p. 381.

[143] Additional sources cited in support of this proposition include Page, Benjamin I., *Who Deliberates* (Chicago: University of Chicago Press, 1996); Rowse, Edward, *Slanted News: A Case Study of the Nixon and Stevenson Fund Stories* (Boston: Beacon, 1957).

[144] McManus, J., "How Objective is Local Television News?", *Mass Communications Review*, 1991.

[145] Snider, James H., and Benjamin I. Page, "Does Media Ownership Affect Media Stands? The Case of the Telecommunications Act of 1996," Paper delivered at the Annual Meeting of the Midwest Political Science Association, April 1997.

[146] Id., pp. 7-8.

[147] Carter, Sue, Frederick Fico, and Joycelyn A. McCabe, "Partisan and Structural Balance in Local Television Election Coverage," *Journalism and Mass Communications Quarterly*, 79, 2002, p. 50.

[148] The FCC's minimal effort to address the issue of bias (Pritchard, David, *Viewpoint Diversity in Cross-Owned Newspapers and Television Stations: A Study of News Coverage of the 2000 Presidential Campaign* (Federal Communications Commission, September 2002), involved a very small number of observations and no effort to introduce a comparison group. It found that half of the newspapers and television stations that were cross-owned shared a bias. On re-examination, Baker, Dean, *Democracy Unhinged: More Media Concentration Means Less Public Discourse, A Critique of the FCC Studies on Media Ownership* (Washington, DC: Department of Professional Employees, AFL-CIO, December 2002), p. 6, concluded that "seven of the ten combinations had a common slant, and only three had a different slant in their coverage." This is a remarkably high bias and, in our view, only underscores the problem of ownership across the media.

[149] Alger, Dean, *MEGAMEDIA: How Giant Corporations Dominate Mass Media, Distort Competition and Endanger Democracy* (Lanham, MD: Rowman & Littlefield, 1998), Chapter 6; Alger, Dean, *The Media and Politics* (New York: Wadsworth Publishing, 2nd edition, 1996). Alger provided analysis for "Initial Comments of Consumer Federation," et al., *Cross Ownership of Broadcast Stations and Newspapers*, MM Docket No. 01-235, December 4, 2001 (hereafter, Alger, CFA).

[150] Also see Karr.

[151] Journal Broadcasting Corporation, "Initial Comments of the Journal Broadcasting Corporation," *In the Matter of Cross Ownership of Broadcast Stations and Newspaper; Newspaper/Radio Cross-Ownership Waiver Policy* (MM Docket Nos. 01-235, 96-197), December 4, 2001, p. 2.

[152] Cited in Alger, CFA, p. 63.

[153] Cited in Alger, CFA, p. 63.

[154] McConnell.

[155] Cited in Alger, CFA, p. 64.

[156] Cited in Alger, CFA, p. 64.

[157] Beam, 1995; Beam, 2002; Vane; Just, Levine and Regan.

[158] Evidence that increasing variety does not increase diversity can be found in Dejong, A. S. and B. J. Bates, "Channel Diversity in Cable Television," *Journal of Broadcasting and Electronic Media*, 1991; Grant, A. E., "The Promise Fulfilled? An Empirical Analysis of Program Diversity on Television," *The Journal of Media Economics*, 1994; Hellman, Heikki and Martii Soramaki, "Competition and Content in the U.S. Video Market," *Journal of Media Economics*, 7, 1994; Lin, C. A., "Diversity of Network Prime-Time Program Formats During the 1980s," *Journal of Media Economics*, 8, 1995; Kubey, Robert, Mark Shifflet, Niranjala Weerakkody, and Stephen Ukeiley, "Demographic Diversity on Cable: Have the New Cable Channels Made a Difference in the Representation of Gender, Race, and Age?," *Journal of Broadcasting and Electronic Media*, 39, 1995. For other nations see Deakin, Simon and Stephen Pratten, "Reinventing the Market? Competition and Regulatory Change in Broadcasting," *Journal of Law and Society*, 26, 1999; Li, Hairong and Janice L. Bukovac, "Cognitive Impact of Banner Ad Characteristics: an Experimental Study," *Journalism & Mass Communication Quarterly*, 76, 1999; Kilborn, Richard W., "Shaping the Real," *European Journal of Communication*, 13, 1998; Blumer, Jay G. and Carolyn Martin Spicer, "Prospects for Creativity in the New Television Marketplace: Evidence form Program-Makers," *Journal of Communications*, 40, 1990, p. 78.

[159] McConnell and Ault.

[160] Trigoboff, 2001.

[161] Trigoboff, 2002.

[162] Just, Levine and Regan, p. 2.

[163] Just, Levine and Regan, p. 2.

[164] Napoli, Philip, "Audience Valuation and Minority Media: An Analysis of the Determinants of the Value of Radio Audiences," *Journal of Broadcasting and Electronic Media*, 46, 2002, pp. 180-181.

[165] The author notes agreement with Ofori, K. A., *When Being No. 1 is not Enough: The Impact of Advertising Practices on Minority-Owned and Minority-Targeted Broadcast Stations* (Civil Rights Forum on Communications Policy, 1999); Webster, J. G. and P. F. Phalen, *The Mass Audience: Rediscovering the Dominant Model* (New Jersey: Erlbaum, 1997); Baker, C. Edwin, *Advertising and a Democratic Press* .

[166] The author cites Owen, Bruce and Steven Wildman, *Video Economics* (Cambridge, MA: Harvard University Press, 1992); Waldfogel, Preference Externalities.

[167] Hamilton, J. T., *Channeling Violence: the Economic Market for Violent Television Programming* (Princeton: Princeton University Press, 1998); Wildman, Steven, "One-way Flows and the Economics of Audience Making," in J. Entema and D.C. Whitney (eds.), *Audiencemaking: How the Media Create the Audience* (Thousand Oaks CA: Sage Publications, 1994); Wildman, Steven and T. Karamanis, "The Economics of Minority Programming," in A. Garner (ed.) *Investing in Diversity: Advancing Opportunities for Minorities in Media* (Washington, DC: Aspen Institute, 1998); and Owen and Wildman.

[168] Fife, M., *The Impact of Minority Ownership on Broadcast Program Content: A Case Study of WGPR-TV's Local News Content* (Washington: National Association of Broadcasters, 1979); Fife, M., *The Impact of Minority Ownership on Broadcast Program Content: A Multi-Market Study* (Washington: National Association of Broadcasters, 1986); Congressional Research Service, *Minority Broadcast Station Ownership and Broadcast Programming: Is There a Nexus?* (Washington: Library of Congress, 1988); Hart, T. A., Jr., "The Case for Minority Broadcast Ownership," *GannettCenter Journal*, 1988; Wimmer, K. A., "Deregulation and the Future of Pluralism in the Mass Media: The Prospects for Positive Policy Reform," *Mass Communications Review*, 1988; Gauger, T. G., "The Constitutionality of the FCC's Use of Race and Sex in Granting Broadcast Licenses," *Northwestern Law Review*, 1989; Klieman, H., "Content Diversity and the FCC's Minority and Gender Licensing Policies," *Journal of Broadcasting and Electronic Media*, 1991; Collins-Jarvis, L. A., "Gender Representation in an Electronic City Hall: Female Adoption of Santa Monica's PEN System," *Journal of Broadcasting and Electronic Media*, 1993; Lacy, Stephen, Mary Alice Shaver, and Charles St. Cyr, "The Effects of Public Ownership and Newspaper Competition on the Financial Performance of Newspaper Corporation: A Replication and Extension," *Journalism and Mass Communications Quarterly*, Summer 1996.

[169] Empirical studies demonstrating the link between minority presence in the media and minority-oriented programming include Fife, 1979; Fife, 1986; Congressional Research Service; Hart; Wimmer; Evans, Akousa Barthewell, "Are Minority Preferences Necessary? Another Look at the Radio Broadcasting Industry," *Yale Law and Policy Review*, 8, 1990; Dubin, Jeff and Matthew L. Spitzer, "Testing Minority Preferences in Broadcasting," *Southern California Law Review*, 68, 1995; Bachen, Christine, Allen Hammond, Laurie Mason, and Stephanie Craft, *Diversity of Programming in the Broadcast Spectrum: Is There a Link Between Owner Race or Ethnicity and News and Public Affairs Programming?* (Santa Clara University, December 1999); Mason, Laurie, Christine M. Bachen and Stephanie L. Craft, "Support for FCC Minority Ownership Policy: How Broadcast Station Owner Race or Ethnicity Affects News and Public Affairs Programming Diversity," *Communications Law Policy*, 6, 2001.

[170] A similar line of empirical research dealing with gender exists. See Lacy, Shaver and St. Cyr; Gauger; Klieman; Collins-Jarvis; Lauzen, Martha M. and

David Dozier, "Making a Difference in Prime Time: Women on Screen and Behind the Scenes in 1995-1996 Television Season, *Journal of Broadcasting and Electronic Media*, Winter 1999; O'Sullivan, Patrick B., *The Nexus Between Broadcast Licensing Gender Preferences and Programming Diversity: What Does the Social Scientific Evidence Say?* (Santa Barbara, CA: Department of Communication, 2000).

[171] Kim, Sei-Hill, Dietram A. Scheufele and James Shanahan, "Think About It This Way: Attribute Agenda Setting Function of the Press and the Public's Evaluation of a Local Issue," *Journalism and Mass Communications Quarterly*, 79, 2002, p. 7; Chaffee, Steven and Stacy Frank, "How Americans Get Their Political Information: Print versus Broadcast News," *The Annals of the American Academy of Political and Social Science*, 546, 1996; McLeod, Jack M., Dietram A. Scheufele, and Patricia Moy, "Community, Communications, and Participation: The Role of Mass Media and Interpersonal Discussion in Local Political Participation," *Political Communication*, 16, 1999.

[172] Waldfogel, Television; Waldfogel and George; Waldfogel, Comments on Consolidation and Localism.

[173] Stone, V. A., "Deregulation Felt Mainly in Large-Market Radio and Independent TV," *Communicator*, April 1987, p. 12; Aufderheide, P., "After the Fairness Doctrine: Controversial Broadcast Programming and the Public Interest," *Journal of Communication*, 1990, pp. 50-51; McKean, M. L. and V. A. Stone, "Why Stations Don't Do News," *Communicator*, 1991, pp. 23-24; Stone, V. A., "New Staffs Change Little in Radio, Take Cuts in Major Markets TV, *RNDA*, 1988; Slattery, K. L. and E. A. Kakanen, "Sensationalism Versus Public Affairs Content of Local TV News: Pennsylvania Revisited," *Journal of Broadcasting and Electronic Media*, 1994; Bernstein, J. M. and S. Lacy, "Contextual Coverage of Government by Local Television News," *Journalism Quarterly*, 1992; Carrol, R. L., "Market Size and TV News Values," *Journalism Quarterly*, 1989; Scott, D. K. and R. H. Gopbetz, "Hard News/Soft News Content of the National Broadcast Networks: 1972-1987," *Journalism Quarterly*, 1992; Ferrall, V. E., "The Impact of Television Deregulation," *Journal of Communications*, 1992; pp. 21... 28... 30.

[174] Slattery, Karen L., Ernest A. Hakanen and Mark Doremus, "The Expression of Localism: Local TV News Coverage in the New Video Marketplace," *Journal of Broadcasting and Electronic Media*, 40, 1996; Carroll, Raymond L. and C.A. Tuggle, "The World Outside: Local TV News Treatment of Imported News," *Journalism and Mass Communications Quarterly*, Spring 1997; Fairchild, Charles, "Deterritorializing Radio: Deregulation and the Continuing Triumph of the Corporatist Perspective in the USA," *Media, Culture & Society*, 1999, 21; Layton, Charles and Jennifer Dorroh, "Sad State," *American Journalism Review,* June 2002; Olson, Kathryn, "Exploiting the Tension between the New Media's "Objective" and Adversarial Roles: The Role Imbalance Attach and its Use of the Implied Audience," *Communications Quarterly* 42:1, 1994, pp. 40-41; Stavitsky, A. G., "The Changing Conception of Localism in U.S. Public Radio," *Journal of Broadcasting and Electronic Media*, 1994.

[175] Bagdikian, Media Monopoly, pp. 182...188; Clarke, P. and E. Fredin, "Newspapers, Television, and Political Reasoning," *Public Opinion Quarterly*, 1978; Pfau, M., "A Channel Approach to Television Influence," *Journal of Broadcasting and Electronic Media*, 1990; Cundy, D. T., "Political Commercials and Candidate Image," in Lynda Lee Kaid (ed.), *New Perspectives in Political Advertising* (Carbondale, IL: Southern Illinois University Press, 1986); O'Keefe, G. J., "Political Malaise and Reliance on the Media," *Journalism Quarterly*, 1980; Becker, S. and H. C. Choi, "Media Use, Issue/Image Discrimination," *Communications Research*, 1987; Robinson, J. P. and D. K. Davis, "Television News and the Informed Public: An Information Process Approach," *Journal of Communication*, 1990; Voakes, Paul S., Jack Kapfer, David Kurpius, and David Shano-yeon Chern, "Diversity in the News: A Conceptual and Methodological Framework," *Journalism and Mass Communications Quarterly*, Autumn 1996; Bishop, Ronald and Ernest A. Hakanen, "In the Public Interest? The State of Local Television Programming Fifteen Years After Deregulation," *Journal of Communications Inquiry*, 26, 2002.

[176] McManus, J. H., "What Kind of a Commodity is News?", *Communications Research*, 1992; Olson.

[177] Bagdikian, pp. 220-221; Paletz, D. L. and R. M. Entmen, *Media, Power, Politics*, (New York: Free Press, 1981); Postman, Neil, *Amusing Ourselves to Death: Public Discourse in the Age of Show Business* (New York: Penguin Press, 1985); Lacy, Stephen, "The Financial Commitment Approaches to News Media Competition," *Journal of Media Economics*, 1992.

[178] Bass, Jack, "Newspaper Monopoly," in Gene Roberts, Thomas Kunkel, and Charles Clayton (eds.), *Leaving Readers Behind* (Fayetteville: University of Arkansas Press, 2001); Gish, Pat and Tom Gish, "We Still Scream: The Perils and Pleasures of Running a Small-Town Newspaper," and Shipp, E. R., "Excuses, Excuses: How Editors and Reporters Justify Ignoring Stories," in William Serrin (ed.), *The Business of Journalism* (New York: New Press, 2000). Complaints about the failure to cover larger national and international stories also abound (see Phillips, Peter and Project Censored, *Censored 2003* (New York: Seven Stories, 2002); Borjesson, Kristina, *Into the BUZZSAW* (Amherst, New York: Prometheus Books, 2002)).

[179] Waldfogel, Television, p. 13.

[180] Krotoszynski and Blaiklock, pp. 866:

"Given economies of scale, it might be inefficient to cover the hog competition at the state fair. Perhaps Jerry Springer or Montel Williams would generate higher ratings or cost less to broadcast. From a purely economic point of view, covering a debate between candidates for local office might be a complete disaster. Many local television and radio stations nevertheless provide such coverage on a voluntary basis. Perhaps local commercial television broadcasters do not provide such coverage solely out of the goodness of their hearts or a keen sense of civic responsibility. Nevertheless, the fact remains that a national television channel generally would not cover the lieutenant governor's race in South Dakota absent the most extraordinary and unlikely of circumstances."

[181] Waldfogel, Localism, p. 9.

[182] Id., p. 9.

[183] Project for Excellence in Journalism, *Does Ownership Matter in Local Television News: A Five-Year Study of Ownership and Quality,* February 17, 2003, executive summary.

[184] Fairchild, pp. 557-559; Bachman, Kathy, "Music Outlets Tune in More News Reports," *MediaWeek*, October 29, 2001.

[185] Network Affiliated Stations Alliance, "Petition for Inquiry into Network Practices," Federal Communications Commission, March 8, 2001 (hereafter NASA, Petition).

[186] Lacy, Stephen, David C. Coulson, and Charles St. Cyr, "The Impact of Beat Competition on City Hall Coverage," *Journalism & Mass Communication Quarterly*, 76, 1999.

[187] Mathews, Anna Wilde, "A Giant Radio Chain is Perfecting the Art of Seeming Local," *Wall Street Journal*, February 25, 2002, p. A1.

[188] Staples, Brent, "The Trouble with Corporate Radio: The Day the Protest Music Died," *The New York Times*, February 20, 2003 p. A30.

[189] Kim, Scheufele and Shanahan, p. 7.

[190] In support of the proposition that media plays a key role in informing the citizenry about local issues, the authors cite, Chaffee and Frank; McLeod, Scheufele and Moy. In support of the more specific agenda setting functions the authors cite Scheufele, Dietram A., "Agenda-Setting, Priming and Framing Revisited: Another Look at Cognitive Effects of Political Communications," *Mass Communications & Society*, 3 (2000) and McCombs, Maxwell and Donald L. Shaw, "The Agenda-Setting Function of Mass Media," *Public Opinion Quarterly*, 36, 1972.

[191] Valentino, Nicholas A., Vincent L. Hutchings, and Ismail K. White, " Cues that Matter: How Political Ads Prime Racial Issues During Campaigns," *American Political Science Review,* 96, 2002, p. 75.

[192] The references cited in support of this proposition include Edsall, Thomas B. and Mary D. Edsall, *Chain Reaction: The Impact of Race, Rights and Taxes on American Politics* (New York: Norton, 1991); Jamieson, Kathleen Hall, *Dirty Politics: Deception, Distraction and Democracy,* (New York: Oxford University Press, 1992); Gilens, Martin, "Race Coding and White Opposition to Welfare," *American Political Science Review,* 90, 1996; Mendelberg, Tali, "Executing Hortons: Racial Crime in the 1988 Presidential Campaign," *Public Opinion Quarterly,* 61, 1997; Mendelberg, Tali, *The Race Card: Campaign Strategy, Implicit Messages and the Norm of Equality* (Princeton: Princeton University Press, 2001); Valentino, Nicholas A., "Crime News and the Priming of Racial Attitudes During the Evaluation of the President," *Public Opinion Quarterly,* 63, 1999.

[193] The references cited in support of this proposition include Mendelberg, 2001; Coltrane, Scott and Melinda Messineo, "The Perpetuation of Subtle Prejudice: Race and Gender Imagery in the 1990's Television Advertising," *Sex Roles*, 42, 1990; Entman, Robert M., and Andrew Rojecki, *The Black Image in the White Mind: Media and Race in America* (Chicago: University of Chicago Press, 2000); Gray, Herman, *Watching Race Television and the Struggle for Blackness* (Chicago: University of Chicago Press, 1995); Dixon, Travis L. and Daniel Linz, "Overrepresentation and Underrepresentation of African Americans and Latinos as Lawbreakers on Television News," *Communications Research*, 50, 2000; Gilliam, Franklin D., Jr., and Shanto Iyengar, "Prime Suspects: The Influence of Local Television News on the Viewing Public," *American Journal of Political Science*, 44, 2000; Peffley, Mark, Todd Shields and Bruce Williams, "The Intersection of Race and Television," *Political Communications*, 13, 1996.

[194] Kim, Shefuele and Shanahan, p. 381.

[195] The sources cited in support of this proposition include, Graber, Doris, *Mass Media and American Politics* (Washington, DC: Congressional Quarterly, 1997); Paletz, David L., *The Media in American Politics: Contents and Consequences* (New York: Longman, 1999); Just, Marion R., Ann N. Crigler, Dean F. Alger, Timothy E. Cook, Montague Kern, and Darrell M. West, *Crosstalk: Citizens, Candidates and the Media in a Presidential Campaign* (Chicago: University of Chicago Press, 1996); Kahn, Kim F. and Patrick J. Kenney, *The Spectacle of U.S. Senate Campaign* (Chicago: University of Chicago Press, 1999).

[196] The sources cited in support of this proposition include Iyengar, Shanto and Donald R. Kinder, *News That Matters: Television and American Opinion* (Chicago: University of Chicago Press, 1987); McCombs and Shaw.

[197] Mutz, Diana C., "Cross-Cutting Social Networks: Testing Democratic Theory in Practice," American *Political Science Review*, 96, 2002, p. 111.

[198] Mutz, identifies rich traditions in political philosophy and social psychology as general support for this view and offers a long tradition of empirical research bearing directly on the relationship, including Stouffer, Samuel, *Communism, Conformity, and Civil Liberties* (New York: Doubleday, 1955); Nunn, Clyde Z., Harry J. Crockett and J. Allen Williams, *Tolerance for Nonconformity* (San Francisco: Josey-Bass, 1978); Sullivan, John L., James Pierson, and George E. Marcus, *Political Tolerance and American Democracy* (Chicago: University of Chicago Press, 1982); Marcus, George E., John L. Sullivan, Elizabeth Theiss-Morse, and Sandra L. Wood, *With Malice Toward Some: How People Make Civil Liberties Judgments* (New York: Cambridge University Press, 1995); Altemeyer, Bob, *The Authoritarian Specter* (Cambridge, MA: Harvard University Press, 1997); Gibson, James L., *Social Networks, Civil Society, and the Prospects for Consolidating Russia's Democratic Transition* (St. Louis: Department of Political Science, Washington University, 1999).

[199] Valentino, Hutchings and White, p. 75.

[200] Scheufele; Geiger, Wendy, Jon Bruning and Jake Harwood, "Talk About TV: Television Viewer's Interpersonal Communications About Programming," *Communications Reports,* 14, 2001.

[201] The author underscores the significance of this process by reminding the reader (p. 57) that de Toqueville offered the "notion that political talk is the soul of democracy."

[202] Albarran, Alan B. and John W. Dimmick, "An Assessment of Utility and Competitive Superiority in the Video Entertainment Industries," *Journal of Media Economics,* 6, 1993; Bennett, W. Lance and Regina G. Lawrence, "News Icons and the Mainstreaming of Social Change," *Journal of Communication,* 45, 1995; McLeod, Douglas M., "Communicating Deviance: The Effects of Television News Coverage of Social Protests," *Journal of Broadcasting & Electronic Media,* 39, 1995; Dimmick, John B., "The Theory of the Niche and Spending on Mass Media: The Case of the Video Revolution," *Journal of Media Economics,* 10, 1997; Sparks, Glenn G., Marianne Pellechia, and Chris Irvine, "Does Television News About UFOs Affect Viewers' UFO Beliefs?: An Experimental Investigation," *Communication Quarterly,* 46, 1998; Walma, Julliete, H. Tom H. A. Van Der Voort, "The Impact of Television, Print, and Audio on Children's Recall of the News," *Human Communication Research,* 26, 2001.

[203] Wilkins, Karin Gwinn, "The Role of Media in Public Disengagement from Political Life," *Journal of Broadcasting & Electronic Media,* 44, 2000.

[204] Clarke and Fredin; Robinson, John P. and Mark R. Levy, "New Media Use and the Informed Public: A 1990s Update," *Journal of Communications,* Spring 1996.

[205] The role of radio talk shows is the new development. Johnson, Thomas J., Mahmoud A. M. Braima, and Jayanthi Sothirajah, "Doing the Traditional Media Sidestep: Comparing Effects of the Internet and Other Nontraditional Media with Traditional Media in the 1996 Presidential Campaign," *Journalism & Mass Communication Quarterly,* 76, 1999, find that nontraditional media do not have an impact on a variety of measures of knowledge and perceptions about the 1996 presidential campaign and to the extent they do, it was specifically radio talk shows, influencing views of Clinton negatively (see also Moy, Patricia, Michael Pfau, and LeeAnn Kahlor, "Media Use and Public Confidence in Democratic Institutions," *Journal of Broadcasting & Electronic Media,* 43, 1999); Johnson, Thomas J., Mahmoud A. M. Braima, Jayanthi Sothirajah, "Measure for Measure: The Relationship Between Different Broadcast Types, Formats, Measures and Political Behaviors and Cognitions," *Journal of Broadcasting & Electronic Media,* 44, 2000, juxtapose the earlier finding of a lack of influence for radio with more recent findings that radio talk shows have an impact. See also Stamm, K., M. Johnson, and B. Martin, "Differences Among Newspapers, Television and Radio in their Contribution to Knowledge of the Contract with America," *Journalism and Mass Communications Quarterly,* 74, 1997.

[206] Berkowitz, D. and D. Pritchard, "Political Knowledge and Communication Resources," *Journalism Quarterly,* 66, 1989; Chaffee, S. H., X. Zhao and G. Leshner, "Political Knowledge and the Campaign Media of 1992," *Communications Research,* 21, 1994; Drew, D. and D. Weaver, "Voter Learning in the 1988 Presidential Election: Did the Media Matter?" *Journalism Quarterly,* 68, 1991.

[207] Stepp, Carl Sessions, "Whatever Happened to Competition," *American Journalism Review,* June 2001:

"Wasn't it television and radio that were going to kill newspapers? 'I don't really consider them competition in that old-school way,' stresses Florida Sun-Sentinel editor Earl Maucker. 'They reach a different kind of audience with a different kind of news…'

"Publisher Gremillion, a former TV executive himself, seconds the point, 'I don't believe people are watching TV as a substitute for reading the newspaper…'

"…Many newspapers are increasingly writing off local TV news as a serious threat, treating local stations instead as potential partners who can help spread the newspapers' brand name to new and bigger audiences."

[208] Sinclair, Jon R., "Reforming Television's Role in American Political Campaigns: Rationale for the Elimination of Paid Political Advertisements," *Communications and the Law,* March 1995.

[209] Coulson, David C. and Stephen Lacy, "Newspapers and Joint Operating Agreements," in E. David Sloan and Emily Erickson Hoff, (eds.) *Contemporary Media Issues* (Northport: Vision Press, 1998); Lacy, Coulson and Cyr.

[210] Cornfield, Michael, "What is Historic About Television?", Journal *of Communications,* 21, 1994, pp. 110-111.

[211] Kunkel and Roberts, citing Walter Williams, "The Journalist's Creed" (1914).

[212] Hansen, Glenn J. and William Benoit, "Presidential Television Advertising and Public Policy Priorities, 1952–2002," *Communications Studies,* 53, 2002, p. 285.

[213] The studies cited in support of this proposition include Patterson, T. E., and R. D. McClure, *The Unseeing Eye: The Myth of Television Power in National Politics* (New York: Putnam Books, 1976); Kern, M., *30 Second Politics: Political Advertising in the Eighties* (New York: Praeger, 1988); Brians, C.L. and M. P. Wattenberg, "Campaigns Issue Knowledge and Salience: Comparing Reception for TV Commercials, TV News, and Newspapers, *American Journal of Political Science,* 40, 1996.

[214] Carter, Fico and McCabe, p. 42.

[215] Brazeal, LeAnn M, and William L. Benoit, "A Functional Analysis of congressional Television Spots," *Communications Quarterly,* 49, 2001, pp. 346-437.

[216] In support of this proposition the authors cite Zhao, X. and G. L. Bleske, "Measurement Effects in Comparing Voter Learning From Television News and Campaign Advertisements," *Journalism and Mass Communications Quarterly*, 72, 1995; Zhao, X. and S. H. Chaffee, "Campaign Advertisements Versus Television News as Sources of Political Issue Information," *Public Opinion Quarterly*, 59, 1995; Patterson and McClure;, Kern; Brians and Wattenberg.

[217] In support of this statement the authors cite campaign spending numbers on the order of a quarter of a billion dollars per election. See Jenkins, K., "Learning to Love those Expensive Campaigns," *U.S. News and World Report*, 122, 1007; Sinclair.

[218] In support of this statement the authors cite Joslyn, R., "The Impact of Campaign Spot Advertising Ads, *Journalism Quarterly*, 7, 1981; Mulder, R., "The Effects of Televised Political Ads in the 1995 Chicago Mayoral Election," *Journalism Quarterly*, 56, 1979; and Pfau, M., and H. C. Kenski, *Attack Politics* (New York: Praeger, 1990).

[219] Domke, David, David Perlmutter and Meg Spratt, "The Primes of Our Times? An Examination of the 'Power' of Visual Images," *Journalism*, 3, 2002, p. 131.

[220] The authors present a detailed social psychological and even neurological discussion of the reasons why and ways in which visual images have a greater impact, but the politically oriented research that they cite as consistent with their findings include Krosnick, J. A. and D. R. Kinder, "Altering the Foundation of Support for the President Through Priming," *American Political Science Review*, 84, 1990; Pan, Z. and G. M. Kosicki, "Priming and Media Impact on the Evaluation the President's Performance," *Communications Research*, 24, 1997; Just, M. R., A. N. Crigler and W. R. Neuman, "Cognitive and Affective Dimensions of Political Conceptualization," in A. N. Crigler (ed.) *The Psychology of Political Communications* (Ann Arbor: University of Michigan Press, 1996); Iyengar and Kinder.

[221] Gwiasda, Gregory W., "Network News Coverage of Campaign Advertisements: Media's Ability to Reinforce Campaign Messages," *American Politics Research*, 29, 2001, p. 461.

[222] Sources cited in support of the subtle interaction between advertising and coverage of advertising include: Kaid, L. L., et al., "Television News and Presidential Campaigns: The Legitimation of Televised Political Advertising," *Social Science Quarterly*, 74, 1993; Ansolabehere, Stephen and Shanto Iyengar, "Riding the Wave and Claiming Ownership Over Issues: The Joint Effect of Advertising and News Coverage in Campaigns," *Public Opinion Quarterly*, 58, 1994; Lemert, James B., William R. Elliott, and James M. Bernstein, *News Verdicts, the Debates, and Presidential Campaigns* (New York: Praeger, 1991).

[223] Gwiasda, p. 461; Hansen and Benoit, p. 284.

[224] While Zaller, J. R., *The Nature and Origins of Mass Opinion* (New York: Cambridge University Press, 1992) is cited as the origin of the hypothesis on effect, the author does note that Joslyn, M. and S. Cecolli, "Attentiveness to Television News and Opinion Change in the Fall of 1992 Election Campaign," *Political Behavior*, 18, 1996, find that the most attentive are most influenced.

[225] Benoit, William L. and Glenn Hansen, "Issue Adaptation of Presidential Television Spots and Debates to Primary and General Audiences," *Communications Research Reports*, 19, 2002.

[226] Federal Communications Commission, Initial Notice.

[227] Notice, p. 32, provides the innovation discussion. "Further Notice of Proposed Rulemaking." In the Matter of Implementation of Section 11 of the Cable Television Consumer Protection and Competition Act of 1992, Implementation of Cable Act Reform Provisions of the Telecommunications Act of 1996, The Commission's Cable Horizontal and Vertical Ownership Limits and Attribution Rules, Review of the Commission's Regulations Governing Attribution Of Broadcast and Cable/MDS Interests, Review of the Commission's Regulations and Policies Affecting Investment In the Broadcast Industry, Reexamination of the Commission's Cross-Interest Policy, CS Docket No. 98-82, CS Docket No. 96-85, MM Docket No. 92-264, MM Docket No. 94-150, MM Docket No. 92-51, MM Docket No. 87-154, September 13, 2001, Para 36, issued on the same day as the original notice in the media ownership proceedings makes reference to Schumpeter in this discussion. The Chairman had made similar references to monopoly and innovation in his Broadband Migration speech and the argument appears word for word in the FCC's draft strategic plan (October 1, 2002).

[228] Information Policy Institute, "Comments of the Information Policy Institute," *In the Matter of 2002 Biennial Regulatory Review – Review of the Commission's Broadcast Ownership Rules and Other Rules Adopted Pursuant to Section 202 of the Telecommunications Act of 1996, Cross Ownership of Broadcast Stations and Newspapers, Rules and Policies Concerning Multiple Ownership of Radio Broadcast Stations in Local Markets, Definition of Radio Markets,* MB Docket No. 02-277, MM Dockets 02-235, 01-317, 00-244, January 2, 2003 (hereafter, Information Policy Institute), pp. 53-59.

[229] Id., pp. 46-52.

[230] Consumers Union, et al., "Initial Comments of Consumer Federation," et al., *Cross Ownership of Broadcast Stations and Newspapers*, MM Docket No. 01-235, December 4, 2001.

[231] Cooper, Mark, *Cable Mergers and Monopolies: Market Power Digital Media and Communications Networks* (Washington, DC: Economic Policy Institute, 2002).

[232] Baker, Media Markets, p. 120.

[233] Baker, Democracy, p. 75, describes the loss of valuable content as the result of mergers as follows:

"The idea is, for example, that the merged entertainment company can benefit by presenting the same highly promoted fictional character in new mediums – in a theatre released movie, a television show, a book, a magazine excerpt, a musical CD based on the movie sound track, and especially in the case of children oriented media, as material representations or as characters in computer games. By clever placements, the enterprise can cross promote its various products – the broadcast news division or the magazine can do stories about the release of the enterprise's outstanding new movie or television show, or do in depth reports about the program's star characters, or about the Oscar or Academy award competitions, or other related matters of "great public concern." Or the combined local broadcast station and newspaper can share reporters, thereby reducing the outlays necessary to report on local affairs, or can at least require its reporting staffs to cooperate, thereby reducing the cost of each entity doing the reporting from scratch.

"Profitable, however, does not mean in the public interest. Often these 'synergies' or efficiency 'gains' occur by creating market-dominating media goods that, although profitable for the firm, may provide less value to the public than would the media goods they drive out of existence. In other cases, these synergies result from eliminating alternative pre-merger productive activities that provided significant positive externalities."

[234] Id., p. 85:

"To perform these, different societal subgroups need their own media. Admittedly, these subgroups (or their members) may not *necessarily* need to own or control their own independent media. Avenues of regular and effective media access might suffice. Still, much greater confidence that the media will serve the democratic needs of these groups would be justified if ownership or control was so distributed."

[235] Id., p. 87:

"This plurality of media structures may provide security in that neither corruption that comes from government nor corruption that comes from the market is likely to be equally powerful within or equally damaging to all the organizational forms. For this reason, such a plurality of organizational structures will likely advance the media's checking function. Moreover, this diversity of media structures is likely to enable the media to better perform its multiple democratic assignments."

[236] Berry, Steven and Joel Waldfogel, *Mergers, Station Entry, and Programming Variety in Radio Broadcasting* (Washington, DC: National Bureau of Economic Research, 1999); George, Lisa, *What's Fit to Print: The Effect of Ownership Concentration on Product Variety in Daily Newspaper Markets* (unpublished manuscript, University of Michigan, 2001). The Berry and Waldfogel analysis shows that radio market suffered a much larger loss of owners than they gained in

formats and the gain in formats were hybrids (close to existing formats). There was no increase in listening. Similarly, the loss of owners exceeds the gain in variety in the newspaper markets with a very small increase in circulation. The variety gains in the newspaper study appear to have been limited to the largest, least concentrated markets.

[237] Downie, Leonard, Jr., and Robert Kaiser, *The News About the News* (New York: Alfred A. Knopf, 2002), p. 13.

[238] Sparrow, Bartholomew H., *Uncertain Guardians* (Baltimore: Johns Hopkins, 1999), p. 103.

[239] Davis and Craft, pp. 222-223.

[240] See "Reply Comments of Consumers Union, Consumer Federation of America, Media Access Project and Center For Digital Democracy" *In the Matter of Cross-Ownership of Broadcast Stations and Newspaper Newspaper/Radio Cross-Ownership Waiver Policy*, Federal Communications Commission, MM Dockets No. 01-235, 96-197, February 15, 2002.

[241] Auletta, Ken, "The State of the American Newspaper," *American Journalism Review*, June 1998.

[242] Media Studies Center Survey, University of Connecticut, January 18, 1999.

[243] Rabasca, Lisa, "Benefits, Costs and Convergence," *Presstime*, 2001, p. 3.

[244] Kunkel and Roberts.

[245] Strupp, p. 23.

[246] Media General, p. 6.

[247] Belo, pp. 8-9.

[248] Moses, p. 22.

[249] Roberts, Gene, Thomas Kunkel and Charles Layton "Leaving Readers Behind," in Gene Roberts, Thomas Kunkel and Charles Layton (eds.), *Leaving Readers Behind* (Fayetteville: University of Arkansas Press: 2001), p. 5.

[250] Roberts, Kunkel and Layton, Leaving, p. 9; Rowse, Arthur E., *Drive-By Journalism* (Monroe, ME: Common Courage Press, 2000), pp. 24-25.

[251] Bass, pp. 113, 116.

[252] Tompkins, Al and Aly Colon, "NAB 200: The Convergence Marketplace", *Broadcast and Cable*, April 10, 2000, p. 48, quoting WFLA News Director Bradley.

[253] Colon, Aly, "The Multimedia Newsroom," *Columbia Journalism Review*, June 2000, p. 26.

[254] Rabasca, p. 2.

[255] Strupp, p. 21.

[256] Id., p. 22.

[257] Tompkins and Colon, p. 53.

[258] Friedland, Lewis, "Statement" Attached to "Reply Comments of Consumer Federation," et al., *Cross Ownership of Broadcast Stations and Newspapers*, MM Docket No. 01-235, February 15, 2002.

[259] Rabasca, p. 4.

[260] Id., p. 4; Tompkins and Colon, p. 50; Mitchell, Bill, "Media Collaborations," *Broadcasting and Cable*, April 10, 2000.

[261] Moses, p. 23.

[262] Tompkins and Colon, p. 50.

[263] Strupp, p. 22.

[264] McConnell, The National Acquirers.

[265] Cranberg, Gilbert, Randall Bezanson, and John Soloski, *Taking Stock: Journalism and the Publicly Traded Newspaper Company* (Ames: Iowa State Press, 2001).

[266] Cranberg, Bezanson and Soloski, cite Roberts, Gene, "Corporatism vs. Journalism," *The Press-Enterprise Lecture Series*, 31, February 12, 1996; for recent discussions see also Dugger, Ronald, "The Corporate Domination of Journalism," in William Serrin (ed.), *The Business of Journalism* (New York: New Press, 2000); Sparrow, Chapter 4.

[267] Cranberg, Bezanson and Soloski, p. 11.

[268] Bass, p. 111.

[269] Bass, p. 111.

[270] Cranberg, Bezanson and Soloski, p. 86.

[271] Downie and Kaiser, p. 68.

[272] Id., p. 13.

[273] From this we can easily conclude that "the owners most likely to encourage their editors' ambitions, give them adequate resources and support aggressive, intelligent journalism are companies controlled by a single family" (Downie and Kaiser, p. 76).

[274] Bissinger, Buzz, "The End of Innocence," in Gene Roberts, Thomas Kunkel and Charles Layton (eds), *Leaving Readers Behind* (Fayetteville: University of Arkansas Press: 2001), p. 83.

[275] Bissinger, p. 103.

[276] Roberts, Kunkel and Layton, Leaving, p. 5.

[277] Id., Leaving, p. 2.

[278] Cranberg, Bezanson and Soloski, p. 42.

[279] Id., p. 42.

[280] Id., p. 42.

[281] Id., p. 108.

[282] Id., p. 78.

[283] Id., p. 64.

[284] Id., p. 86.

[285] Cranberg, Bezanson and Soloski, p. 89; *The Business of News, the News About Business,* Neiman Reports, Summer 1999.

[286] Downie and Kaiser, p. 93.

[287] Id., p. 68; Layton.

[288] Downie and Kaiser, p. 81.

[289] Cranberg, Bezanson, Soloski, p. 38

[290] Downie and Kaiser, p. 97.

[291] Id., p. 97.

[292] Id., p. 109.

[293] Layton, p. 143.

[294] Cranberg, Bezanson, and Soloski, p. 13.

[295] Downie and Kaiser, p. 69.

[296] Id., p. 87.

[297] Id., p. 91.

[298] Bass, p. 145.

[299] Roberts, Kunkel and Clayton, Leaving, p. 10.

[300] Walton, Mary and Charles Layton, "Missing the Story at the Statehouse," in Roberts, Gene and Thomas Kunkel (eds.), *Breach of Faith: A Crisis of Coverage in the Age of Corporate Newspapering* (Fayetteville: University of Arkansas Press, 2002), p. 14.

[301] Id., p. 21.

[302] Rowse, p. 163:

"*USA Today* goes one step farther, offering to redo its front page for any advertiser who is willing to pay top dollar. The page remains similar to a normal *USA Today* front page but is complete with stories promoting whatever firm is in question. The revised edition is then circulated as a promotional piece."

[303] According to Rowse, p. 49, in 1994, *The Washington Post* ran a huge story urging the approval of GATT without admitting that it was a subsidiary of

American Personnel Communications and stood to profit $1.3 billion if GATT went through. Similarly, p. 159, the *Post* runs ads for the Nuclear Energy Institute, a large supplier of advertising revenue, and neglected to run a story about a report by Public Citizen which said 90 percent of nuclear reactors had been operating in violation of government safety rules.

[304] According to Street, John, *Mass Media, Politics, and Democracy* (New York: Palgrave, 2001), p. 141, "*The New York Times* changed an article about Tiffany's, a huge advertiser, and accompanied it by a bland editorial, to avoid damaging their relationship with the company." Similarly, Rowse, p. 162, notes that Chrysler, an enormous source of ad revenue for whomever it deals with, demands to see the content in the pages accompanying its ads to ensure that it is 'positive' and 'light.'

[305] Cranberg, Bezanson and Soloski, p. 93.

[306] Id., p. 96.

[307] Id., p. 10.

[308] Id., p. 95.

[309] Williams, Vanessa, "Black and White and Red All Over: The Ongoing Struggle to Integrate America's Newsrooms," in William Serrin (ed.), *The Business of Journalism* (New York: New York Press, 2000), p. 100.

[310] Bagdikian, Mchesney, 1999; Esslin.

[311] Mosco, Chp.. 2; Levy, 109; Levine, Peter, *The Internet and Civil Society*, Report from the University of Maryland, Institute for Philosophy & Public Policy, vol. 20, no. 4, Fall 2000, p. 3; Liberty, Chp. 8.

[312] Mosco, p. 43.

[313] Levine, Peter, "Can the Internet Rescue Democracy? Toward an On-line Commons," in Ronald Hayuk and Kevin Mattson (eds.), *Democracy's Moment: Reforming the American Political System for the 21st Century* (Lanham, ME: Rowman and Littlefield, 2002); Levine, *The Internet*, p. 3.

[314] Mosco, p. 11.

[315] Meyer, Thomas, *Media Democracy* (Cambridge: Polity Press, 2002), pp. 37-38; McManus, 1994.

[316] Levy, p. 197.

[317] Street, p. 9, citations to Habermas, Jurgen, *The Structural Transformation of the Public* (Cambridge: Polity Press, 1989), *Between Facts and Norms* (Cambridge: Polity Press, 1996).

[318] Meyer, p. 38.

[319] Esslin, p. viii.

[320] Meyer, p. x, citing Barber, B. R., *Jihad v. McWorld* (New York: Ballentine, 1996), pp. 88-99 and Postman.

[321] Kovach, Bill and Tom Rosenstiel, *Warp Speed: America in the Age of Mixed Media* (New York: The Century Foundation Press, 1999).

[322] Gans, Herbert, J., *Democracy and the News* (Oxford: Oxford University Press, 2003), p. 50; Kovach and Rosentsteil, p. 6.

[323] Gans, p. 49.

[324] Street, pp. 36-52.

[325] Graber, Doris, *Processing Politics* (Chicago: University of Chicago Press, 2001), pp. 113-114.

[326] Kovach and Rosentsteil, pp. 21, 44.

[327] Meyer, pp. 32-35.

[328] Id., p. 67; Graber, pp. 112-114; Jones, Nicholas, *Soundbites and Spindoctors: How Politicians Manipulate the Media – and Visa Versa* (London: Cassel, 1995).

[329] Kovach and Rosentsteil, pp. 7-8.

[330] Street, pp. 47-49; Meyerowitz, J., *No Sense of Place: The Effect of Electronic Media on Social Behavior* (New York: Oxford, 1985).

[331] Street, p. 47; Graber, pp. 111-112; Gitlin, T., "Bits and Blips: Chunk News, Savvy Talk and the Bifurcation of American Politics," in P. Dahlgren and C. Sparks (eds), *Communications and Citizenship: Journalism and the Public Sphere* (London: Routledge, 1991), pp. 119-136.

[332] Meyer, p. 35; Kovach and Rosenstiel, Chapter 7; Street, p. 44.

[333] Barker, David, C., *Rushed to Judgment* (New York: Columbia University Press, 2002).

[334] Mosco, p. 26

[335] Levin, Can, p. 124.

[336] Meyer, p. 133; Gans, pp. 47-48.

[337] Sparrow, pp. 28-38.

[338] Gans, p. 49.

[339] Meyer, p. 53; Dorner, A., *Politainment* (Frankfurt/Main: Surhkamp, 2001).

[340] Graber, p. 84.

[341] Id., p. 88.

[342] Kovach and Rosentstiel, Chapters 4, 5.

[343] Gans, pp. 50-51.

[344] Street, pp. 57-58, 83, 90.

[345] Gans, p. 83; Cook, Timothy E., *Governing with the New: The News Media as a Political Institution* (Chicago: University of Chicago Press, 1998).

[346] Meyer, p. 58.

[347] Id., p. xi.

[348] Id., p. 15.

[349] Curran, James, *Media and Power* (Routledge, London: 2002), p. 150.

[350] Id., p. 138.

[351] Gans, pp. 45-46, 79-80; Curran p. 220.

[352] Curran, p. 138.

[353] Meyer, p. 24.

[354] Id., p. 106.

[355] Id., p. 104.

[356] Patterson, Thomas E., *The Vanishing Voter* (New York: Alfred A. Knopf, 2002); Crenson, Matthew A. and Benjamin Ginsberg, *Downsizing Democracy* (Baltimore, Johns Hopkins University Press, 2002).

[357] Id., p. 25.

[358] Bimber, Bruce, "The Internet and Political Transformation: Populism, Community and Accelerated Pluralism," *Polity,* 31, 1998; Grossman, Lawrence, *The Electronic Republic: Reshaping Democracy in the Information Age* (New York: Penguin, 1996); Weston, Tracy, "Can Technology Save Democracy," *National Civic Review,* 87, 1998.

[359] Wise, Richard, *Multimedia: A Critical Introduction* (London: Routledge, 2000), p. 26.

[360] Levy, Pierre, *Cyberculture* (Minneapolis: University of Minnesota, 2001), p. 106.

[361] Id., p. 166.

[362] Saco, Diana, *Cybering Democracy* (Minneapolis: University of Minnesota Press, 2002), p. 44.

[363] Levy, p. 176

[364] Mosco, Vincent, *The Pay-Per Society: Computers & Communications in the Information Age* (Norwood, NJ: Ablex, 1989), p. 24.

[365] Lessig, Future.

[366] Levine, Peter, "Can the Internet Rescue Democracy? Toward an On-Line Commons," in Ronald Hayuk and Kevin Mattson (eds.), *Democracy's Moment: Reforming the American Political System for the 21st Century* (Lanham, ME: Rowman and Littlefield, 2002).

[367] Levine, Can, p. 137.

[368] Concerns about establishing a public sphere, or commons, as the key to a significant enrichment of democratic discourse are echoed by other, see Blumler, Jay G., and Michael Gurevitch, "The New Media and Our Political Communication Discontents: Democratizing Cyberspace," *Information, Communications and Society*, 4, 2001; O'Loughlin, Ben, "The Political Implications of Digital Innovations: Trade-Offs of Democracy and Liberty in the Developed World," *Information, Communications and Society*, 4, 2001; Agre, Philip E., "Real-Time Politics: The Internet and the Political Process," *Information Society*, 18, 2002.

[369] Levine, Peter, "The Internet and Civil Society: Dangers and Opportunities," *Information Impacts Magazine*, May 2001, p. 1.

[370] Liberty (National Council for Civil Liberties), *Liberating Cyberspace* (London: Pluto Press, 1999), Introduction.

[371] Mosco, Chps. 2 and 4; Wise, p. 5

[372] Wise, p. 126; Miller, Steven E, *Civilizing Cyberspace* (New York: ACM Press, 1998), Ch. 2

[373] Lessig, Future.

[374] Cooper, *Cable*, 2002.

[375] Firestone and Schement, p. 45; Stempell, Guido H. III, and Thomas Hargrove, "Mass Media Audiences in a Changing Media Environment," *Journalism and Mass Communications Quarterly*, Autumn 1996; Gunther, Albert C., "The Persuasive Press Inference: Effects of Mass Media on Perceived Public Opinion," *Communications Research*, October 1998; American Civil Liberties Union v. Janet Reno, 929 F. Supp. 824 (E. D. Pa. 1996), 117 S. Ct. 2329 (1997); Iosifides.

[376] Loudon, K. C. "Promise versus Performances of Cable," in Dutton, H.W. et al. (ed.), *Wired Cities: Shaping the Future of Communications* (Boston: K. G. Hall, 1987); Le Duc, D., *Beyond Broadcasting* (New York: Longman, 1987); Streeter, T., "The Cable Fable Revisited; Discourse, Policy, and the Making of Cable Television," *Critical Studies in Mass Communications*, 1987; Winston, B., "Rejecting the Jehovah's Witness Gambit," *Intermedia*, 1990; Sine, N. M., et al., "Current Issues in Cable Television: A Re-balancing to Protect the Consumer," *Cardozo Arts & Entertainment Law Journal*, 1990; Wicks, R. H. and M. Kern, "Factors Influencing Decisions by Local Television News Directors to Develop New Reporting Strategies During the 1992 Political Campaign," *Communications Research*, 1995; Massimo, Motta and Michele Polo, "Concentration and Public Policies in the Broadcasting Industry," *Communications Law and Policy*, Spring 1997; Lubunski, Richard, "The First Amendment at the Crossroads: Free Expression and New Media Technology," *Communications Law and Policy*, Spring 1997; Chan-Olmsted, Sylvia and Jung Suk Park, "From On-Air to Online World: Examining the Content and Structures of Broadcast TV Stations' Web Sites," *Journalism & Mass Communication Quarterly*, 77 2000.

[377] Ofori, asserts a bias in advertising rates; Bradford, William D., "Discrimination in Capital Markets, Broadcast/Wireless Spectrum Service

Providers and Auction Outcomes" (School of Business Administration, Univ. of Washington, December 5, 2000), asserts a bias in capital markets.

[378] Jordan, Tim, *Cyberpower* (London: Routledge, 1998), Ch. 5

[379] Mosco, p. 26; Miller, Ch. 13

[380] Van Orden, Bob, "Top Five Interactive Digital-TV Applications," *Multichannel News*, June 21, 1999, p. 143; Kearney, Chapter 4.

[381] Menezes, Bill, "Replay, TiVo Get Cash for Consumer Push," *Multichannel News*, April 5, 1999, p. 48.

[382] Cooper, Mark, "Inequality in Digital Society," *Cardozo Journal On Media and the Arts*, 73, 2002.

[383] The cost of early HDTV equipment has been exorbitant with current prices in the range of $2,000 to $4,000. "Profile with Bob Wright: The Agony Before the Ecstasy of Digital TV," *Digital Television*, April 1999, p. 40; Maxwell, Kim, *Residential Broadband: An Insider's Guide to the Battle for the Last Mile* (New York: John Wiley, 1999), pp. 9-10.

[384] Sakar, Jayati, "Technological Diffusion: Alternative Theories and Historical Evidence," *Journal of Economic Surveys*, 12:2, 1998; Martinez, Evan, Yolanda Polo and Carlos Flavian, "The Acceptance and Diffusion of New Consumer Durables: Differences Between First and Last Adopters," *Journal of Consumer Marketing*, 15:4, 1998.

[385] Meeks, Carol B. and Anne L. Sweaney, "Consumer's Willingness to Innovate: Ownership of Microwaves, Computers and Entertainment Products," *Journal of Consumer Studies and Home Economics*, 16, 1992; Savage, Scott, Gary Madden and Michael Simpson, "Broadband Delivery of Educational Services: A Study of Subscription Intentions in Australian Provincial Centers," *Journal of Media Economics*, 10:1, 1997; Atkin, David J., Leo W. Jeffres and Kimberly A. Neuendorf, "Understanding Internet Adoption as Telecommunications Behavior," *Journal of Broadcasting and Electronic Media*, 42:4, 1998; Neuendorf, Kimberly A., David J. Atkin and Leo W. Jeffres, "Understanding Adopters of Audio Information Innovations," *Journal of Broadcasting and Electronic Media*, 42:4, 1998; Lin, Carolyn A., "Exploring Personal Computer Adoption Dynamics," *Journal of Broadcasting and Electronic Media*, 42:4, 1998.

[386] Sultan, Fareena, "Consumer Preferences for Forthcoming Innovations: The Case of High Definition Television," *Journal of Consumer Marketing*, 16, 1999, p. 37.

[387] Levine, Peter, *Building the Electronic Commons* (Democracy Collaborative, April 5, 2002).

[388] Mosco, p. 38.

[389] Dahlberg, Lincoln, "The Internet and Democratic Discourse," *Information, Communications and Society,* 4, 2001.

[390] Chyi, Hsiang Iris and Dominic L. Lasora, "An Exploratory Study on the Market Relation Between Online and Print Newspapers," *The Journal of Media Economics,* 15, 2002.

[391] Foot, Kirsten A. and Steven M. Schneider, "Online Action in Campaign 2000: An Exploratory Analysis of the U.S. Political Web Sphere," *Journal of Broadcasting and Electronic Media,* 46, 2002.

[392] Levine, Can, p. 125.

[393] Id., p. 125.

[394] Levine, The Internet, p. 2.

[395] Jordan, Chs. 3 and 4.

[396] Levine, The Internet, p. 2.

[397] Levine, Can, p. 127.

[398] Id., p. 23.

[399] Levine, The Internet, p. 8.

[400] Id., p. 7.

[401] Levine, Can, p. 127.

[402] Id., p. 127.

[403] Id., p. 123.

[404] Saco, p. 47, quoting Arendt.

[405] Levine, Can, p. 125.

[406] Mosco, p. 38; Miller, Chs. 1, 8; Liberty, Introduction.

[407] Mosco, p. 38.

[408] Mosco, Ch. 3; Wise, Chs. 1, 5, 9; Miller, Ch. 4, 5, 6.

[409] Cooper, Inequality; Miller, Chs. 1 and 8; Liberty, Introduction; Levy, Introduction; Levine, The Internet.

[410] Levine, Can, p. 122.

[411] Mosco, p. 35.

[412] Levy, p. x.

[413] Morgan Stanley Dean Whitter Reynolds, *Digital Decade* (New York, 1999).

[414] Ploskina, Brian and Dana Coffield, "Regional Bells Ringing Up Higher DSL Rates," *Interactive Week,* February 18, 2001; Braunstein, Yale, *Market Power and Price Increases in the DSL Market* (July 2001). "Cable Industry Comment," *Banc of*

America Securities, May 7, 2001; Ames, Sam, "Study: Broadband Fees Climbed in 2001," *Yahoo News,* January 18, 2002; Spangler, Todd, "Crossing the Broadband Divide," *PC Magazine,* February 12, 2002; Office of Technology Policy, *Understanding Broadband Demand* (Washington, D.C.: U.S. Department of Commerce, September 23, 2002), p. 14.

[415] Cooper, Inequality.

[416] Levine, The Internet, p. 2.

[417] Levy, p. 12.

[418] Miller, Chs. 1 and 2.

[419] Cooper, Inequality.

[420] Mosco, pp. 71.

[421] Cooper, Inequality.

[422] Levine, Building, p. 16.

[423] Miller, Ch. 1; Liberty, Introduction; Cooper, Inequality.

[424] Mosco, Ch. 2; Levine, The Internet.

[425] Mosco, p. 78.

[426] Levine, Can, p. 135.

[427] Mosco, p. 115.

[428] Levy, p. 97.

[429] Wise, Ch. 1; Mosco, Ch. 2.

[430] Wise, p. 8.

[431] Levine, Building, p. 17.

[432] Levine, Can, p. 135.

[433] Levy, p. 191.

[434] Mosco, p. 73.

[435] Saco, p. xv.

[436] Wise, p. 197.

[437] Id., p. 202.

[438] Levine, Can, pp. 124

[439] Levy, p. xv.

[440] Fahri, Paul, "For Broadcast Media, Patriotism Pays: Consultants Tell, Radio, TV Clients that Protest Coverage Drives Viewers Off," *Washington Post,* March 28, 2003, C2.

[441] Fahri, C1.

[442] Kurtz, Howard, "The 'Beeb' in Their Bonnet; BBC Is Taking Flak for Its Cover-All-Sides Approach," *Washington Post*, March 27, 2003, p. C1.

[443] Waldfogel, Joel, *Consumer Substitution Among Media* (Federal Communications Commission, Media Bureau Staff Research Paper, September 2002); Nielsen Media Research, *Consumer Survey on Media Usage* (Federal Communications Commission, Media Bureau Staff Research Paper, September 2002).

[444] The advertising studies lend little support to the claim of substitutability; see Brown, Keith and George Williams, *Consolidation and Advertising Prices in Local Radio Markets* (Federal Communications Commission, Media Bureau Staff Research Paper, September 2002); Bush, C. Anthony, *On the Substitutability of Local Newspaper, Radio, and Television Advertising in Local Business Sales* (Federal Communications Commission, Media Bureau Staff Research Paper, September 2002).

[445] Brown, Allan, "Public Service Broadcasting in Four Countries: Overview," *The Journal of Media Economics,* 9, 1996; Moy, Patricia and Dietram A. Scheufele, "Media Effects on Political and Social Trust," *Journalism and Mass Communications Quarterly*, 77, 2000, pp. 746...751:

"The general trend of effects is one in which reliance on television news leads to lower levels of trust in government, while newspaper reading results in higher levels of trust...

"While the mass media have been blamed for diminishing levels of trust among the citizenry, we have shown that it is crucial to distinguish not only between types of media, but also between types of trust. Our analysis shows that use of different types of media has different effects on political and social trust."

[446] *In the Matter of Cross Ownership of Broadcast Stations and Newspaper; Newspaper/Radio Cross-Ownership Waiver Policy* (MM Docket Nos. 01-235, 96-197), p. 5.

[447] Newspaper Notice, pp. 6-9.

[448] *Horizontal Merger Guidelines*, at section 0.1.

[449] Friedman, J.W., *Oligopoly Theory* (Cambridge: Cambridge University Press, 1983), p. 8-9.

[450] *Horizontal Merger Guidelines.*

[451] Shepherd, William G., *The Economics of Industrial Organization* (Englewood Cliffs, NJ: Prentice Hall, 1985), p. 389, gives the following formulas for the Herfindahl-Hirschman Index (HHI) and the Concentration Ratio (CR):

$$H = \sum_{i=1}^{n} S_i{}^2$$

$$CR = \sum_{i=1}^{m} S_i$$

where

n = the number of firms

m= the market share of the largest firms (4 for the four firm concentration ratio)

S_i = the share of the ith firm.

[452] Shepherd, p. 4.

[453] *Horizontal Merger Guidelines*, at section 0.1:

"The rule of thumb reflected in all iterations of the Merger Guidelines is that the more concentrated an industry, the more likely is oligopolistic behavior by that industry.... Still, the inference that higher concentration increases the risks of oligopolistic conduct seems well grounded. As the number of industry participants becomes smaller, the task of coordinating industry behavior becomes easier. For example, a ten-firm industry is more likely to require some sort of coordination to maintain prices at an oligopoly level, whereas the three-firm industry might more easily maintain prices through parallel behavior without express coordination."

[454] Taylor, John B., *Economics* (Boston: Houghton Mifflin, 2001); Viscusi, W. Kip, John M. Vernon, and Joseph E. Harrington, Jr., *Economics of Regulation and Antitrust* (Cambridge: MIT Press, 2000), Chapter 5; Fudenberg, Jean and Jean Tirole, "Noncooperative Game Theory for Industrial Organization: An Introduction and Overview," in Richard Schmalensee and Robert D. Willig, (eds.) *Handbook of Industrial Organization* (New York: North-Holland, 1989).

[455] *Horixontal Merger Guidelines*, section 1.51.

[456] *Id.*, section .01.

[457] Nielsen, Study Number 8.

[458] Roper Reports, *Consuming More News and Believing It Less*, February 28, 2002.

[459] Pew Research Center, "Internet Sapping Broadcast News Audience," June 11, 2000.

[460] Federal Communications Commission, *National Cable Horizontal Ownership Limits, Further Notice of Proposed Rulemaking*, CS Docket Nos 98-82, et al., Federal Communications Commission (hereafter, Notice), p. 8.

266

[461] Lebo, Harlan, *Surveying the Digital Future* (UCLA Center for Communication Policy, November 2001).

[462] Norris, Pippa, "Revolution, What Revolution? The Internet and U.S. Elections, 1992-2000," in Elaine Ciulla Kamarch and Joseph S. Nye Jr. (eds.), *governance.com* (Washington, DC: Brookings, 2002).

[463] Waldfogel, Consumer Substitution, p. 3.

[464] Id., p. 3.

[465] Id., p. 3.

[466] Id., p. 3.

[467] Id., p. 40.

[468] Id., p. 40.

[469] Id., p. 40.

[470] Since the study is proprietary, we report only the summary result. The results of the statistical runs are stored in confidential computers at the Federal Communications Commission and available upon request.

[471] Brown and Williams.

[472] Cunningham, Brendan C. and Peter J. Alexander, *A Theory of Broadcast Media Concentration and Commercial Advertising,* Federal Communications Commission, Staff Report 6, September 2002.

[473] This is how CEO Sumner Redstone is reported to have referred to Viacom/CBS, *Communications Daily*, December 5, 2000 cited in NASA, Petition.

[474] Levy, Jonathan, Marcelino Ford-Livene and Anne Levin, *Broadcast Television: Survivor in a Sea of Competition,* Federal Communications Commission, OPP Working Paper, No. 37, September 2002.

[475] NASA, Petition.

[476] Stone,, *News Operations.*

[477] Stone refers to "viable commercial TV stations."

[478] "Sinclair Issues a Challenge to FCC, Powell," *Electronic Media*, October 15, 2001, p. 9.

[479] Owen, Bruce, M. Kent W Mikkelsen and Allison Ivory, "News and Public Affairs Offered by the Four Top-Ranked Versus Lower-Ranked Television Stations," Economic Study A, Attachment to the Joint Comments of Fox, et al.

[480] Crandall, Robert W., *The Economic Impact of Providing Service to Multiple Local Broadcast Stations Within a Single Geographic Market,"* attached to Sinclair Comments, Exhibit 1.

[481] Id.

[482] Id.

483 Mundy, Alicia, "The Price of Freedom," *MediaWeek,* March 29, 1999, p. 32.

484 Federal Communications Commission, *Pricing Analysis,* February 2001, did find a weak subscriber effect. Even though satellite is not cross elastic on price, larger satellite subscribership does have a small effect in taking subscribers away from cable. There is also evidence that satellite is much more effective where cable quality is weak. Neither of these observations is inconsistent with our argument that satellite is not sufficiently competitive to discipline cable pricing.

485 Pub. L. 104-104, Conference Report, p. 148.

486 Title II, part 5.

487 Federal Communications Commission, *In the Matter of Annual Assessment of the Status of Competition in the Market for the Delivery of Video Programming, Seventh Annual Report.* CS Docket No. 00-132, January 2001 (hereafter, FCC, Seventh Annual Report).

488 Id.

489 Id.

490 Id.

491 Id.

492 U.S. Bureau of Labor Statistics, *Consumer Price Index.*

493 Contrast Federal Communications Commission, Federal Communications Commission, *In the Matter of Annual Assessment of Competition in Markets for the Delivery of Video Programming,* Fifth Annual Report, 1998, Appendix B, and Federal Communications Commission, Federal Communications Commission, *In the Matter of Annual Assessment of Competition in Markets for the Delivery of Video Programming.* Eight Annual Report, CS Docket No. 01-129, January 14, 2002. Appendix B.

494 Waterman, David and Michael Zhaoxu Yan, "Cable Advertising and the Future of Basic Cable Networking," *Journal of Electronic Media and Broadcasting,* Fall 1999. Survey evidence indicates that advertisers think cable and broadcast are "substitutes" for each other, but the market shares do not (see Reid, Leonard N. and Karen Whitehill King, "A Demand-Side View of Media Substitutability in National Advertising: A Study of Advertiser Opinions about Traditional Media Options," *Journalism & Mass Communication Quarterly,* 77, 2000).

495 The following discussion is based on Nielson ratings from Spring 2001.

496 Wolzien, Tom, *Returning Oligopoly of Media Content Threatens Cable's Power.* The Long View, Bernstein Research (February 7, 2003), emphasis added.

497 Diversity and Competition Supporters, "Supplemental Comments of Diversity and Competition Supporters," *Cross-Ownership of Broadcast Stations and Newspapers, MM Docket No. 01-235; Newspaper/Radio Cross Ownership Waiver Policy,*

MM No. 98-82; *Rules and Policies Concerning Multiple Ownership of Radio Broadcast Stations in Local Markets*, MM Docket No. 01-317, January 27, 2003.

[498] Federal Communications Commission, Ninth Annual Report, In the Matter of Annual Assessment of the Status of Competition in the Market for the Delivery of Video Programming, MB docket No. 02-145 (December 31, 2002).

[499] Sinclair, Exhibit 15.

[500] Anon, "Comcast Rejects Antiwar TV Spots," *Washington Post,* January 29, 2003, p. A7.

[501] Since Baltimore is the 24th largest DMA and Milwaukee is the 34th, we can generally expect the vast majority of (smaller) DMAs to be more concentrated.

[502] Reid and King.

[503] Busterna, John, "The Cross Elasticity of Demand for National Newspaper Advertising," *Journalism Quarterly,* 64, 1987; Sentman, Mary Alice, "When the Newspaper Closes," *Journalism Quarterly,* 63, 1986.

[504] Nowak, Glen J., Glen T. Cameron, and Dean M. Krugman, "How Local Advertisers Choose and Use Advertising Media," *Journal of Advertising Research,* Nov/Dec 1993, find that targeting is the critical factor for local advertising. When interactive video media develop an effective targeting approach, an issue that is receiving significant attention, it could infringe more on the local revenue stream of radio and newspapers. The failure of the Internet to develop that local focus may account for the slow growth of advertising revenue garnered by that medium.

[505] Schwartzman, Andrew J. and Andrew Blau, *What's Local About Local Broadcasting* (Washington, DC: Media Access Project and the Benton Foundation, 1998), found virtually no local public affairs programming and what little there was aired at times that it was not likely to attract much of an audience.

[506] *Editor and Publisher International Yearbook,* various years. We have calculated the total number of owners by treating all groups listed in the yearbook as a single owner.

[507] Kanniss, Phyllis, *Making Local News* (Chicago: University of Chicago Press, 1991), p. 154.

[508] Kaniss, p. 159.

[509] Downie and Kaiser, p. 125.

[510] Comments of Gannett.

[511] Spavins, et al., Appendix C.

[512] Schwartz, Marius and Daniel R. Vincent, "The Television Ownership Cap and Localism: Reply Comments," February 3, 2003, Attached to *Reply Comments of the National Association of Broadcsters and the Network Affiliated Stations Alliance,* In the Matter of 2002 Biennial Regulatory Review – Review of the Commission's

Broadcast Ownership Rules and Other Rules Adopted Pursuant to Section 202 of the Telecommunications Act of 1996, Cross Ownership of Broadcast Stations and Newspapers, Rules and Policies Concerning Multiple Ownership of Radio Broadcast Stations in Local Markets, Definition of Radio Markets, MB Docket No. 02-277, MM Dockets 02-235, 01=317, 00-244, February 3, 2003. See also Schwartz, Marius and Daniel R. Vincent, "The Television Ownership Cap and Localism," February 3, 2003, Attached to *Reply Comments of the National Association of Broadcsters and the Network Affiliated Stations Alliance,* In the Matter of 2002 Biennial Regulatory Review – Review of the Commission's Broadcast Ownership Rules and Other Rules Adopted Pursuant to Section 202 of the Telecommunications Act of 1996, Cross Ownership of Broadcast Stations and Newspapers, Rules and Policies Concerning Multiple Ownership of Radio Broadcast Stations in Local Markets, Definition of Radio Markets, MB Docket No. 02-277, MM Dockets 02-235, 01=317, 00-244, January 2, 2003.

[513] Johnson, Thomas J., Mahmoud A. M. Braima, Jayanthi Sothirajah, "Measure for Measure: The Relationship Between Different Broadcast Types, Formats, Measures and Political Behaviors and Cognitions," *Journal of Broadcasting & Electronic Media,* 44, 2000, p. 45; see also Chaffee and Frank.

[514] Stempell, Hargrove and Bernt, p. 77, point out that the different demand may enable radio to continue its role even as the new media expand:

"Information seekers can listen to the radio while they are using the Internet. Obviously, they are not going to be paying full attention to both, but one involves seeing and the other involves listening, so both can be used at the same time."

[515] The Pew Research Center reports that fewer than half of all respondents to a mid-2000 survey listened to the radio for news regularly compared to two-thirds who read a newspaper and three-quarters who watched TV.

[516] Stone, New Operations.

[517] Bachman. The article notes that these music stations are adding news, but it takes the form of a minute an hour from national services, hardly representing either an independent or local voice.

[518] Schwartzman, Andrew J., "Viacom-CBS Merger: Media Competition and Consolidation in the New Millenium," *Federal Communications Law Journal* 52, 2000, p. 516.

[519] Brown and Williams, p. 10.

[520] DiCola, Peter and Kristin Thomson, *Radio Deregulation: Has It Served Citizens and Musicians* (Future of Music Coalition, 2002), pp. 37-39. Nineteen of 30 self reported formats are tight oligopolies, while 13 of 19 BIA formats are and 8 of 13 *Radio and Records* categories are.

[521] Self-reported CR4 is 64%; BIA CR4 is 61%; R&R CR4 is 65%.

[522] For these purposes, duopolies were defined as markets in which the two largest firms had market shares in excess of 40%/40% or 50%/30%.

[523] For these purposes, monopolies are defined as markets with a dominant firm with a market share of 65% or more.

[524] For purposes of this analysis, loose oligopolies were defined as markets with a four firm concentration ratio less than 60 percent.

[525] Stempell, Hargrove and Bernt, p. 75, present the results of a unique longitudinal study that allowed for careful elaboration of research findings. They emphatically reject the notion that the Internet is stealing attention from other media:

"Our finding seems consistent with the speculation from many quarters that the Internet has taken people away form other media. However, [it] tells a different story. Almost exactly half of our sample indicated they are using the Internet at least once a week, so we compared use of other media by those who use the Internet and those who do not. Users and non-users of the Internet both used network TV news to about the same extent. Those who use the Internet were slightly less likely to use local TV news, but the difference was not statistically significant. Those who use the Internet were more likely than those who don't use it to be regular newspaper readers and regular radio news listeners. So the Internet is not stealing readers from newspapers or listeners from radio."

[526] It can be argued that before the advent of TV, radio occupied this product space (see Tankel, Johnathan David and Wenmouth Williams, Jr., "The Economics of Contemporary Radio," *Media Economics: Theory and Practice*, 2nd ed., Alison Alexander, James Owers and Rod Carveth, Eds. (Lawrence Erlbaum Associates, 1998).

[527] A low estimate of AOL subscription revenues is $8 billion. Internet Advertising revenue is estimated in the range of $1-2 billion.

[528] Wall Street analysts praised the merger on these grounds; see Consumers Union, et al., *In the Matter of Application of America Online Inc. and Time Warner, Inc., for Transfer of Control*, Federal Communications Commission, Docket No. CS-00-30, April 26, 2000.

[529] Stempel, Hargrove and Bernt, p. 78:

"Clearly an information seeking device helps explain the greater newspaper use by Internet users, and this information-seeking behavior may run two ways. Internet users may turn to their newspapers or newspaper readers may go to the Internet for more information on a given topic. Either is possible sequentially as a supplemental information-seeking behavior. What is at least not practical is going from either the Internet or the newspaper to TV news to seek additional information on a given topic. TV news is not organized in a way that makes this practical or even possible in many cases."

[530] This discussion is based on Nielson ratings for May and June 2001.

[531] Cooper, 2001, reviews the evidence.

[532] A leading or dominant firm proviso was included in the 1982 Merger Guidelines but was subsequently dropped. Shepherd talks about firms with a 50 percent or more market share as leading firm and a source of concern.

[533] Jupiter Research, *Online Media Consolidation Offers No Argument for Media Deregulation*, 2001.

[534] Rutenberg, Jim "Fewer Media Owners, More Media Choices," *New York Times*, December 2, 2002, p. C-1.

[535] Sinclair v. FCC, p. 148.

[536] Id., p. 5.

[537] Federal Communications Commission, "Report and Order," In the Matter of 2002 Biennial Regulatory Review – Review of the Commission's Broadcast Ownership Rules and Other Rules Adopted Pursuant to Section 202 of the Telecommunications Act of 1996, Cross Ownership of Broadcast Stations and Newspapers, Rules and Policies Concerning Multiple Ownership of Radio Broadcast Stations in Local Markets, Definition of Radio Markets, MB Docket No. 02-277, MM Dockets 02-235, 01-317, 00-244 July 2, 2003, (hereafter, Order), at para. 391, states that "In order to provide our media ownership framework with an empirical footing, we developed a method for analyzing and measuring the availability of outlets that contribute to viewpoint diversity in local markets."

[538] Order, para. 442.

[539] Consumer Federation, et al, First Initial Comments, made this very point, p. 103, noting that

For economic analysis eyeballs are what should be counted, not stations. In other markets the number of competitors is not the central issue, it is their market share that matters. Recently, Microsoft asserted that there were seven different operating systems in the marketplace with over twenty thousand applications available and at least three different computing environments (handhelds, PCs and the Internet) and therefore Microsoft could not possible be a monopoly. Even a conservative appeals court resoundingly rejected that argument.

[540] The FCC asserts (para. 433) that "Based on an analysis of a large sample of markets of various sizes, the Diversity Index suggests that the vast majority of local media markets are healthy, well-functioning and diverse."

[541] Order, para. 422, "We believe that the overall impact of a medium is substantially determined by the physical attributes of its distribution technology, along with user preferences."

[542] Shepherd, William G., *The Economics of Industrial Organization* (Englewood Cliffs, NJ: Prentice Hall, 1985); Scherer, F. Michael and David Ross, *Industrial Market Structure and Economic Performance* (New York: Houghton Mifflin Company, 1990). Viscusi, W. Kip, John M. Vernon, and Joseph E. Harrington, Jr., *Economics of Regulation and Antitrust* (Cambridge: MIT Press, 2000).

[543] Order, para. 357.

[544] Order, para. 359.

[545] Order, para 360.

[546]Order, para. 366.

[547] Order, paras. 187… 420.

[548] Order, para. 230.

[549] Order, paras. 273-274.

[550] Consumer Federation of America, Consumers Union, Center for Digital Democracy and Media Access Project In the Matter of 2002 Biennial Regulatory Review – Review of the Commission's Broadcast Ownership Rules and Other Rules Adopted Pursuant to Section 202 of the Telecommunications Act of 1996, Cross Ownership of Broadcast Stations and Newspapers, Rules and Policies Concerning Multiple Ownership of Radio Broadcast Stations in Local Markets, Definition of Radio Markets, MB Docket No. 02-277, MM Dockets 02-235, 01=317, 00-244, January 2, 2003 (hereafter Second Initial Comments), noted that the coverage of newspapers is much smaller than the DMA.

[551] Order, paras. 429-430.

[552] Id., para. 167.

[553] Consumer Federation of America, et al., First Initial Comments, p.77.

[554] Cooper, Mark, Ex Parte presentation in Docket No. 02-277, March 24, 2003, Principles Of Market Structure Analysis For Media Based On Economic Fundamentals And The Unique Importance Of Civic Discourse; Ex Parte presentation in Docket No. 02-277, Promoting The Public Interest Through Media Ownership Limits: A Critique Of The FCC's Draft Order Based On Rigorous Market Structure Analysis And First Amendment Principles, May 2003.

[555] Order, para. 167.

[556] Id., para, 399, cites Media Ownership Working Group Study No. 3 to the effect that "the record contains evidence that most people can and do substitute among different media for news and information," Para. 423, claims that current usage is not a predictor of future usage.

[557] Consumer Federation of America, et al., Second Initial Comments.

[558] Order, paras. 197… 604.

[559] Id., paras. 195…608.

[560] Id., paras. 605, 602.

[561] Id., paras., 200, 196… 608.

[562] Id., paras., 198… 611.

[563] Cooper, Ex parte.

[564] Order, para., 420.

[565] Id., para., 183.

[566] Id., para., 32, 78.

[567] Id., para., 343, 344,

[568] Id., paras., 157-164.

[569] Id., , para. 198.

[570] Id., para. 198.

[571] Id., para. 420.

[572] Id., para. 353.

[673] Id., para. 410, "Unfortunately, we do not have data on this question

specifically with regard to local news and current affairs."

[574] Nielsen Media Research, *Consumer Survey,* question no. 10.

[575] Id., question no. 1.

[578] Id., question no. 2.

[577] Order, para. 407, citing PEW, *Internet Sapping Broadcast News Audience* (June 11, 2000), para. 417, citing Pew Center for the People and the Press, *Sources for Campaign News, Fewer Turn to Broadcast TV and Papers* (Apr. 27, 2003).

[578] Trenton newspapers are included in the New York analysis, when it is in the Philadelphia DMA. The New York analysis includes no Connecticut newspapers, when several are in the New York DMA.

[579] In this analysis I assume the number one TV station buys the number one newspaper and the maximum number of radio stations. The number two TV station forms a duopoly with the largest available TV station and acquires the maximum number of radio stations. The process continues until no more TV mergers are allowed.

[580] *U.S. v. Microsoft Corp.,* 253 F. 3d 34, 49 (D.C. Circ. 2001) (hereafter, *Appeals*), pp. 19-20. See also the *Conclusions of Law,* United States v. Microsoft Corp., 87 F. Supp. 2d 30, 44 (D.D.C. 2000) (hereafter, *Conclusions)* and the *Findings of Fact,* United States v. Microsoft Corp., 84 F. Supp. 2d 9 (D.D.C. 1999) (hereafter, *Findings,* citations are to paragraphs). Establishing the existence of a monopoly is central to the case, so both the District Court (*Findings,* 18-27, 30, 33-43, 54-55, 141, 166; *Conclusions,* 4,5, 6) and the Appeals Court (14-25) devote a great deal of attention to the monopoly and barriers to entry into the market..

[581] *Appeals,* p.1.

[582] Sinclar, p. 5.

Bibliography

Abate, Janet , 1999, *Inventing the Internet* (Cambridge: MIT Press).

Ackerman, Seth, 2002, *"Cable News Wars: Interviews* (PBS, Online Newshour, March)..

Ackerman, Seth, 2002, The Most Biased Name in News: Fox Channel's Extraordinary Right-wing Tilt." (FAIR, August)..

Adelstein, Jonathan S., 2003, "Big Macs and Big Media: The Decision to Supersize," The Media Institute, May 20.

Agre, Philip E., 2002, "Real-Time Politics: The Internet and the Political Process," *Information Society, 18.*

Albarran, Alan B. and John W. Dimmick, 1993, "An Assessment of Utility and Competitive Superiority in the Video Entertainment Industries," *Journal of Media Economics,* 6.

Alger, Dean E., 1996, *The Media and Politics* (New York: Wadsworth Publishing, 2nd edition)..

Alger, Dean E., 1998, *MEGAMEDIA: How Giant Corporations Dominate Mass Media, Distort Competition and Endanger Democracy* (Lanham, MD: Rowman & Littlefield)..

Altemeyer, 1997, Bob, *The Authoritarian Specter* (Cambridge, MA: Harvard University Press)..

American Civil Liberties Union v. Janet Reno, 929 F. Supp. 824 (E. D. Pa. 1996), 117 S. Ct. 2329 (1997)..

Ames, Sam, 2002, "Study: Broadband Fees Climbed in 2001," *Yahoo News,* January 18.

Anon, 1999 "Profile with Bob Wright: The Agony Before the Ecstasy of Digital TV," *Digital Television,* April.

Anon, 1999, "Profile with Bob Wright: The Agony Before the Ecstasy of Digital TV," *Digital Television,* April.

Anon, 2001, "Sinclair Issues a Challenge to FCC, Powell," *Electronic Media,* October 15..

Anon, 2001, "On Media Bias, Network Stars Are Rather Clueless," *Wall Street Journal,* May 24..

Anon, 2002, "The Fox News Presidential Advisor," *Washington Post,* November 21, p. A36.

Anon, 2003, "Comcast Rejects Antiwar TV Spots," in *The Washington Post,* January

29, p. A7.

Ansolabehere, Stephen and Shanto Iyengar, 1994, "Riding the Wave and Claiming Ownership Over Issues: The Joint Effect of Advertising and News Coverage in Campaigns," *Public Opinion Quarterly,* 58.

Associated Press v. United States, 326 U.S. 1, 20 (1945)..

Atkin, David J., Leo W. Jeffres and Kimberly A. Neuendorf, 1998, "Understanding Internet Adoption as Telecommunications Behavior," *Journal of Broadcasting and Electronic Media,* 42:4.

Aufderheide, Pat, 1990, "After the Fairness Doctrine: Controversial Broadcast Programming and the Public Interest," *Journal of Communication.*

Auletta, Ken, 1998, "The State of the American Newspaper," *American Journalism Review,* June.

Bachen, Christine, Allen Hammond, Laurie Mason, and Stephanie Craft, 1999, *Diversity of Programming in the Broadcast Spectrum: Is there a Link Between Owner Race or Ethnicity and News and Public Affairs Programming?* (Santa Clara University, December)..

Bachman, Kathy, 2001, "Music Outlets Tune in More News Reports," *MediaWeek,* October 29.

Bagdikian, Ben, 2000, *The Media Monopoly* (Boston: Beacon Press)..

Baker, C. Edwin, 1994, *Advertising and a Democratic Press* (Princeton: Princeton University Press)..

Baker, C. Edwin, 1997, "Giving the Audience What it Wants," *Ohio State Law Journal* 58.

Baker, C. Edwin, 2001, "Giving Up on Democracy: The Legal Regulation of Media Ownership," Attachment C, *Comments of Consumers Union, Consumer Federation of America, Civil Rights Forum, Center for Digital Democracy, Leadership Conference on Civil Rights and Media Access Project,* (before the Federal Communications Commission, *In the Matter of Cross Ownership of Broadcast Station and Newspaper/ Radio Cross-Ownership Waiver Policy,* MM Docket No. 01-235, 96-197, December 3)..

Baker, C. Edwin, 2001 , *Media, Markets and Democracy* (Cambridge: Cambridge University Press)..

Baker, Dean, 2002, *Democracy Unhinged: More Media Concentration Means Less Public Discourse, A Critique of the FCC Studies on Media Ownership* (Washington, DC: Department of Professional Employees, AFL-CIO, December)..

Barber, B. R., 1996, *Jihad v. McWorld* (New York: Ballantine).

Barker, David, C., 2002, *Rushed to Judgment* (New York: Columbia University Press)..

Bass, Jack, 2001, "Newspaper Monopoly," in Roberts, Gene, Thomas Kunkel, and

Charles Clayton (eds.), *Leaving Readers Behind* (Fayetteville: University of Arkansas Press)..

Bates, Benjamin, 1990, "Concentration in Local Television Markets," *Annual Convention of the Association For Education in Journalism and Mass Communications.*

Bates, B. J., 1993, "Station Trafficking in Radio: The Impact of Deregulation," *Journal of Broadcasting and Electronic Media.*

Bates, Benjamin, 1994, "Concentration in Local Television Markets," *Journal of Media Economics.*

Beam, Randal A., 1995, "What it Means to Be a Market-Oriented Newspaper," *Newspaper Research Journal,* 16.

Beam, Randal A., 2002, "Size of Corporate Parent Drives Market Orientation," *Newspaper Research Journal,* 23.

Becker, S. and H. C. Choi, 1987, "Media Use, Issue/Image Discrimination," *Communications Research.*

Belo, 2003, "Comments of Belo Corp., In the Matter of 2002 Biennial Regulatory Review – Review of the Commission's Broadcast Ownership Rules and Other Rules Adopted Pursuant to Section 202 of the Telecommunications Act of 1996, Cross Ownership of Broadcast Stations and Newspapers, Rules and Policies Concerning Multiple Ownership of Radio Broadcast Stations in Local Markets, Definition of Radio Markets, MB Docket No. 02-277, MM Dockets 02-235, 01-317, 00-244, January 2.

Benkler, Yochai, 1999, Free as the Air, *New York University Law Review,* 74.

Benkler, Yochai, 2000, "From Consumers to Users: Shifting the Deeper Structure of Regulation Toward Sustainable Commons and User Access," *Federal Communications Law Journal,* 56.

Benkler, Yochai, 2001, "The Battle Over the Institutional Ecosystem in the Digital Environment," *Communications of the ACM,* 44:2.

Benkler, Yochai, 2002, "Intellectual Property and the Organization of Information Production," *International Review of Law and Economics,* 22.

Benkler, Yochai, 2002, "Coase's Penguin, or Linux and the Nature of the Firm," *Yale Law Journal,* 112.

Bennett, W. Lance and Regina G. Lawrence, 1995, "News Icons and the Mainstreaming of Social Change," *Journal of Communication,* 45.

Bennett, W. Lance, 1988, *News: The Politics of Illusion* (New York: Longmans).

Benoit, William L. and Glenn Hansen, 2002, "Issue Adaptation of Presidential Television Spots and Debates to Primary and General Audiences," *Communications Research Reports,* 19.

Berkowitz, D., and D. Pritchard, 1989, "Political Knowledge and Communication Resources," *Journalism Quarterly,* 66.

Bernstein, J. M. and S. Lacy, 1992, "Contextual Coverage of Government by Local Television News," *Journalism Quarterly*.

Berry, Steven and Joel Waldfogel, 1999, *Mergers, Station Entry, and Programming Variety in Radio Broadcasting* (Washington, DC: National Bureau of Economic Research)..

Berry, Steven T. and Joel Waldfogel, 1999, "Public Radio in the United States: Does it Correct Market Failure or Cannibalize Commercial Stations?," *Journal of Public Economics, 71.*

BIA Financial, 2002, *Television Market Report* (Chantilly, VA: BIA Financial).

Bimber, Bruce, 1998, "The Internet and Political Transformation: Populism, Community and Accelerated Pluralism," *Polity, 31.*

Bishop, Ronald and Ernest A. Hakanen, 2002, "In the Public Interest? The State of Local Television Programming Fifteen Years After Deregulation," *Journal of Communications Inquiry, 26.*

Bissinger, Buzz, 2001, "The End of Innocence, in Roberts, Gene, Thomas Kunkel, and Charles Clayton (eds.), *Leaving Readers Behind* (Fayetteville: University of Arkansas Press).

Blumer, Jay G. and Carolyn Martin Spicer, 1990, "Prospects for Creativity in the New Television Marketplace: Evidence form Program-Makers," *Journal of Communications*, 40.

Blumler, Jay G., and Michael Gurevitch, 2001, "The New Media and Our Political Communication Discontents: Democratizing Cyberspace," *Information, Communications and Society, 4.*

Boardwatch Magazine, annual, "North American ISPs," midyear.

Boliek, Brooks, 2002, "FCC's Copps to Conduct Hearings," *Hollywood Reporter*, November 22.

Borjesson, Kristina, 2002, *Into the BUZZSAW* (Amherst, New York: Prometheus Books.

Bourdieu, Pierre, 1998, *On Television* (New York: The New Press).

Bradford, William D., 2000, "Discrimination in Capital Markets, Broadcast/Wireless Spectrum Service Providers and Auction Outcomes" (School of Business Administration, Univ. of Washington, December 5).

Braunstein, Yale, *2001, Market Power and Price Increases in the DSL Market* (July).

Banc of America, 2002, "Cable Industry Comment," *Banc of America Securities*, May 7.

Braunstein, Yale, *2001, Market Power and Price Increases in the DSL Market*, July .

Brazeal, LeAnn M, and William L. Benoit, 2001, "A Functional Analysis of Congressional Television Spots," *Communications Quarterly*, 49.

Brians, C. L. and M. P. Wattenberg, 1996, "Campaigns Issue Knowledge and Salience: Comparing Reception for TV Commercials, TV News, and Newspapers, *American Journal of Political* Science, 40.

Brown, Allan, 1996, "Public Service Broadcasting in Four Countries: Overview," *The Journal of Media Economics*, 9.

Brown, Duncan H., 1994," The Academy's Response to the Call for a Marketplace Approach to Broadcast Regulation," 11 *Critical Studies in Mass Communications*, 257.

Brown, Keith and George Williams, *Consolidation and Advertising Prices in Local Radio Markets* (Federal Communications Commission, Media Bureau Staff Research Paper, September 2002).

Bush, C. Anthony, 2002, *On the Substitutability of Local Newspaper, Radio, and Television Advertising in Local Business Sales* (Federal Communications Commission, Media Bureau Staff Research Paper, September).

Busterna, John, 1987, "The Cross Elasticity of Demand for National Newspaper Advertising," *Journalism Quarterly*, 64.

Busterna, J. C. 1988, "Television Ownership Effects on Programming and Idea Diversity: Baseline Data," *Journal of Media Economics*.

Busterna, John C., 1988, "Trends in Daily Newspaper Ownership," *Journalism Quarterly*, Winter.

Cable News Wars: Interviews, 2002, PBS, Online Newshour, March).

Carey, John, 1999, "The First Hundred Feet for Households: Consumer Adoption Patterns," in Deborah Hurley and James H. Keller (Eds.), *The First Hundred Feet* (Cambridge: MIT Press).

Carrol, Raymond, L., 1989, "Market Size and TV News Values," *Journalism Quarterly*.

Carroll, Raymond L. and C.A. Tuggle, 1997, "The World Outside: Local TV News Treatment of Imported News," *Journalism and Mass Communications Quarterly*, Spring.

Carter, Sue, Frederick Fico, and Joycelyn A. McCabe, 2002, "Partisan and Structural Balance in Local Television Election Coverage," *Journalism and Mass Communications Quarterly*, 79.

Chaffee, Steven and Stacy Frank, 1996, "How Americans Get Their Political Information: Print versus Broadcast News," *The Annals of the American Academy of Political and Social Science*, 546.

Chaffee, Steven, X. Zhao and G. Leshner, 1994, "Political Knowledge and the Campaign Media of 1992," *Communications Research*, 21.

Chan-Olmsted, Sylvia and Jung Suk Park, 2000, "From On-Air to Online World: Examining the Content and Structures of Broadcast TV Stations' Web Sites," *Journalism & Mass Communication Quarterly*, 77.

Ching, Frank, 1997, "Misreading Hong Kong," *Foreign Affairs*, May.

Chyi, Hsiang Iris and Dominic L. Lasora, "An Exploratory Study on the Market Relation Between Online and Print Newspapers," *The Journal of Media Economics*, 15, 2002.

Clarke, Pere and Eric Fredin, 1978, "Newspapers, Television and Political Reasoning," *Public Opinion Quarterly*, Summer.

Clear Channel, Inc., 2003, *Comments of Clear Channel*, In the Matter of 2002 Biennial Regulatory Review – Review of the Commission's Broadcast Ownership Rules and Other Rules Adopted Pursuant to Section 202 of the Telecommunications Act of 1996, Cross Ownership of Broadcast Stations and Newspapers, Rules and Policies Concerning Multiple Ownership of Radio Broadcast Stations in Local Markets, Definition of Radio Markets, MB Docket No. 02-277, MM Dockets 02-235, 01=317, 00-244, January 2.

Coalition for Program Diversity, 2003, "Supplemental Comments of Diversity and Diversity and Competition Supporters," *Cross-Ownership of Broadcast Stations and Newspapers, MM Docket No. 01-235; Newspaper/Radio Cross Ownership Waiver Policy*, MM No. 98-82; *Rules and Policies Concerning Multiple Ownership of Radio Broadcast Stations in Local Markets*, MM Docket No. 01-317, January 27.

Collins-Jarvis, L. A., 1993, "Gender Representation in an Electronic City Hall: Female Adoption of Santa Monica's PEN System," *Journal of Broadcasting and Electronic Media*.

Colon, Aly, 2000, "The Multimedia Newsroom," *Columbia Journalism Review*, June.

Coltrane, Scott and Melinda Messineo, 1990, "The Perpetuation of Subtle Prejudice: Race and Gender Imagery in the 1990's Television Advertising," *Sex Roles*, 42.

Congressional Research Service, 1988, *Minority Broadcast Station Ownership and Broadcast Programming: Is There a Nexus?* (Washington: Library of Congress).

Consumer Federation of America and Center for Media Education, , 1995, *Mergers and Deregulation on the Information Superhighway: The Public Takes a Dim View: Results of a National Opinion Poll*.

Consumer Federation of America, 2002, *Media Policy Goals Survey*, September.

Consumer Federation of America, Consumers Unions, Center for Media Education and the Media Access Project, "Initial Comments," In the Matter of 2002 Biennial Regulatory Review – Review of the Commission's Broadcast Ownership Rules and Other Rules Adopted Pursuant to Section 202 of the Telecommunications Act of 1996, Cross Ownership of Broadcast Stations and Newspapers, Rules and Policies Concerning Multiple Ownership of Radio Broadcast Stations in Local Markets, Definition of Radio Markets, MB Docket No. 02-277, MM

Dockets 02-235, 01-317, 00-244, January 2, 2003.

Consumer Federation of America, Consumers Unions, Center for Media Education and the Media Access Project, "Initial Comments," In the Matter of 2002 Biennial Regulatory Review – Review of the Commission's Broadcast Ownership Rules and Other Rules Adopted Pursuant to Section 202 of the Telecommunications Act of 1996, Cross Ownership of Broadcast Stations and Newspapers, Rules and Policies Concerning Multiple Ownership of Radio Broadcast Stations in Local Markets, Definition of Radio Markets, MB Docket No. 02-277, MM Dockets 02-235, 01-317, 00-244, February 3, 2003.

Consumers Union, et al., 2000, *In the Matter of Application of America Online Inc. and Time Warner, Inc., for Transfer of Control,* Federal Communications Commission, Docket No. CS-00-30, April 26.

Consumer Union, Consumer Federation of America, Center for Digital Democracy and Media Access Project, 2001, "Comments of the Consumer Federation of America, et al," *In the Matter of Cross Ownership of Broadcast Stations and Newspaper; Newspaper/Radio Cross-Ownership Waiver Policy* (MM Docket Nos. 01-235, 96-197), December 4..

Consumers Union, et al., 2002, "Reply Comments of Consumers Union, Consumer Federation of America, Media Access Project and Center For Digital Democracy," *In the Matter of Cross-Ownership of Broadcast Stations and Newspaper Newspaper/Radio Cross-Ownership Waiver Policy,* Federal Communications Commission, MM Dockets No. 01-235, 96-197, February 15.

Cook, Timothy E., 1998, *Governing with the New: The News Media as a Political Institution* (Chicago: University of Chicago Press).

Cooper, Mark, N., 1990, *Expanding the Information Age for the 1990s: A Pragmatic Consumer View* (Consumer Federation of America, American Association of Retired Persons, January 11).

Cooper, Mark, 1995, "Economic Concentration and Diversity in the Broadcast Media: Public Policy and Empirical Evidence (Washington, D.C.: Consumer Federation of America, Center for Media Education, November).

Cooper, Mark N., 2001, "Antitrust as Consumer Protection in the New Economy: Lessons from the Microsoft Case," *Hasting Law Journal,* 52, April.

Cooper, Mark, N., 2002, "Inequality in Digital Society," *Cardozo Journal On Media and the Arts,* 73.

Cooper, Mark, N., 2002, *Cable Mergers and Monopolies: Market Power Digital Media and Communications Networks* (Washington, DC: Economic Policy Institute).

Cooper, Mark, 2003, Ex Parte presentation in Docket No. 02-277,, Principles Of Market Structure Analysis For Media Based On Economic Fundamentals And The Unique Importance Of Civic Discourse, March 24.

Cooper, Mark, 2003, Ex Parte presentation in Docket No. 02-277, Promoting The Public Interest Through Media Ownership Limits: A Critique Of The FCC's

Draft Order Based On Rigorous Market Structure Analysis And First Amendment Principles, May 2003.

Copps, Michael J., 2003, "Statement of Commissioner Michael J. Copps, Dissenting," *Federal Communications Commission,* June 2.

Cornfield, Michael, 1994, "What is Historic About Television?", *Journal of Communications,* 21.

Coulson, D. C., "Impact of Ownership on Newspaper Quality," *Journalism Quarterly,* 1994.

Coulson, D. C. and Anne Hansen, 1995, "The Louisville Courier-Journal's News Content After Purchase by Gannet," *Journalism and Mass Communications Quarterly.*

Coulson, David C. and Stephen Lacy, 1998, "Newspapers and Joint Operating Agreements," in E. Sloan David and Emily Erickson Hoff, (eds.) *Contemporary Media Issues* (Northport: Vision Press).

Cranberg, Gilbert, Randall Bezanson, and John Soloski, 2001', *Taking Stock: Journalism and the Publicly Traded Newspaper Company* (Ames: Iowa State Press).

Crandall, Robert W., 2003, *The Economic Impact of Providing Service to Multiple Local Broadcast Stations Within a Single Geographic Market,"* attached to Sinclair Broadcasting, *Comments of Sinclair,* In the Matter of 2002 Biennial Regulatory Review – Review of the Commission's Broadcast Ownership Rules and Other Rules Adopted Pursuant to Section 202 of the Telecommunications Act of 1996, Cross Ownership of Broadcast Stations and Newspapers, Rules and Policies Concerning Multiple Ownership of Radio Broadcast Stations in Local Markets, Definition of Radio Markets, MB Docket No. 02-277, MM Dockets 02-235, 01=317, 00-244, January 2.

Crenson, Matthew A. and Benjamin Ginsberg, 2002, *Downsizing Democracy* (Baltimore, Johns Hopkins University Press).

Crigler, Ann N., (ed.), 1996, *The Psychology of Political Communications* (Ann Arbor: University of Michigan Press).

Cundy, D. T., 1986, "Political Commercials and Candidate Image," in Lynda Lee Kaid, (ed.) *New Perspectives in Political Advertising* (Carbondale, IL: Southern Illinois University Press).

Cunningham, Brendan C. and Peter J. Alexander, 2002, *A Theory of Broadcast Media Concentration and Commercial Advertising,* Federal Communications Commission, Staff Report 6, September.

Curran, James, 2002, *Media and Power* (London: Routledge).

Dahlberg, Lincoln, 2001, "The Internet and Democratic Discourse," *Information, Communications and Society,* 4.

Dahlgren, P. and C. Sparks (eds) , 1991, *Communications and Citizenship: Journalism and the Public Sphere* (London: Routledge).

David, E. Sloan and Emily Erickson Hoff, (eds.), 1998, *Contemporary Media Issues* (Northport: Vision Press).

Davidson, Paul, 2002, "FCC Could Alter Rules Affecting TV, Telephone, Airwaves," *USA Today*, February 6.

Davie, W. R. and J. S. Lee, 1993, "Television News Technology: Do More Sources Mean Less Diversity," *Journal of Broadcasting and Electronic Media*.

Davis, Charles and Stephanie Craft, 2000, "New Media Synergy: Emergence of Institutional Conflict of Interest," *Journal of Mass Media Ethics*, 15.

Deakin, Simon and Stephen Pratten, 1999, "Reinventing the Market? Competition and Regulatory Change in Broadcasting," *Journal of Law and Society*, 26.

Dejong, A. S. and B. J. Bates, 1991, "Channel Diversity in Cable Television," *Journal of Broadcasting and Electronic Media*.

DiCola, Peter and Kristin Thomson, 2002, *Radio Deregulation: Has It Served Citizens and Musicians* (Future of Music Coalition).

Digital Media Forum, 2000, *Survey Findings on Media Mergers and Internet Open Access*, September 13.

Dimmick, John B. 1997, "The Theory of the Niche and Spending on Mass Media: The Case of the Video Revolution," *Journal of Media Economics*, 10.

Diversity and Competition Supporters, 2003, "Supplemental Comments of Diversity and Competition Supporters," *Cross-Ownership of Broadcast Stations and Newspapers*, MM Docket No. 01-235; *Newspaper/Radio Cross Ownership Waiver Policy*, MM No. 98-82; *Rules and Policies Concerning Multiple Ownership of Radio Broadcast Stations in Local Markets*, MM Docket No. 01-317, January 27.

Dixon, Travis, L. and Daniel Linz, 2000, "Overrepresentation and Underrepresentation of African Americans and Latinos as Lawbreakers on Television News," *Communications Research*, 50.

Domke, David, David Perlmutter and Meg Spratt, 2002, "The Primes of Our Times? An Examination of the 'Power' of Visual Images," *Journalism*, 3.

Dorner, A., 2001, *Politainment* (Frankfurt/Main: Surhkamp).

Downie, Leonard, Jr., and Robert G. Kaiser, 2002, *The News About the News* (New York: Alfred A. Knopf).

Drew, D. and D. Weaver, 1991, "Voter Learning in the 1988 Presidential Election: Did the Media Matter?" *Journalism Quarterly*, 68.

Dubin, Jeff and Matthew L. Spitzer, 1995, "Testing Minority Preferences in Broadcasting," *Southern California Law Review*, 68.

Dugger, Ronald, 2000 "The Corporate Domination of Journalism," in William Serrin (ed.), *The Business of Journalism* (New York: New Press).

Dutton, H. W. et al. (ed.), 1987, *Wired Cities: Shaping the Future of Communications*

(Boston: K. G. Hall).

Economists, Inc., 1995, "An Economic Analysis of the Broadcast Television, National Ownership, Local Ownership, and Radio Cross-ownership Rules," before the Federal Communications Commission, *In Re: Review of the Commission's Regulations Governing Television Broadcasting*, MM Docket No. 91-221, May 17.

Editor And Publisher, various, *International Yearbook*, annual issues.

Edsall, Thomas B. and Mary D. and Edsall, 1991, *Chain Reaction: The Impact of Race, Rights and Taxes on American Politics* (New York: Norton).

Edwards, E. S. and N. Chomsky, 1988, *Manufacturing Consent* (New York: Pantheon).

Entema, J. and D.C. Whitney (eds.), 1994, *Audience Making: How the Media Create the Audience* (Thousand Oaks, CA: Sage Publications).

Entman, Robert M., and Andrew Rojecki, 2000, *The Black Image in the White Mind: Media and Race in America* (Chicago: University of Chicago Press).

Epstein, Mara, 2000, *Prime Time Power and Politics: The Financial Interest and Syndication Rules and Their Impact on the Structure and Practices of the Television Industry* (Ph.D. Dissertation, Department of Culture and Communications, New York University).

Epstein, Mara, 2002, *Program Diversity and the Program Selection Process on Broadcast Network Television* (Federal Communications Commission, Media Bureau Staff Research Paper, No. 5, September 2002).

Esslin, Martin, 2002, *The Age of Television* (New Brunswick: Transaction).

Evans, Akousa Barthewell, 1990, "Are Minority Preferences Necessary? Another Look at the Radio Broadcasting Industry," *Yale Law and Policy Review*, 8.

Fahri, Paul, 2003, "For Broadcast Media, Patriotism Pays: Consultants Tell, Radio, TV Clients that Protest Coverage Drives Viewers Off," *The Washington Post*, March 28, C2.

Fairchild, Charles, 1999, "Deterritorializing Radio: Deregulation and the Continuing Triumph of the Corporatist Perspective in the USA," *Media, Culture & Society*, 21.

FCC v. National Citizens Committee for Broadcasting, 436 U.S. 775 (1978).

Federal Communications Commission, 2001, "Further Notice of Proposed Rulemaking." *In the Matter of Implementation of Section 11 of the Cable Television Consumer Protection and Competition Act of 1992, Implementation of Cable Act Reform Provisions of the Telecommunications Act of 1996, The Commission's Cable Horizontal and Vertical Ownership Limits and Attribution Rules, Review of the Commission's Regulations Governing Attribution Of Broadcast and Cable/MDS Interests, Review of the Commission's Regulations and Policies Affecting Investment In the Broadcast Industry, Reexamination of the Commission's Cross-Interest Policy*, CS Docket No. 98-82, CS Docket No. 96-85, MM Docket No. 92-264, MM Docket No.

94-150, MM Docket No. 92-51, MM Docket No. 87-154, September 13.

Federal Communications Commission, 2002, In the Matter of 2002 Biennial Regulatory Review – Review of the Commission's Broadcast Ownership Rules and Other Rules Adopted Pursuant to Section 202 of the Telecommunications Act of 1996, Cross Ownership of Broadcast Stations and Newspapers, Rules and Policies Concerning Multiple Ownership of Radio Broadcast Stations in Local Markets, Definition of Radio Markets, MB Docket No. 02-277, MM Dockets 02-235, 01-317, 00-244, September 23.

Federal Communications Commission, 2003, "Report and Order," In the Matter of 2002 Biennial Regulatory Review – Review of the Commission's Broadcast Ownership Rules and Other Rules Adopted Pursuant to Section 202 of the Telecommunications Act of 1996, Cross Ownership of Broadcast Stations and Newspapers, Rules and Policies Concerning Multiple Ownership of Radio Broadcast Stations in Local Markets, Definition of Radio Markets, MB Docket No. 02-277, MM Dockets 02-235, 01-317, 00-244 (hereafter, Order), July 2.

Federal Communications Commission, various issues, *In the Matter of Annual Assessment of Competition in Markets for the Delivery of Video Programming*, Annual Report.

Federal Communications Commission, various issues, *High-Speed Services for Internet Access,*, Annual Report.

Federal Communications Commission, various issues, *Pricing Analysis,* Annual Report..

Ferrall, V. E., 1992, "The Impact of Television Deregulation," *Journal of Communications*.

Fife, M., 1979, The Impact of Minority Ownership on Broadcast Program Content: A Case Study of WGPR-TV's Local News Content (Washington: National Association of Broadcasters).

Fife, M., 1986, The Impact of Minority Ownership on Broadcast Program Content: A Multi-Market Study (Washington: National Association of Broadcasters).

Findings of Fact, United States v. Microsoft Corp., 84 F. Supp. 2d 9 (D.D.C. 1999).

Firestone, C. M. and J. M. Schement, 1995, *Toward an Information Bill of Rights and Responsibilities* (Washington, DC: Aspen Institute).

Fiss, Owen, 1987, "Essays Commemorating the One Hundredth Anniversary of the Harvard Law Review: Why the State?" *Harvard Law Review* 100.

Foot, Kirsten A. and Steven M. Schneider, 2002, "Online Action in Campaign 2000: An Exploratory Analysis of the U.S. Political Web Sphere," *Journal of Broadcasting and Electronic Media,* 46.

Fox, Entertainment Group, et al., 2003, *Comments of Fox Entertainment Group and Fox Television Stations, Inc., National Broadcasting Company, Inc. and Telemundo Group, Inc., and Viacom,* In the Matter of 2002 Biennial Regulatory Review –

Review of the Commission's Broadcast Ownership Rules and Other Rules Adopted Pursuant to Section 202 of the Telecommunications Act of 1996, Cross Ownership of Broadcast Stations and Newspapers, Rules and Policies Concerning Multiple Ownership of Radio Broadcast Stations in Local Markets, Definition of Radio Markets, MB Docket No. 02-277, MM Dockets 02-235, 01=317, 00-244, January 2.

Fox Television Stations, Inc., v. FCC, 280 F.3d 1027.

Frank, Robert H. and Phillip J. Cook, 1996, *The Winner-Take-All Society* (New York: Penguin).

Friedland, Lewis, 2002, "Statement" Attached to "Reply Comments of Consumer Federation," et al., *Cross Ownership of Broadcast Stations and Newspapers*, MM Docket No. 01-235, February 15.

Friedman, J. W., 1983, *Oligopoly Theory* (Cambridge: Cambridge University Press).

Fudenberg, Jean and Jean Tirole, 1989, "Noncooperative Game Theory for Industrial Organization: An Introduction and Overview," in Richard Schmalensee and Robert D. Willig, (eds.) *Handbook of Industrial Organization* (New York: North-Holland).

Gannet, 2003, *Initial Comments,* In the Matter of 2002 Biennial Regulatory Review – Review of the Commission's Broadcast Ownership Rules and Other Rules Adopted Pursuant to Section 202 of the Telecommunications Act of 1996, Cross Ownership of Broadcast Stations and Newspapers, Rules and Policies Concerning Multiple Ownership of Radio Broadcast Stations in Local Markets, Definition of Radio Markets, MB Docket No. 02-277, MM Dockets 02-235, 01=317, 00-244, January 2.

Gans, Herbert J., 2003, *Democracy and the News* (Oxford: Oxford University Press).

Garner, A., 1998, (ed.) *Investing in Diversity: Advancing Opportunities for Minorities in Media* (Washington, DC: Aspen Institute).

Gauger, T. G., 1989, "The Constitutionality of the FCC's Use of Race and Sex in Granting Broadcast Licenses," *Northwestern Law Review*.

Geiger, Weny, Jon Bruning and Jake Harwood, 2001, "Talk About TV: Television Viewer's Interpersonal Communications About Programming," *Communications Reports*, 14.

George, Lisa, 2001, *What's Fit to Print: The Effect of Ownership Concentration on Product Variety in Daily Newspaper Markets* (unpublished manuscript, University of Michigan).

Gibson, James L., 1999, *Social Networks, Civil Society, and the Prospects for Consolidating Russia's Democratic Transition* (St. Louis: Department of Political Science, Washington University).

Gilens, Martin, 1996, "Race Coding and White Opposition to Welfare," *American Political Science Review*, 90.

Gilens, Martin and Craig Hertzman, 1997, "Corporate Ownership and News Bias: Newspaper Coverage of the 1996 Telecommunications Act," Paper delivered at the Annual Meeting of the American Political Science Association, August.

Gilliam, Franklin D., Jr., and Shanto Iyengar, 2000, "Prime Suspects: The Influence of Local Television News on the Viewing Public," *American Journal of Political Science*, 44.

Gish, Pat and Tom Gish, 2000, "We Still Scream: The Perils and Pleasures of Running a Small-Town Newspaper," in William Serrin (ed.), *The Business of Journalism* (New York: New Press).

Gitlin, T., 1991, "Bits and Blips: Chunk News, Savvy Talk and the Bifurcation of American Politics," in P. Dahlgren and C. Sparks (eds), *Communications and Citizenship: Journalism and the Public Sphere* (London: Routledge).

Glasser, Theodore L., David S. Allen and S. Elizabeth Banks, 1989, "The Influence of Chain Ownership on News Play: A Case Study," *Journalism Quarterly*, 66.

Goldberg, Bernard, 2002, *Bias* (Washington, DC: Regnery).

Goodman, James, 2003, "Statement of James Goodman," presented at *Media Monopoly: Should the FCC Permit the Consolidation of Media Ownership*, New America Foundation, May 9.

Graber, Doris, 1997, *Mass Media and American Politics* (Washington, DC: Congressional Quarterly).

Graber, Doris, 2001, *Processing Politics* (Chicago: University of Chicago Press).

Grant, A. E., 1994, "The Promise Fulfilled? An Empirical Analysis of Program Diversity on Television," *The Journal of Media Economics*.

Gray, Herman, 1995, *Watching Race Television and the Struggle for Blackness* (Chicago: University of Chicago Press).

Grossman, Lawrence, 1996, *The Electronic Republic: Reshaping Democracy in the Information Age* (New York: Penguin).

Grove, Lloyd, 2002, "The Reliable Source," *The Washington Post*, November 19, p. C3.

Gunther, Albert C., 1998, "The Persuasive Press Inference: Effects of Mass Media on Perceived Public Opinion," *Communications Research*, October.

Gwiasda, Gregory W., 2001, "Network News Coverage of Campaign Advertisements: Media's Ability to Reinforce Campaign Messages," *American Politics Research*, 29.

Habermas, Jurgen, 1996, *Between Facts and Norms* (Cambridge: Polity).

Habermas, Jurgen, 1989, *The Structural Transformation of the Public* (Cambridge: Polity).

Hamilton, J. T., 1998, *Channeling Violence: the Economic Market for Violent Television*

Programming (Princeton: Princeton University Press).

Hansen, Glenn J. and William Benoit, 2002, "Presidential Television Advertising and Public Policy Priorities, 1952 –2002," *Communications Studies*, 53.

Hart, Jr., T. A. , 1988, "The Case for Minority Broadcast Ownership," *Gannet Center Journal*.

Hayuk, Ronald and Kevin Mattson (eds.) , 2002, *Democracy's Moment: Reforming the American Political System for the 21ˢᵗ Century* (Lanham, ME: Rowman and Littlefield).

Hearst Corporation, 2001, "Initial Comments of Hearst Argyle," *In the Matter of Cross Ownership of Broadcast Stations and Newspaper; Newspaper/Radio Cross-Ownership Waiver Policy* (MM Docket Nos. 01-235, 96-197), December 4.

Hearst Corporation, 2003, *Comments of Hearst,* In the Matter of 2002 Biennial Regulatory Review – Review of the Commission's Broadcast Ownership Rules and Other Rules Adopted Pursuant to Section 202 of the Telecommunications Act of 1996, Cross Ownership of Broadcast Stations and Newspapers, Rules and Policies Concerning Multiple Ownership of Radio Broadcast Stations in Local Markets, Definition of Radio Markets, MB Docket No. 02-277, MM Dockets 02-235, 01=317, 00-244, January 2.

Hellman, Heikki and Martii Soramaki, 1994, "Competition and Content in the U.S. Video Market," *Journal of Media Economics*, 7.

Hopkins, Wat W., 1996, "The Supreme Court Defines the Forum for Democratic Discourse," *Journalism and Mass Communications Quarterly*, Spring.

Hudson Eileen Davis, and Mark Fitzgerald, 201, "Capturing Audience Requires a Dragnet," *Editor and Publisher*, October 22.

Hurley Deborah, 1999, and James H. Keller (Eds.), *The First Hundred Feet* (Cambridge: MIT Press).

Information Policy Institute, 2003, In the Matter of 2002 Biennial Regulatory Review – Review of the Commission's Broadcast Ownership Rules and Other Rules Adopted Pursuant to Section 202 of the Telecommunications Act of 1996, Cross Ownership of Broadcast Stations and Newspapers, Rules and Policies Concerning Multiple Ownership of Radio Broadcast Stations in Local Markets, Definition of Radio Markets, MB Docket No. 02-277, MM Dockets 02-235, 01=317, 00-244, January 2.

Iosifides, Petros, Spring 1999, "Diversity versus Concentration in the Deregulated Mass Media," *Journalism and Mass Communications Quarterly*.

Iyengar, Shanto and Donald R. Kinder, 1987, *News That Matters: Television and American Opinion* (Chicago: University of Chicago Press).

Jamieson, Kathleen Hall, 1992, *Dirty Politics: Deception, Distraction and Democracy,* (New York: Oxford University Press).

Jenkins, K. , 1997, "Learning to Love those Expensive Campaigns," *U.S. News and*

World Report, 122.

Johnson, T. J. and W. Wanta, 1993, "Newspaper Circulation and Message Diversity in an Urban Market," *Mass Communications Review.*

Johnson, Thomas J., Mahmoud A. M. Braima, and Jayanthi Sothirajah, 1999, "Doing the Traditional Media Sidestep: Comparing Effects of the Internet and Other Nontraditional Media with Traditional Media in the 1996 Presidential Campaign," *Journalism & Mass Communication Quarterly,* 76.

Johnson, Thomas J., Mahmoud A. M. Braima, Jayanthi Sothirajah, 2000, "Measure for Measure: The Relationship Between Different Broadcast Types, Formats, Measures and Political Behaviors and Cognitions," *Journal of Broadcasting & Electronic Media,* 44.

Jones, Nicholas, 1995, *Soundbites and Spindoctors: How Politicians Manipulate the Media – and Visa Versa* (London: Cassel).

Jordan, Tim, 1998, *Cyberpower* (London: Routledge).

Joslyn, M. and S. Cecolli, 1996, "Attentiveness to Television News and Opinion Change in the Fall of 1992 Election Campaign," *Political Behavior,* 18.

Joslyn, R., 1981, "The Impact of Campaign Spot Advertising Ads, *Journalism Quarterly,* 7.

Journal Broadcasting Corporation, 2001, "Initial Comments of the Journal Broadcasting Corporation," *In the Matter of Cross Ownership of Broadcast Stations and Newspaper; Newspaper/Radio Cross-Ownership Waiver Policy* (MM Docket Nos. 01-235, 96-197), December 4.

Jupiter Research, *Online Media Consolidation Offers No Argument for Media Deregulation,* 2001.

Jurkowitz, Mark, 2002, "FCC Chairman: Consolidation Hasn't Inhibited Variety, Fairness," *Boston Globe,* April 17.

Just, M. R., A. N. Crigler and W. R. Neuman, 1996, "Cognitive and Affective Dimensions of Political Conceptualization," in A. N. Crigler (ed.) *The Psychology of Political Communications* (Ann Arbor: University of Michigan Press).

Just, Marion, R., Ann N. Crigler, Dean F. Alger, Timothy E. Cook, Montague Kern, and Darrell M. West, 1996, *Crosstalk: Citizens, Candidates and the Media in a Presidential Campaign* (Chicago: University of Chicago Press).

Just, Marion, Rosalind Levine and Kathleen Regan, 2001, "News for Sale: Half of Stations Report Sponsor Pressure on News Decision," *Columbia Journalism Review-Project for Excellence in Journalism,* November/December.

Kahn, Kim F. and Patrick J. Kenney, 1999, *The Spectacle of U.S. Senate Campaign* (Chicago: University of Chicago Press).

Kahn, Kim Fridkin and Patrick J. Kenny, 2002, "The Slant of News: How Editorial Endorsements Influence Campaign Coverage and Citizens' Views of Candi-

289

dates," *American Political Science Review*, 96.

Kaid, Lynda Lee (ed.) , 1986, *New Perspectives in Political Advertising* (Carbondale, IL: Southern Illinois University Press).

Kaid, L. L., et al. , 1993, "Television News and Presidential Campaigns: The Legitimation of Televised Political Advertising," *Social Science Quarterly*, 74.

Kamarch, Elaine Ciulla and Joseph S. Nye Jr. (eds.) , 2002., *governance.com* (Washington, DC: Brookings

Kaniss, Phyllis, 1991, *Making Local News* (Chicago: University of Chicago Press).

Karr, Albert, 1996, "Television News Tunes Out Airwaves Auction Battle," *Wall Street Journal*, May 1, p. B1.

Katz, J. , 1990, "Memo to Local News Directors," *Columbia Journalism Review*.

Kelly, Michael, 2002, "Left Everlasting," *The Washington Post*, December 11, p. A33.

Kelly, Michael, 2002, "Left Everlasting (Cont'd)," *The Washington Post*, December 18, p. A35.

Kern, M. , 1988, *30 Second Politics: Political Advertising in the Eighties* (New York: Praeger).

Kilborn, Richard W., 1998, "Shaping the Real," *European Journal of Communication*, 13.

Kim, Sei-Hill, Dietram A. Scheufele and James Shanahan, 2002, "Think About It This Way: Attribute Agenda Setting Function of the Press and the Public's Evaluation of a Local Issue," *Journalism and Mass Communications Quarterly*, 79.

Klieman, H., 1991, "Content Diversity and the FCC's Minority and Gender Licensing Policies," *Journal of Broadcasting and Electronic Media*.

Klugman, Paul, 2002, "In Media Res," *New York Times*, November 29, p. A-39.

Kovach, Bill and Tom Rosenstiel, 1999, *Warp Speed: America in the Age of Mixed Media* (New York: The Century Foundation Press).

Krosnick, J. A. and D. R. Kinder, 1990, "Altering the Foundation of Support for the President Through Priming," *American Political Science Review*, 84.

Krotoszynski, Ronald J., Jr. and A. Richard M. Blaiklock, 2000, "Enhancing the Spectrum: Media Power, Democracy, and the Marketplace of Ideas, *University of Illinois Law Review*.

Kubey, Robert, Mark Shifflet, Niranjala Weerakkody, and Stephen Ukeiley, 1995, "Demographic Diversity on Cable: Have the New Cable Channels Made a Difference in the Representation of Gender, Race, and Age?," *Journal of Broadcasting and Electronic Media*, 39.

Kunkel, Thomas, and Gene Roberts, 2001, "The Age of Corporate Newspapering; Leaving Readers Behind," *American Journalism Review*.

Kurtz, Howard, 2003, "The 'Beeb' in Their Bonnet; BBC Is Taking Flak for Its

Cover-All-Sides Approach," *Washington Post*, March 27.

Labaton, Stephen, 2002, "A Lone Voice for Regulation at the F.C.C.." *New York Times*, September 30.

Labaton, Stephen, "Give and Take, FCC Aims to Redraw Media Map," *New York Times*, May 11, 2003.

Lacy, Stephen, 1989, "A Model of Demand for News: Impact of Competition on Newspaper Content," *Journalism Quarterly*.

Lacy, Stephen, 1992, "The Financial Commitment Approaches to News Media Competition," *Journal of Media Economics*.

Lacy, Stephen and Todd F. Simon, 1993, "Competition in the Newspaper Industry," in Stephen Lacy and Todd F. Simon (eds.), *The Economics and Regulation of United States Newspapers* (Norwood, NJ: Ablex).

Lacy Stephen and Todd F. Simon, 1993, [eds] *The Economics and Regulation of United States Newspapers* (Norwood, NJ: Ablex).

Lacy, Stephen, Mary Alice Shaver and Charles St. Cyr, 1996, "The Effects of Public Ownership and Newspaper Competition on the Financial Performance of Newspaper Corporation: A Replication and Extension," *Journalism and Mass Communications Quarterly*, Summer.

Lacy, Stephen, David C. Coulson, and Charles St. Cyr, 1999, "The Impact of Beat Competition on City Hall Coverage," *Journalism & Mass Communication Quarterly*, 76.

Lacy, Shaver and St. Cyr; Gauger; Klieman; Collins-Jarvis; Lauzen, Martha M. and David Dozier, 1999, "Making a Difference in Prime Time: Women on Screen and Behind the Scenes in 1995-1996 Television Season, *Journal of Broadcasting and Electronic Media*, Winter.

Lauzen, Martha M. and David Dozier, 1999, "Making a Difference in Prime Time: Women on Screen and Behind the Scenes in 1995-1996 Television Season, *Journal of Broadcasting and Electronic Media*, Winter.

Layton, Charles, 1999, "What do Readers Really Want?", *American Journalism Review*, March.

Layton, Charles and Jennifer Dorroh, 2002, "Sad State," *American Journalism Review*, June.

Le Duc, D, ,1987, *Beyond Broadcasting* (New York: Longman).

Lebo, Harlan, 2001, Surveying *the Digital Future* (UCLA Center for Communication Policy, November).

Lemert, James B. 1991, William R. Elliott, and James M. Bernstein, *News Verdicts, the Debates, and Presidential Campaigns* (New York: Praeger).

Lessig, Lawrence, 1999, *Code and Other Laws of Cyberspace* (New York: Basic Books).

Lessig, Lawrence, 2001, *Code and The Future of Ideas: The Fate of the Commons in a Connected World* (New York: Random House).

Levin, H. J., 1971, "Program Duplication, Diversity, and Effective Viewer Choices: Some Empirical Findings," *American Economic Review.*

Levine, Peter, 2000, *The Internet* and *Civil Society,* Report from the University of Maryland, Institute for Philosophy & Public Policy, 20, 4, Fall. [369]

Levine, Peter, 2001, "The Internet and Civil Society: Dangers and Opportunities," *Information Impacts Magazine,* May .

Levine, Peter, 2002, "Can the Internet Rescue Democracy? Toward an On-Line Commons," in Ronald Hayuk and Kevin Mattson (eds.), *Democracy's Moment: Reforming the American Political System for the 21st Century* (Lanham, ME: Rowman and Littlefield).

Levine, Peter, 2002, *Building the Electronic Commons* (Democracy Collaborative, April 5).

Levy, Jonathan, 2002, Marcelino Ford-Livene and Anne Levin, *Broadcast Television: Survivor in a Sea of Competition,* Federal Communications Commission, OPP Working Paper, No. 37, September.

Levy, Pierre, 2001, *Cyberculture* (Minneapolis: University of Minnesota).

Li, Hairong and Janice L. Bukovac, 1999, "Cognitive Impact of Banner Ad Characteristics: an Experimental Study," *Journalism & Mass Communication Quarterly,* 76.

Liberty (National Council for Civil Liberties), 1999, *Liberating Cyberspace* (London: Pluto Press).

Lichter, S. Robert, 2002, "Depends on How You Define 'Bias'," *The Washington Post,* December 18, A19.

Lin, Carolyn A., 1995, "Diversity of Network Prime-Time Program Formats During the 1980s," *Journal of Media Economics,* 8.

Lin, Carolyn A., 1998, "Exploring Personal Computer Adoption Dynamics," *Journal of Broadcasting and Electronic Media,* 42:4.

Loudon, K. C., 1987, "Promise versus Performances of Cable," in Dutton, H. W. et al. (ed.), *Wired Cities: Shaping the Future of Communications* (Boston: K. G. Hall).

Lubunski, Richard, 1997, "The First Amendment at the Crossroads: Free Expression and New Media Technology," *Communications Law and Policy,* Spring.

Marcus, George E., John L. Sullivan, Elizabeth Theiss-Morse, and Sandra L. Wood, 1995, *With Malice Toward Some: How People Make Civil Liberties Judgments* (New York: Cambridge University Press).

Martinez, Evan, Yolanda Polo and Carlos Flavian, 1998, "The Acceptance and Diffusion of New Consumer Durables: Differences Between First and Last Adopters," *Journal of Consumer Marketing,* 15:4.

Mason, Laurie, Christine M. Bachen and Stephanie L. Craft, 2001, "Support for FCC Minority Ownership Policy: How Broadcast Station Owner Race or Ethnicity Affects News and Public Affairs Programming Diversity," *Comm. Law Policy*, 6.

Massimo, Motta and Michele Polo, 1997, "Concentration and Public Policies in the Broadcasting Industry," *Communications Law and Policy*, Spring.

Mathews, Anna Wilde, 2002, "A Giant Radio Chain is Perfecting the Art of Seeming Local," *Wall Street Journal*, February 25, p. A1.

Matos, F., 1988, *Information Service Report* (Washington, D.C.: National Telecommunications Information Administration, August).

Maxwell, Kim, 1999, *Residential Broadband: An Insider's Guide to the Battle for the Last Mile* (New York: John Wiley).

McChesney, Robert, 2000, *Rich Media, Poor Democracy: Communication Politics in Dubious Times* (New York: New Press)

McChesney Robert W. and John Nichols, 2002, *Our Media, Not Theirs* (New York: Seven Stories Press).

McCombs, Maxwell E. and Donald Shaw, 1972, "The Agenda-Setting Function of the Mass Media," *Public Opinion Quarterly*, 36.

McConnell, Bill and Susanne Ault, 2001, "Fox TV's Strategy: Two by Two, Duopolies are Key to the Company's Goal of Becoming a Major Local Presence," *Broadcasting and Cable*, July 30.

McConnell, Bill, 2001, "The National Acquirers: Whether Better for News or Fatter Profits, Media Companies want in on TV/Newspaper Cross-ownership," *Broadcasting and Cable*, December 10.

McConnell, Bill, 2003, "Deregulation Foes Plan to Fight On," *Broadcasting and Cable*, June 2.

McKean, M. L. and V. A. Stone, 1991, "Why Stations Don't Do News," *Communicator*.

McLeod, Douglas M. , 1995, "Communicating Deviance: The Effects of Television News Coverage of Social Protests," *Journal of Broadcasting & Electronic Media*, 39.

McLeod, Jack M., Dietram A. Scheufele, and Patricia Moy, 1999, "Community, Communications, and Participation: The Role of Mass Media and Interpersonal Discussion in Local Political Participation," *Political Communication*, 16.

McManus, J., 1990, "Local News: Not a Pretty Picture," *Columbia Journalism Review*.

McManus, J., 1991, "How Objective is Local Television News?", *Mass Communications Review*.

McManus, J., 1992, "What Kind of a Commodity is News?", *Communications Research*.

Media General, 2001, Comments of Media General, *In the Matter of Cross Ownership of Broadcast Stations and Newspaper; Newspaper/Radio Cross-Ownership Waiver Policy* (MM Docket Nos. 01-235, 96-197), December 4.

Media Studies Center Survey, 1999, University of Connecticut, Jan. 18.

Meeks, Carol B. and Anne L. Sweaney, 1992, "Consumer's Willingness to Innovate: Ownership of Microwaves, Computers and Entertainment Products," *Journal of Consumer Studies and Home Economics*, 16.

Mendelberg, Tali, 1997, "Executing Hortons: Racial Crime in the 1988 Presidential Campaign," *Public Opinion Quarterly*, 61.

Mendelberg, Tali, 2001, *The Race Card: Campaign Strategy, Implicit Messages and the Norm of Equality* (Princeton: University Press, Princeton).

Menezes, Bill, 1999, "Replay, TiVo Get Cash for Consumer Push," *Multichannel News*, April 5.

Meyer, Thomas, 2002, *Media Democracy.* (Cambridge: Polity Press).

Meyerowitz, J., 1985, No *Sense of Place: The Effect of Electronic Media on Social Behavior* (New York: Oxford).

Miller, Steven E., 1998, *Civilizing Cyberspace* (New York: ACM Press).

Mitchell, Bill, 2000, "Media Collaborations," *Broadcasting and Cable*, April 10.

Morgan Stanley Dean Whitter Reynolds, *Digital Decade* (New York, 1999).

Mosco, Vincent, 1989, *The Pay-Per Society: Computers & Communications in the Information Age* (Norwood, NJ: Ablex).

Moses, Lucia, 2000, "TV or not TV? Few Newspapers are Camera Shy, But Sometimes Two Into One Just Doesn't Go," *Editor and Cable*, August 21.

Moy, Patricia, Michael Pfau, and LeeAnn Kahlor, 1999, "Media Use and Public Confidence in Democratic Institutions," *Journal of Broadcasting & Electronic Media*, 43.

Moy, Patricia and Dietram A. Scheufele, 2000, "Media Effects on Political and Social Trust," *Journalism and Mass Communications Quarterly*, 77.

Mulder, R., 1979, "The Effects of Televised Political Ads in the 1995 Chicago Mayoral Election," *Journalism Quarterly*, 56.

Mundy, Alicia, 1999, "The Price of Freedom," *MediaWeek*, March 29.

Mutz, Diana C., 2002, "Cross-cutting Social Networks: Testing Democratic Theory in Practice," American *Political Science Review*, 96.

Napoli, Philip, 2002, "Audience Valuation and Minority Media: An Analysis of the Determinants of the Value of Radio Audiences," *Journal of Broadcasting and Electronic Media*, 46.

National Association of Broadcasters, 2002, "Early Submission of the National Association of Broadcasters and the Network Affiliated Stations Alliance," *In the*

Matter of 2002 Biennial Regulatory Review – Review of the Commissions' Broadcast Ownership Rules and Other Rules Adopted Pursuant to Section 202 of the Telecommunications Act of 1996, Cross Ownership of Broadcast Stations and Newspapers, Rules and Policies Concerning Multiple Ownership of Radio Broadcast Stations in Local Markets, Definition of Radio Markets, MB Docket NO. 02-277; MM Docket Nos. 01-235, 01-317, 00-244, December 9.

National Broadcasting Co., Inc. et al. v. United States, et. al., 319 U.S. 190 (1943) 70.

National Telecommunications Information Administration, 2002, *A Nation Online* (U.S. Department of Commerce).

Neiman Reports, 1999, *The Business of News, the News About Business,* Neiman Reports, Summer.

Netanal, Neil, 2001, *Is the Commercial Mass Media Necessary, or Even Desirable, for Liberal Democracy,* TPRC Conference on Information, Communications, and Internet Policy, October.

Network Affiliated Stations Alliance, 2001, "Petition for Inquiry into Network Practices, "(Federal Communications Commission, March 8).

Neuendorf, Kimberly A., David Atkin and Leo W. Jeffres, 1998, "Understanding Adopters of Audio Information Innovations," *Journal of Broadcasting and Electronic Media,* 42:4.

Nielsen Media Research, 2002, *Consumer Survey on Media Usage* (Federal Communications Commission, Media Bureau Staff Research Paper, September).

Norris, Pippa, 2002, "Revolution, What Revolution? The Internet and U.S. Elections, 1992-2000," in Ellaine Ciulla Kamarch and Joseph S. Nye Jr. (eds.), *governance.com* (Washington, DC: Brookings).

Nowak, Glen J., Glen T. Cameron, and Dean M. Krugman, 1993, "How Local Advertisers Choose and Use Advertising Media," *Journal of Advertising Research,* Nov/Dec.

Nunn, Clyde Z., Harry J. Crockett and J. Allen Williams, 1978, *Tolerance for Nonconformity* (San Francisco: Josey-Bass).

O'Keefe, G. J., 1980, "Political Malaise and Reliance on the Media," *Journalism Quarterly.*

O'Loughlin, Ben, 2001, "The Political Implications of Digital Innovations: Trade-Offs of Democracy and Liberty in the Developed World," *Information, Communications and Society,* 4.

O'Sullivan, Patrick B., 2000, "The Nexus Between Broadcast Licensing Gender Preferences and Programming Diversity: What Does the Social Scientific Evidence Say?" (Santa Barbara: Department of Communication, U.C. Santa Barbara, CA).

Oberholzer-Gee, Felix and Joel Waldfogel, 2001, *Electoral Acceleration: The Effect of Minority Population on Minority Voter Turnout,* NBER Working Paper 8252 (Cambridge, MA: National Bureau of Economic Research).

Oberholzer-Gee, Felix and Joel Waldfogel, 2001, *Tiebout Acceleration: Political Participation in Heterogeneous Jurisdictions*, NBER).

Office of Technology Policy, 2002, *Understanding Broadband Demand* (Washington, DC: U.S. Department of Commerce, September 23).

Ofori, K. A., 1999, *When Being No. 1 is not Enough: The Impact of Advertising Practices on Minority-Owned and Minority-Targeted Broadcast Stations* (Civil Rights Forum on Communications Policy

Olson, Kathryn, 1994, "Exploiting the Tension between the New Media's "Objective" and Adversarial Roles: The Role Imbalance Attach and its Use of the Implied Audience," *Communications Quarterly* 42:1.

Owen, Bruce and Steven Wildman, 1992, *Video Economics* (Cambridge, MA: Harvard University Press).

Owen, Bruce M. and Michael G. Baumann, 2003, "Economic Study E; Concentration Among National Purchasers of Video Entertainment Programming," *Comments of Fox Entertainment Group and Fox Television Stations, Inc., National Broadcasting Company, Inc. and Telemundo Group, Inc., and Viacom,* In the Matter of 2002 Biennial Regulatory Review – Review of the Commission's Broadcast Ownership Rules and Other Rules Adopted Pursuant to Section 202 of the Telecommunications Act of 1996, Cross Ownership of Broadcast Stations and Newspapers, Rules and Policies Concerning Multiple Ownership of Radio Broadcast Stations in Local Markets, Definition of Radio Markets, MB Docket No. 02-277, MM Dockets 02-235, 01-317, 00-244, January 2, 2003.

Owen, Bruce and Kent W. Mikkelsen, 2003, "Counting Outlets and Owners in Milwaukee: An Illustrative Example," Economic Study F: Attachment to *Comments of Fox Entertainment Group and Fox Television Stations, Inc., National Broadcasting Company, Inc. and Telemundo Group, Inc., and Viacom,* In the Matter of 2002 Biennial Regulatory Review – Review of the Commission's Broadcast Ownership Rules and Other Rules Adopted Pursuant to Section 202 of the Telecommunications Act of 1996, Cross Ownership of Broadcast Stations and Newspapers, Rules and Policies Concerning Multiple Ownership of Radio Broadcast Stations in Local Markets, Definition of Radio Markets, MB Docket No. 02-277, MM Dockets 02-235, 01-317, 00-244, January 2.

Owen, Bruce M., 2003, "Statement on Media Ownership Rules," Attachment to *Comments of Fox Entertainment Group and Fox Television Stations, Inc., National Broadcasting Company, Inc. and Telemundo Group, Inc., and Viacom,* In the Matter of 2002 Biennial Regulatory Review – Review of the Commission's Broadcast Ownership Rules and Other Rules Adopted Pursuant to Section 202 of the Telecommunications Act of 1996, Cross Ownership of Broadcast Stations and Newspapers, Rules and Policies Concerning Multiple Ownership of Radio Broadcast Stations in Local Markets, Definition of Radio Markets, MB Docket No. 02-277, MM Dockets 02-235, 01-317, 00-244, January 2.

Owen, Bruce, Kent W. Mikkelsen and Allison Ivory, 2003, "News and Public Affairs Offered by the Four Top-Ranked Versus Lower-Ranked Television Stations," Economic Study A, Attachment to *Comments of Fox Entertainment Group and Fox Television Stations, Inc., National Broadcasting Company, Inc. and Telemundo Group, Inc., and Viacom,* In the Matter of 2002 Biennial Regulatory Review – Review of the Commission's Broadcast Ownership Rules and Other Rules Adopted Pursuant to Section 202 of the Telecommunications Act of 1996, Cross Ownership of Broadcast Stations and Newspapers, Rules and Policies Concerning Multiple Ownership of Radio Broadcast Stations in Local Markets, Definition of Radio Markets, MB Docket No. 02-277, MM Dockets 02-235, 01-17, 00-244, January 2.

Page, Benjamin I., 1996, *Who Deliberates* (Chicago: University of Chicago Press).

Paletz, D. L. and R. M. Entmen, 1981, *Media, Power, Politics,* (New York: Free Press).

Paletz, David L., 1999, *The Media in American Politics: Contents and Consequences* (New York: Longman).

Pan, Z. and G. M. Kosicki, 1997, "Priming and Media Impact on the Evaluation the President's Performance," *Communications Research,* 24.

Patterson, T. E., and McClure, R. D., 1976, *The Unseeing Eye: The Myth of Television Power in National Politics* (New York: Putnam Books).

Patterson, Thomas E., 2002, *The Vanishing Voter* (New York: Alfred A. Knopf).

Peffley, Mark, Todd Shields and Bruce Williams, 1996, "The Intersection of Race and Television," *Political Communications,* 13.

Pew Center for the People and the Press, 2000, *Sources for Campaign News, Fewer Turn to Broadcast TV and Papers,* Feb.

Pew Research Center, 2000, "Internet Sapping Broadcast News Audience," June 11.

Pew Center for the People and the Press, 20003, *Modest Increase in Internet Use for Campaign 2002,* Jan.

Pew Center for the People and the Press, 2003, *Sources for Campaign News, Fewer Turn to Broadcast TV and Papers,* Apr. 2.

People for Better TV, 1999, *Project on Media Ownership, People for Better TV, Findings of a National Survey,* Lake Snell Perry & Associates, May.

Pfau, M. , 1990, "A Channel Approach to Television Influence," *Journal of Broadcasting and Electronic Media.*

Pfau, M., and H. C. Kenski, 1990, *Attack Politics* (New York: Praeger).

Phillips, Peter and Project Censored, 2002, *Censored 2003* (New York: Seven Stories).

Ploskina, Brian and Dana Coffield, 2001, "Regional Bells Ringing Up Higher DSL

Rates," *Interactive Week,* February 18.

Postman, Neil, 1985, *Amusing Ourselves to Death: Public Discourse in the Age of Show Business* (New York: Viking).

Powell, Michael K., 1998, *The Public Interest Standard: A New Regulator's Search for Enlightenment,* 17th Annual Legal Forum on Communications Law, Las Vegas, April 5.

Powell, Michael, K., 1999, "Law in the Internet Age," D.C. Bar Association Computer and Telecommunications Law Section and the Federal Communications Bar Association, September 29.

Powell, Michael K., 2000, "The Great Digital Broadband Migration," Progress and Freedom Foundation, December 8.

Powell, Michael K., 2001, "Digital Broadband Migration: Part II," Press Conference, October 32.

Price, Monroe E., 1999, "Public Broadcasting and the Crisis of Corporate Governance," *Cardozo Arts & Entertainment,* 17.

Pritchard, David, 2002, *Viewpoint Diversity in Cross-Owned Newspapers and Television Stations: A Study of News Coverage of the 2000 Presidential Campaign* (Federal Communications Commission, September).

Project for Excellence in Journalism, 2003, *Does Ownership Matter in Local Television News: A Five-Year Study of Ownership and Quality,* February 17.

Project on Media Ownership, People for Better TV, *Findings of a National Survey,* Lake Snell Perry & Associates, May 1999.

Quincy Illinois Visitors Guide, 2001 edition.

Rabasca, Lisa, 2001, "Benefits, Costs and Convergence," *Presstime.*

Ray, W. B., 1990, "FCC: The Ups and Downs of Radio-TV Regulation (Iowa: Iowa State University Press

Red Lion Broadcasting v. FCC, 395 US 367 (1969).

Reid, Leonard N. and Karen Whitehill King, 2000, "A Demand-Side View of Media Substitutability in National Advertising: A Study of Advertiser Opinions about Traditional Media Options," *Journalism & Mass Communication Quarterly,* 77.

Rifkin, Jeremy, 2000, *The Age of Access* (New York: J.P. Tarcher).

Riskin, Victoria, 2003, President of Writers Guild of America, West, *Remarks at FCC EnBanc Hearing, Richmond, VA* (Feb. 27).

Roberts, Gene and Thomas Kunkel (eds.), 2002, *Breach of Faith: A Crisis of Coverage in the Age of Corporate Newspapering* (Fayetteville: University of Arkansas Press).

Roberts, Gene, 1996, "Corporatism vs. Journalism," *The Press-Enterprise Lecture Series,* 31, February 12.

Roberts, Gene, Thomas Kunkel, and Charles Clayton (eds.) , 2001, *Leaving Readers Behind* (Fayetteville: University of Arkansas Press).

Roberts, Gene, Thomas Kunkel, and Charles Clayton, 2001, "Leaving Readers Behind," in Roberts, Gene, Thomas Kunkel, and Charles Clayton (eds.), *Leaving Readers Behind* (Fayetteville: University of Arkansas Press).

Roberts, Gene, Thomas Kunkel, and Charles Clayton (eds.), 2001, *Leaving Readers Behind* (Fayetteville: University of Arkansas Press).

Roberts, Scott, Jane Frenette and Dione Stearns, *A Comparison of Media Outlets and Owners for Ten Selected Markets (1960, 1980, 2000)* (Federal Communications Commission, Media Bureau Staff Research Paper, 2002).

Robinson, J. P. and D. K. Davis, 1990, "Television News and the Informed Public: An Information Process Approach," *Journal of Communication*.

Robinson, John P. and Mark R. Levy, 1996, "New Media Use and the Informed Public: A 1990s Update," *Journal of Communications*, Spring.

Roper, 1990, *America's Watching: 30th Anniversary 1959-1989*.

Roper Reports, 2001, 01-2.

Roper Reports, 2002, *Consuming More News and Believing It Less*, February 28.

Rowse, Edward, 1975, *Slanted News: A Case Study of the Nixon and Stevenson Fund Stories* (Boston; Beacon).

Rowse, Arthur E., 2000, *Drive-By Journalism* (Monroe, ME: Common Courage Press).

Rubinovitz, R., 1991, *Market Power and Price Increases for Basic Cable Service Since Deregulation*, (Economic Analysis Regulatory Group, Department of Justice, August 6).

Rutenberg, Jim 2002, "Fewer Media Owners, More Media Choices," *New York Times*, December 2.

Saco, Diana, 2002, *Cybering Democracy* (Minneapolis: University of Minnesota Press).

Sakar, Jayati, 1998, "Technological Diffusion: Alternative Theories and Historical Evidence," *Journal of Economic Surveys*, 12:2.

Savage, Scott, 1997, Gary Madden and Michael Simpson, "Broadband Delivery of Educational Services: A Study of Subscription Intentions in Australian Provincial Centers," *Journal of Media Economics*, 10:1.

Scherer, F. Michael and David Ross, 1990, *Industrial Market Structure and Economic Performance* (New York: Houghton Mifflin Company).

Scheufele, Dietram A., 2000, "Agenda-setting, Priming and Framing Revisited: Another Look at Cognitive Effects of Political Communications," *Mass Communications & Society*, 3.

Scheufele, Dietram A., 2002, "Examining Differential Gains from Mass Media and Their Implications for Participatory Behavior," *Communications Research,* 29.

Schmalensee, Richard and Robert D. Willig (eds.), 1989, *Handbook of Industrial Organization* (New York: North-Holland).

Schumpeter, Joseph, 1976, *Capitalism, Socialism and Democracy,* 3rd. ed., (New York: Harper Torchbooks).

Schwartz, Marius and Daniel R. Vincent, 2003, "The Television Ownership Cap and Localism," February 3, 2003, Attached to *Reply Comments of the National Association of Broadcsters and the Network Affiliated Stations Alliance,* In the Matter of 2002 Biennial Regulatory Review – Review of the Commission's Broadcast Ownership Rules and Other Rules Adopted Pursuant to Section 202 of the Telecommunications Act of 1996, Cross Ownership of Broadcast Stations and Newspapers, Rules and Policies Concerning Multiple Ownership of Radio Broadcast Stations in Local Markets, Definition of Radio Markets, MB Docket No. 02-277, MM Dockets 02-235, 01=317, 00-244, January 2.

Schwartz, Marius and Daniel R. Vincent, 2003, "The Television Ownership Cap and Localism: Reply Comments," February 3, 2003, Attached to *Reply Comments of the National Association of Broadcsters and the Network Affiliated Stations Alliance,* In the Matter of 2002 Biennial Regulatory Review – Review of the Commission's Broadcast Ownership Rules and Other Rules Adopted Pursuant to Section 202 of the Telecommunications Act of 1996, Cross Ownership of Broadcast Stations and Newspapers, Rules and Policies Concerning Multiple Ownership of Radio Broadcast Stations in Local Markets, Definition of Radio Markets, MB Docket No. 02-277, MM Dockets 02-235, 01=317, 00-244, February 3.

Schwartzman, Andrew J. and Andrew Blau, 1998, *What's Local About Local Broadcasting* (Washington, DC: Media Access Project and the Benton Foundation).

Schwartzman, Andrew J., 1998, "Viacom-CBS Merger: Media Competition and Consolidation in the New Millenium," *Federal Communications Law Journal* 52.

Scott, D. K. and R. H. Gopbetz, 2000, "Hard News/Soft News Content of the National Broadcast Networks: 1972-1987," *Journalism Quarterly,* 1992.

Seattle Post Intelligenser, PI-Daily Poll, May, 2003.

Sentelle, Circuit Judge, 2002, Concurring and Dissenting in Part," *Sinclair Broadcast Group, Inc. v. Federal Communications Commission,* April 2.

Sentman, Mary Alice, 1986, "When the Newspaper Closes," *Journalism Quarterly,* 63.

Sezter, Florence, and Jonathan Levy, 1991, *Broadcast Television in Multichannel Marketplace,* (Office of Plans and Policy, Federal Communications Commission, June).

Shah, Rajiv, J. Jay and P. Kesan, *The Role of Institutions in the Design of Communications Technologies,* Telecommunications Policy Research Conference, Conference on Information, Communications, and Internet Policy, October 2001.

Shepherd, William G., 1985,, *The Economics of Industrial Organization* (Englewood Cliffs, NJ: Prentice Hall).

Shipp, E. R., 2000, "Excuses, Excuses: How Editors and Reporters Justify Ignoring Stories," in William Serrin (ed.), *The Business of Journalism* (New York: New Press, 2000).

Sinclair Broadcast Group, Inc. v. Federal Communications Commission, D.C.C., No. 01-1079, April 2 .

Simon, Bernard, 2000, "Some Bet the Future of Broadband Belongs to Regional Bells, Not Cable," *New York Times*, July.

Simon, J., W. J. Primeaux and E. Rice, "The Price Effects of Monopoly Ownership in Newspapers," *Antitrust Bulletin*, 1986

Sinclair, Jon R., 1995, "Reforming Television's Role in American Political Campaigns: Rationale for the Elimination of Paid Political Advertisements," *Communications and the Law*, March.

Sine, N. M., et al., 1990, "Current Issues in Cable Television: A Re-balancing to Protect the Consumer," *Cardozo Arts & Entertainment Law Journal*.

Slattery, K. L. and E. A. Kakanen, 1994, "Sensationalism Versus Public Affairs Content of Local TV News: Pennsylvania Revisited," *Journal of Broadcasting and Electronic Media*.

Slattery, Karen L., Ernest A. Hakanen and Mark Doremus, 1996 ,"The Expression of Localism: Local TV News Coverage in the New Video Marketplace," *Journal of Broadcasting and Electronic Media*, 40.

Snider, James H., and Benjamin I. Page, 1997, "Does Media Ownership Affect Media Stands? The Case of the Telecommunications Act of 1996," Paper delivered at the Annual Meeting of the Midwest Political Science Association, April.

Soloski, John, 1979, "Economics and Management: The Real Influence of Newspaper Groups," *Newspaper Research Journal*, 1.

Spangler, Todd, 2002, "Crossing the Broadband Divide," *PC Magazine*, February 12.

Sparks, Glenn G., Marianne Pellechia, and Chris Irvine, 1998, "Does Television News About UFOs Affect Viewers' UFO Beliefs?: An Experimental Investigation," *Communication Quarterly*, 46.

Sparrow, Bartholomew H., 1999, *Uncertain Guardians: The News Media as A Political Institution* (Baltimore, Johns Hopkins).

Spavins, Thomas C., et al., *The Measurement of Local Television News and Public Affairs Programs* (Federal Communication Commission, Media Bureau Staff Research Paper, No. 7, September 2002), Appendices B and C.

Stamm, K., M Johnson and B. Martin, 1997, "Differences Among Newspapers, Television and Radio in their Contribution to Knowledge of the Contract with

America," *Journalism and Mass Communications Quarterly*, 74.

Staples, Brent, 2003, "The Trouble with Corporate Radio: The Day the Protest Music Died," *The New York Times*, February 20, p. A30.

Stavitsky, A. G. , 1994, "The Changing Conception of Localism in U.S. Public Radio," *Journal of Broadcasting and Electronic Media*.

Steiner, Peter, O., 1952, "Program Patterns and the Workability of Competition in Radio Broadcasting," *Quarterly Journal of Economics,* 66.

Stempell, Guido H. III, and Thomas Hargrove, 1996, "Mass Media Audiences in a Changing Media Environment," *Journalism and Mass Communications Quarterly*, Autumn.

Stepp, Carl Sessions, 2001, *"Whatever Happened to Competition,"* *American Journalism Review*, June.

Stone, V. A., 1987, "Deregulation Felt Mainly in Large-Market Radio and Independent TV," *Communicator*, April.

Stone, V. A., 1988, "New Staffs Change Little in Radio, Take Cuts in Major Markets TV, *RNDA*.

Stone, Vernon, 2002, *News Operations at U.S. TV Stations*, University of Missouri, School of Journalism.

Stouffer, Samuel, 1955, *Communism, Conformity, and Civil Liberties* (New York: Doubelday).

Street, John, 2001, *Mass Media, Politics and Democracy* New York: Palgrave).

Streeter, T. , 1987, "The Cable Fable Revisited; Discourse, Policy, and the Making of Cable Television," *Critical Studies in Mass Communications*.

Strupp, Joe, 2000, "Three Point Play," *Editor and Publisher*, August 21.

Stucke, Maurice E. and Allen P. Grunes, 2001, "Antitrust and the Forum for Democratic Discourse," *Antitrust Law Journal*, 69.

Sullivan, John L., James Pierson, and George E. Marcus, 1982, *Political Tolerance and American Democracy* (Chicago: University of Chicago Press).

Sullivan, Lawrence, 1977, "Economics and More Humanistic Disciplines: What are the Sources of Wisdom for Antitrust," *University of Pennsylvania Law Review*.

Sultan, Fareena, 1999, "Consumer Preferences for Forthcoming Innovations: The Case of High Definition Television," *Journal of Consumer Marketing*, 16.

Sunstein, Cass, 1999, "Television and the Public Interest," *California Law Review,* 8.

Sunstein, Cass, 2001, *Republic.com* (Princeton: Princeton University Press).

Tankel, Johnathan David and Wenmouth Williams, Jr., 1998, "The Economics of Contemporary Radio," *Media Economics: Theory and Practice*, 2nd ed., Alison Alexander, James Owers and Rod Carveth, eds. (Lawrence Erlbaum Associates).

Taylor, John B., 2001, *Economics* (Boston: Houghton Mifflin).

Telecommunications Act of 1996, Pub. LA. No. 104-104, 110 Stat. 56 (1996).

Time Warner Entertainment Co., L.P. v. FCC, 240 F.3d 1126 (D.C. Cir. 2001).

Tompkins, Al and Aly Colon, 2000, "NAB 200: The Convergence Marketplace," *Broadcasting and Cable*, April 10.

Trigoboff, Dan, 2001, "Chris-Craft, Fox Moves In: The Duopoly Marriage in Three Markets Comes with Some Consolidation," *Broadcasting and Cable*, August 6.

Trigoboff, Dan, 2002, "Rios Heads KCOP News," *Broadcasting and Cable*, October 14.

Turner Broadcasting System, Inc. v. FCC, 512 U.S. 622, 638-39 (1994).

U.S. Bureau of Labor Statistics, *Consumer Price Index.*, various issues.

U.S. Bureau of the Census, various issues, *Statistical Abstract of the United States* (Washington, D.C.: U.S. Department of Commerce).

U.S. Department of Justice and the Federal Trade Commission, 1997, *Horizontal Merger Guidelines.*

U.S. v. Microsoft Corp., 253 F. 3d 34, 49 (D.C. Circ. 2001).

U. S. v. Microsoft Corp., *Conclusions of Law* , 87 F. Supp. 2d 30, 44 (D.D.C. 2000)

Valentino, Nicholas A., 1999, "Crime News and the Priming of Racial Attitudes During the Evaluation of the President," *Public Opinion Quarterly*, 63.

Valentino, Nicholas A., Vincent L. Hutchings and Ismail K. White, 2002, "Cues that Matter: How Political Ads Prime Racial Issues During Campaigns," *American Political Science Review*, 96.

Van Der Molen, Juliette H. Walma, Tom H. A. Van Der Voort, 2001, "The Impact of Television, Print, and Audio on Children's Recall of the News," *Human Communication Research*, 26.

Van Orden, Bob, 1999, "Top Five Interactive Digital-TV Applications," *Multichannel News*, June 21.

Vane, Sharyn, 2002, "Taking Care of Business," *American Journalism Review*, March.

Viscusi, W. Kip, John M. Vernon, and Joseph E. Harrington, Jr., 2000, *Economics of Regulation and Antitrust* (Cambridge: MIT Press).

Voakes, Paul S., Jack Kapfer, David Kurpius and David Shano-yeon Chern, 1996, "Diversity in the News: A Conceptual and Methodological Framework," *Journalism and Mass Communications Quarterly*, Autumn.

Vogel, Harold, 1986, *Entertainment Industry Economics* (Cambridge: Cambridge University Press).

Waldfogel, Joel, 1999, *Preference Externalities: An Empirical Study of Who Benefits Whom in Differentiated Product Markets*, NBER Working Paper 7391 (Cambridge,

MA: National Bureau of Economic Research).

Waldfogel, Joel and Lisa George, 2000, *Who Benefits Whom in Daily Newspaper Markets?*, NBER Working Paper 7944 (Cambridge, MA: National Bureau of Economic Research).

Waldfogel, Joel, 2001, Comments on Consolidation and Localism, Federal Communications Commission, Roundtable on Media Ownership (October 29).

Waldfogel, Joel, 2001, *Who Benefits Whom in Local Television Markets?* (Philadelphia: The Wharton School, November).

Waldfogel, Joel, 2002, *Consumer Substitution among Media* (Federal Communications Commission, Media Bureau Staff Research Paper, September).

Walma, Julliete, H. Tom H. A. Van Der Voort, 2001, "The Impact of Television, Print, and Audio on Children's Recall of the News," *Human Communication Research,* 26.

Walton, Mary and Charles Layton, 2001, "Missing the Story at the Statehouse," in Roberts, Gene, Thomas Kunkel, and Charles Clayton (eds.), *Leaving Readers Behind* (Fayetteville: University of Arkansas Press).

Wanta, W. and T. J. Johnson, 1994, "Content Changes in the St. Louis Post-Dispatch During Different Market Situations," *Journal of Media Economics.*

Washington Post (editorial), , 2002 "The Fox News Presidential Advisor," November 21, p. A36.

Waterman, David and Michael Zhaoxu Yan, 1999, "Cable Advertising and the Future of Basic Cable Networking," *Journal of Electronic Media and Broadcasting,* Fall.

Webster, J. G. and P. F. Phalen, 1997, *The Mass Audience: Rediscovering the Dominant Model* (New Jersey: Erlbaum).

Weston, Tracy, 1998, "Can Technology Save Democracy," *National Civic Review,* 87.

Wicks, R. H. and M. Kern, 1995, "Factors Influencing Decisions by Local Television News Directors to Develop New Reporting Strategies During the 1992 Political Campaign," *Communications Research.*

Wildman, Steven, 1994, "One-way Flows and the Economics of Audience Making," in J. Entema and D.C. Whitney (eds.), *Audiencemaking: How the Media Create the Audience* (Thousand Oaks, CA: Sage Publications).

Wildman, Steven and T. Karamanis, 1998, "The Economics of Minority Programming," in A. Garner (ed.) *Investing in Diversity: Advancing Opportunities for Minorities in Media* (Washington, DC: Aspen Institute).

Wilkins, Karin Gwinn, 2000, "The Role of Media in Public Disengagement from Political Life," *Journal of Broadcasting & Electronic Media,* 44.

Williams, Vanessa, 2000, "Black and White and Red All Over: The Ongoing Struggle to Integrate America's Newsrooms," in William Serrin (ed.), *The Busi-*

ness of Journalism (New York: New York Press).

Williams, Walter, "The Journalist's Creed" (1914).

Wimmer, K. A., 1988, "Deregulation and the Future of Pluralism in the Mass Media: The Prospects for Positive Policy Reform," *Mass Communications Review*.

Winston, B. , 1990, "Rejecting the Jehovah's Witness Gambit," *Intermedia*.

Wirth, M. O., 1984, "The Effects of Market Structure on Television News Pricing," *Journal of Broadcasting*.

Wise, Richard, 2000, *Multimedia: A Critical Introduction* (London: Routledge).

Wolzien, Tom, 2003, *Returning Oligopoly of Media Content Threatens Cable's Power.* The Long View, Bernstein Research (February 7).

Woodward, Bob, 2002, *Bush At War* (New York: Simon and Schuster).

Writers guild of America, 2002, "Comments of the Writers Guild of America Regarding Harmful Vertical and Horizontal Integration in the Television Industry, Appendix A. Federal Communications Commission", *In the Matter of Implementation of Section 11 of the Cable Television Consumer Protection and Competition Act of 1992 Implementation of Cable Act Reform Provisions of the Telecommunications Act of 1996 The Commission's Cable Horizontal and Vertical Ownership Limits and Attribution Rules Review of the Commission's Regulations Governing Attribution Of Broadcast and Cable/MDS Interests Review of the Commission's Regulations and Policies Affecting Investment In the Broadcast Industry Reexamination of the Commission's Cross-Interest Policy,* CS Docket No. 98-82, CS Docket No. 96-85, MM Docket No. 92-264, MM Docket No. 94-150, MM Docket No. 92-51, MM Docket No. 87-154, January 4, 2002.

Zaller, J. R., *The Nature and Origins of Mass Opinion* (New York: Cambridge University Press).

Zhao, X and G. L. Bleske, 1992, "Measurement Effects in Comparing Voter Learning From Television News and Campaign Advertisements," *Journalism and Mass Communications Quarterly,* 72, 1995.

Zhao, X and S. H. Chaffee, 1995, "Campaign Advertisements Versus Television News as Sources of Political Issue Information," *Public Opinion Quarterly,* 59.